Resolving Critical Issues in Clinical Supervision

Resolving Critical Issues in Clinical Supervision

A Practical, Evidence-based Approach

Derek L. Milne, PhD
Retired Scholar
Northumberland, England

Robert P. Reiser, PhD
Adjunct Faculty Member
Beck Institute for Cognitive Behavior Therapy
Kentfield, CA

This edition first published 2023
© 2023 John Wiley & Sons Ltd

All rights reserved. No part of this publication may be reproduced, stored in a retrieval system, or transmitted, in any form or by any means, electronic, mechanical, photocopying, recording or otherwise, except as permitted by law. Advice on how to obtain permission to reuse material from this title is available at http://www.wiley.com/go/permissions.

The right of Derek L. Milne and Robert P. Reiser to be identified as the authors of this work has been asserted in accordance with law.

Registered Office
John Wiley & Sons Ltd, The Atrium, Southern Gate, Chichester, West Sussex, PO19 8SQ, UK

For details of our global editorial offices, customer services, and more information about Wiley products visit us at www.wiley.com.

Wiley also publishes its books in a variety of electronic formats and by print-on-demand. Some content that appears in standard print versions of this book may not be available in other formats.

Trademarks: Wiley and the Wiley logo are trademarks or registered trademarks of John Wiley & Sons, Inc. and/or its affiliates in the United States and other countries and may not be used without written permission. All other trademarks are the property of their respective owners. John Wiley & Sons, Inc. is not associated with any product or vendor mentioned in this book.

Limit of Liability/Disclaimer of Warranty
While the publisher and authors have used their best efforts in preparing this work, they make no representations or warranties with respect to the accuracy or completeness of the contents of this work and specifically disclaim all warranties, including without limitation any implied warranties of merchantability or fitness for a particular purpose. No warranty may be created or extended by sales representatives, written sales materials or promotional statements for this work. The fact that an organization, website, or product is referred to in this work as a citation and/or potential source of further information does not mean that the publisher and authors endorse the information or services the organization, website, or product may provide or recommendations it may make. This work is sold with the understanding that the publisher is not engaged in rendering professional services. The advice and strategies contained herein may not be suitable for your situation. You should consult with a specialist where appropriate. Further, readers should be aware that websites listed in this work may have changed or disappeared between when this work was written and when it is read. Neither the publisher nor authors shall be liable for any loss of profit or any other commercial damages, including but not limited to special, incidental, consequential, or other damages.

Library of Congress Cataloging-in-Publication Data
Names: Milne, Derek, 1949- author. | Reiser, Robert P., author.
Title: Resolving critical issues in clinical supervision : a practical, evidence-based approach.
Description: Chichester, West Sussex : Wiley-Blackwell, 2023. | Includes bibliographical
    references and index.
Identifiers: LCCN 2022055940 (print) | LCCN 2022055941 (ebook) | ISBN 9781119812456 (paperback) |
    ISBN 9781119812487 (adobe pdf) | ISBN 9781119812463 (epub) | ISBN 9781119812470 (ebook)
Subjects: LCSH: Medical personnel--Supervision of. | Health facilities--Personnel management. |
    Clinical competence. | Medical care--Quality control.
Classification: LCC RA971.35 .M56 2023 (print) | LCC RA971.35 (ebook) | DDC 362.11068/3--dc23/
    eng/20230125
LC record available at https://lccn.loc.gov/2022055940
LC ebook record available at https://lccn.loc.gov/2022055941

Cover image: © agsandrew/Shutterstock
Cover design by Wiley

Set in 9.5/12.5pt STIXTwoText by Integra Software Services Pvt. Ltd, Pondicherry, India

This book represents the completion of a 40-year research and development programme, made possible by many hundreds of people who, since the 1980's, have helped us to research, develop, and implement evidence-based clinical supervision (EBCS). This includes close collaboration with dozens of co-authors, clinical tutors, health service managers, service users, clinical supervisors, supervisees, and others (including hundreds of supervisors who participated in our many workshops). We would like to dedicate this book to them all.

Contents

About the Authors *viii*
Acknowledgements *ix*

1 Introduction: What are the Critical Issues in Supervision? *1*

2 What Is the Appropriate Supervisory Relationship? *22*

3 Who Is Ultimately Responsible for Patient Care? *39*

4 Understanding Unethical Issues in Clinical Supervision *50*

5 Resolving Unethical Issues in Clinical Supervision *68*

6 Resolving Critical Issues in Training for Supervision *88*

7 Skills in Dealing with Incompetent Supervisors *114*

8 Skills in Dealing with Challenging Supervisees *136*

9 Resolving Other Supervisee Challenges: Ineffective Treatment *156*

10 Placing Supervision in Context: How the Organizational System Affects the Quality of Supervision *172*

11 Conclusions: What Do We Now Know about Resolving Critical Issues in Supervision? *196*

Index *204*

About the Authors

Derek L. Milne (Ph.D., FBPS) is a retired clinical psychologist and visiting professor who worked in England's National Health Service (NHS) for 33 years, specialising in staff development. This included a decade as Director of the Doctorate in Clinical Psychology at Newcastle University, preceded by 12 years as a clinical tutor at Leeds and then Newcastle Universities. Clinical supervision was a significant focus for this work, including the organisation and management of placements/practicums for trainee clinical psychologists, together with workshops for clinical supervisors of all mental health disciplines. Since 1979, Derek Milne has published several books on clinical supervision, and over 100 papers in peer-reviewed scientific journals. Many of these addressed practical issues in enhancing clinical supervision, such as clarifying conceptual models, improving measurement (especially through direct observation), conducting single-subject ($n = 1$) and other evaluations, and developing supervisor training. This activity has been guided by a commitment to evidence-based practice, drawing on a scientist–practitioner orientation.

Robert P. Reiser (Ph.D.) maintains an active clinical practice as a licensed clinical psychologist in California and provides training to clinicians as an Adjunct Faculty member at the Beck Institute for Cognitive Behavior Therapy. Since 2006, he has been delighted to collaborate with Derek Milne on a series of research projects including a manualized account of evidence-based CBT supervision in 2017. He has written and co-authored journal articles and has contributed book chapters focusing on evidence-based approaches to clinical supervision in conjunction with Derek Milne. He has provided CBT training to VA clinicians within the CBT-D national training program with the Veterans Administration over several years. Dr. Reiser also leads workshops focused on improving supervision and training through the use of empirically supported practices. Currently, he trains psychiatric residents at the University of California, San Francisco, in the Department of Psychiatry.

Acknowledgements

Derek Milne would like to acknowledge all those who have helped to develop EBCS over four decades. Prominent latterly are the enthusiastic and committed members of National Education Scotland, who gave us priceless support, direction and validation. Particular thanks go to my long-standing (and long-suffering) co-author Robert Reiser, who has since 2006 collaborated closely with me on supervision research, training, and publications. His companionship, energy, and positivity have played a huge part in building EBCS to this stage. Such collaboration has also provided enormous satisfaction, and hopefully this book will contribute to further work on EBCS, and to related improvements in clinical supervision.

Robert Reiser would like to acknowledge the stimulating but sometimes painful journey in moving forward and adopting EBCS in his own practice. Apologies to my students and trainees, as this required many years of probably imperfect supervision. At least one student in his evaluation commented to the effect that I was experimenting with a new form of supervision, and that 'it would probably be quite useful when he eventually gets it right'! The best part of working with Derek has been the many and constant opportunities to review my practice, reflect on challenges and difficulties, formulate how the issues might be tackled, and then plan and deliberately practise how to incorporate this into the body of our work together. This entailed many trips around this experiential learning cycle based especially on our 11-month study of tapes from my supervision (Milne, et al., 2013), so central to our conceptualization of supervision. This book exemplifies this experiential emphasis, and is a fitting milestone on our EBCS journey together. We would both like to acknowledge Wiley for maintaining interest in our approach to clinical supervision, especially to Jake Opie and Monica Rogers in relation to the present book. Graphic Artist Angela Butler provided some of the figures. Helpful guidance on legal aspects of supervision were welcomed from Ken Hunt and an anonymous second lawyer. Big thanks too, to Duncan Gray, consultant physician, and the anonymous colleagues for the case study illustrations. Our partners, Jan Little and Susan Reiser, and granddaughter Lily Reiser, deserve huge thanks for their unfailing social support and encouragement throughout the writing of this book.

1

Introduction: What are the Critical Issues in Supervision?

In this book we identify the main kinds of critical issues that arise in supervision, suggesting how they can best be resolved. Our guidance is practical, and draws on the evidence-based practice approach that we have used to write prior books and academic papers (e.g., Milne & Reiser, 2017). Much of our earlier work addressed the 'formative' function of supervision, studying how supervisors could facilitate the supervisees' learning and professional development (e.g., Milne & Reiser, 2017). Our last book addressed the 'restorative' function of supervision, again adopting a practical emphasis (Milne & Reiser, 2020). To complete the job, in this new book we will be focusing on the final aspect, the 'normative' function of supervision. This concerns the management or administration of supervision, having to do with areas such as quality control, risk management, gatekeeping, and ethical practice.

Critical issues arise regularly within clinical supervision (hereafter 'supervision'), as an inevitable consequence of complex healthcare environments that include constantly shifting and sometimes competing priorities and pressures. Examples include the often-conflicting priorities of managers and supervisees, which can lead to dilemmas in which supervision is a low management priority, yet essential for the professional development of supervisees (Gonge & Buus, 2010). Even when supervision is securely in place, numerous factors can create tensions between healthcare workers and those who manage their clinical services. A further and fundamental source of tension arises from the sometimes divergent formative, normative, and restorative functions of supervision (Kadushin, 1968). Such intrinsic tensions arise from the increasing organisational pressures on clinical supervisors to monitor and scrutinise the work of their supervisees for varied reasons such as quality assurance, administrative accountability, and risk management. In addition, some professions appear to have a general ambivalence or resistance towards clinical supervision, leading to its devaluation or avoidance (e.g., the nursing profession: White & Winstanley, 2014).

In this chapter we set the scene for resolving such issues, taking a constructive and evidence-based perspective that will characterise this book. Our optimism is based on the accumulating evidence that supervision is uniquely valuable in healthcare (Milne & Reiser, 2020; Watkins & Milne, 2014), and on our extensive experience of working with supervisors and supervisees across many professions and contexts since the 1980s (e.g., Milne, 1983). Our ongoing involvement in supervision research and practice is now approaching the 40-year mark, culminating most recently in an evidence-based

Resolving Critical Issues in Clinical Supervision: A Practical, Evidence-based Approach, First Edition.
Derek L. Milne and Robert P. Reiser.
© 2023 John Wiley & Sons Ltd. Published 2023 by John Wiley & Sons Ltd.

supervision manual (Milne & Reiser, 2017), and a book specifically concerned with restorative supervision (Milne & Reiser, 2020). Based on this experience and our distinctively evidence-based perspective, we will now outline this latest book, clarifying what we mean by normative supervision, and reviewing the best-available literature in order to classify the main critical issues that arise within normative supervision. We will close this introductory chapter by describing how our evidence-based approach can lead to the resolution of these issues. Later chapters will examine all the identified critical issues. The result is an exceptionally wide-ranging review of critical issues, together with evidence-based suggestions on how best to understand and resolve them.

What Is Clinical Supervision?

Supervision has a long history, dating back to the beginnings of social work in the eighteenth century (White & Winstanley, 2014). Although the different healthcare professions make variable use of supervision (Hession & Habernicht, 2020), it has become increasingly recognised internationally as an essential part of modern healthcare systems (Watkins & Milne, 2014). In addition to supporting staff (Milne & Reiser, 2020), it contributes to evidence-based practice (Beidas & Kendall, 2010), and it enhances clinical effectiveness, partly through minimising harm (Milne, 2020). These benefits of supervision are further examined later in this chapter.

Although these benefits are widely endorsed, the definition of supervision has proved problematic. One problem is that illogical variants such as 'peer supervision' (Martin et al., 2018) and 'self-supervision' (Basa, 2018) have developed. Among other reasons, these are flawed because they are irrational (i.e., they are self-contradictory terms), and because they remove the hierarchical relationship that is required to oversee and control supervision (see Chapter 2). The other problem is that there are many different ways in which supervision has been conceptualised and practised: 'Clinical supervision has become a synonym for coaching, mentorship, peer review, clinical facilitation, preceptorship, clinical teaching, buddying, debriefing and other oversight... encounters. Not uncommonly, the term is also used as a byword for "personal performance review", case review, and even therapy' (White, 2017, p. 1251). A third problem is that the different health and social care professions define supervision in distinctive ways (Vandette & Gosselin, 2019). This makes it vital that we next clarify what we mean by supervision.

An early and influential account of supervision is given by Dawson (1926), which defined supervision in terms of the three functions mentioned earlier: educational ('formative'), administrative ('normative') and supportive ('restorative'). Formative supervision addresses the professional development of staff members, mainly through refining their clinical competencies. Normative supervision focuses on enhancing quality-control, an administrative or management perspective (e.g., managing waiting lists; organisational issues). Lastly, supportive supervision concerns the well-being of staff, improving their morale and job satisfaction. More recent definitions help us to build on Dawson (1926): Clinical supervision is *a formal process of professional support and learning, which enables individual practitioners to develop knowledge and competence, assume responsibility for their own practice, and enhance consumer protection and safety of care in complex clinical situations*

(Department of Health 1993, p. 15). In turn, this National Health Service (NHS) definition provided a foundation for an empirical definition of clinical supervision: *The formal provision, by approved supervisors, of a relationship-based education and training that is work-focused and which manages, supports, develops and evaluates the work of designated supervisees. The objectives are primarily: quality control (e.g., "gate-keeping" and ethical practice); maintaining and facilitating the supervisees' competence and capability; and helping supervisees to work effectively (e.g., promoting quality control and preserving client safety); accepting developing own professional identity; enhancing self-awareness and resilience/ effective personal coping with the job; critical reflection lifelong learning skills* (Milne, 2007).

Definition of Normative Supervision

We should also define the normative function of supervision. Following Kadushin and Harkness (2002), we define normative supervision as *an aspect of clinical supervision that addresses supervisees' professional functioning in their organisational context, aiming to ensure that workplace arrangements are effective and satisfactory. It is a formal, constructive, work-focussed, and interpersonal process, addressing the supervisee's critical issues and encouraging positive learning opportunities. It is conducted with due authority by a trained, suitably experienced, and appropriate supervisor. The main supervision methods are workload review (e.g., joint problem-solving discussions); education and training (e.g., competence development through guided experiential learning); awareness-raising (e.g., via facilitated reflection on practice); and evaluation, monitoring and feedback, related to work performance (e.g., to ensure quality control).* This definition complements and develops the one we provided for the restorative function of supervision in our recent book on that function (D. Milne & Reiser, 2020), and both elaborate as necessary the empirical definition of supervision explained here.

What are the Most Common Critical Issues?

Ladany et al. (2016) reviewed the literature in relation to psychological therapy, concluding that the most common issues presented to supervisors by their supervisees were skill deficits and competency concerns; interpersonal dilemmas (e.g., role conflicts); problematic attitudes and behaviour; and work-related misunderstandings (e.g., diversity or power issues). Some of these will also affect supervisors, and self-doubt about one's supervisory competence appears to be common (probably linked to the scarcity and brevity of training in supervision). Major textbooks of most relevance to this book (e.g., Beddoe & Davys, 2016; Haarman, 2013) also address similar issues, including:

- *Competence concerns:* inadequate cultural competence among supervisors; fostering clinical/professional competence and capability in supervisees (adherence, skill and appropriateness); defining, evaluating and addressing incompetence.
- *Relationship struggles:* collusion; struggles over authority, accountability, and responsibility; interpersonal dynamics and 'alliance ruptures'; tensions between different styles/ approaches/belief systems, including balancing support versus challenge, and the use of

the different methods of supervision (especially ambivalence concerning experiential learning); personality clashes.
- *Communication problems:* confidentiality; criticism, evaluation, and feedback.
- *Work-related stressors:* personal distress (e.g., burnout); diversity issues; ethical concerns (e.g., boundary issues); organisational matters (e.g., staff morale; training and support for supervisors); coping with change (e.g., new technologies and practices).

The Role of Major Workplace Stressors

The aforementioned issues arise in the context of events at work. The main workplace stressors were identified in a systematic review of 49 studies, concerned with work-related psychological problems, such as occupational burnout (Michie & Williams, 2003). Similar findings were reported in a more recent systematic review (Bhatt & Ramani, 2016). Both reviews included international, multi-disciplinary samples of healthcare workers. The review conclusions were highly consistent, regardless of the different nationalities and professional groups, in reporting major workplace stressors:

- long working hours
- work overload and pressure
- lack of control over work
- lack of participation in decision-making
- inadequate social support
- unclear and conflicting job roles.

We would expect there to be significant individual differences in the extent to which supervisees would raise such stressors for discussion in supervision, reflecting their different work histories, personal appraisals, and coping strategies, alongside the other variables in the personal coping model (described shortly). In addition, if the supervisor is also the supervisee's manager, that may significantly influence the nature of the discussion. For example, supervisees are unlikely to freely disclose their work struggles or competence issues to a supervisor who is also their line manager (McMahon & Errity, 2014; Ladany et al., 1996). In turn, line managers may naturally bias the supervision agenda towards organisational matters, and may take an unsympathetic position in relation to their supervisee's struggles to cope at work.

Common Ethical Concerns

Ethical issues are often identified through supervision, which is sometimes described as an ethical 'hornet's nest' on account of the many intrinsic tensio ns (e.g., support versus evaluation: Beddoe & Davys, 2016). Although ethical conduct may be discussed most frequently in supervision, ethics is incorporated in all areas of our work, representing the accepted conventions guiding how we ought to behave in professional life generally. In addition to being so wide-ranging, ethical involvement in healthcare is often unobservable (e.g., private struggles over stressful working relationships). This means that ethical conduct '…although rarely discussed, affects everything we do in our professional life, helping to regulate, educate and guide us (e.g., with respect to doing no harm, doing what is beneficial, and doing justice'. Watkins & Milne, 2014, p. 684). These moral principles, together with others widely accepted in healthcare, tend to be given varying degrees of importance (e.g., respect for patients' rights, transparency, and honesty). This will depend on the value system of individuals, and of their professional colleagues and organisations, as formalised in their codes of conduct.

Being complex, unobservable, variable, and universal, it is difficult to reduce workplace ethics to a small number of critical issues. One helpful approach is to combine the most common issues, including the codes of conduct and guidelines concerning supervision that have been developed within regulatory bodies and professions internationally. Following this approach, Thomas (2014), defined the most common ethical transgressions as:

- *Blurred relationship boundaries*, including the abuse of power and multiple relationships (e.g., exploitation, oppression, or coercion of the supervisee for personal gain; abuse of power or trust; disrespect and indignities; racial and other forms of discrimination)
- *Lack of informed consent or 'due process'*, failing to protect the rights and welfare of patients and supervisees (e.g., sub-standard supervision, including unclear parameters, vague objectives, and inappropriate methods; misunderstandings over communication, evaluation criteria, confidentiality, and record-keeping)
- *Incompetence in supervisors and supervisees* (e.g., failure to address ethical issues or to develop ethical competence in supervisees; lack of ethical understanding, clinical oversight, or appropriate delegation of responsibilities by the supervisor; lack of supervisor training or consultation; multicultural incompetence, including privilege and oppression).

Similar topics and categories have been described in other supervision texts and journal papers that pay particular attention to resolving critical issues. These include: Barnett and Molzon (2014), Bernard and Goodyear (2014), Ellis et al. (2014), Falender and Shafranske (2008), Haarman (2013), and Ladany et al. (2016).

As far as we know, however, there has not been a clear consensus or classification framework that captures this range of events and associated critical issues in supervision. In some ways, this lack of consensus inevitably follows from the subjectivity implicit in defining critical issues, including the ways that supervisors themselves perceive events. These factors make it problematic to attempt to create an objective and complete list. In addition, critical issues are diverse and wide-ranging (Kadushin & Harkness, 2002). This variability is illustrated by clinicians' misguided efforts at coping with critical issues, leading to disciplinary action in relation to 86 different types of problematic behaviour, as listed by one professional body (ASPPB, 2019). The most common reasons for the actions were 'unprofessional conduct' and 'sexual misconduct', each representing 10% of all disciplinary actions during the 45-year period studied. Despite these difficulties, we attempt to address this diversity of incidents by creating an integrative classification scheme, building on the above summaries. We think that this effort is potentially useful, providing some clarity and order (and a practical basis for identifying which critical issues to prioritise within this book). In addition, there are many common events, such as work overload, which trigger typical reactions, arising from their general features (e.g., their severity, uncontrollability, and unpredictability). This makes it appropriate to try to list the most common events and critical issues with which they are usually linked.

Pulling It All Together: A Classification of Critical Issues

A helpful approach to consider when a literature is unclear is to integrate key ideas from related literatures that have clear relevance, and a stronger evidence-base (extrapolation). We did this successfully when preparing our CBT supervision manual (D.L. Milne & Reiser, 2017), for example, by studying the educational literature in order to better understand how to give effective feedback (e.g., Hattie & Timperley, 2007). We repeat this approach here, to help us to clarify the full range of critical issues in supervision. In particular, the related literature on patient safety is highly relevant, has strong research foundations, and focuses on things that go wrong in healthcare. Things that go wrong are critical issues that have not been addressed or resolved, and have become a greater concern, potentially causing harm. The overlap between patient harm and critical issues in supervision becomes clearer when we consider the definition: Patient harm related to supervision causes lasting damage (psychological and/or physical) due to supervised clinical interventions which have been incorrectly selected or applied, or where unethical events occur. Such harm is understood to arise from clinicians' errors, commonly taking the form of incompetence, unethical behaviour, poor health, and other types of unprofessional conduct (Milne, 2020).

The patient safety literature includes taxonomies covering behavioural interventions in healthcare (e.g., Bellg et al., 2004) and patient safety frameworks (e.g., Chang et al., 2005; Chatburn et al., 2018). In addition, we draw on valuable concepts from the literature on therapy-related harm (e.g., Curran et al., 2019; Hardy et al., 2019; Klatte et al., 2018), and examples of the harm that can be done to supervisors and supervisees within organisations (e.g., due to chronically high stressors: Griffiths et al., 2019). We conducted a theoretical review which integrated these literatures to classify the different sources of harm, in relation to supervision (Milne, 2020). This integrative effort yielded an evidence-based classification system with 10 types of critical issue, as summarised in Table 1.1. These are the critical issues that we address in this book.

The first column in Table 1.1 provides a classification system for 10 kinds of 'adverse triggering events' in supervision, based on the fidelity framework (Bellg et al., 2004). This list starts with individual events with relatively circumscribed implications, such as a supervisor adopting an inappropriate approach to supervision with one supervisee. The list ends with events that affect many people, and which carry huge implications (e.g., a faulty system that leads to a healthcare disaster). Therefore, Table 1.1 incorporates a systemic perspective, one that includes consideration of personal, interpersonal, cultural, organisational, and community issues. The second column in Table 1.1 offers examples of critical events. These examples, such as unstructured supervision or communication problems, are ones that might be expected to occur in conjunction with these adverse triggering events, being a summary of the most frequently mentioned examples in the literature.

By using this extended fidelity framework, we hope to ensure that critical issues are addressed systematically, that supervisors are helped to identify relevant critical issues, and that we provide a properly organised book. For example, in Chapter 2 we next address the power imbalance in supervision, and the tension between autonomy and control. This is consistent with the adverse event in row 1 that is labelled: *1. Faulty 'design' (bad planning*

Table 1.1 A systemic classification of negative critical issues in supervision.

Adverse triggering events	Negative critical issues in supervision (see text for descriptions)
Faulty 'design': The wrong thing is 1. planned or 2. practiced unprofessionally by the supervisor.	Supervisor is unfit for practice: unethical, improper, or illegal acts by the supervisor; professional misconduct; incapacity (physical and mental); personality issues. Lack of due process (e.g., no supervision contract; unclear supervision parameters, such as evaluation).
Faulty 'training': Supervisor training is: 3. done wrong (i.e., lacks adherence to the proper approach).	Supervisor training is unfit for purpose: incompetence due to absent, inadequate or faulty training (or poor training transfer).
Faulty 'delivery': Supervision is: 4. done incompetently by the supervisor (i.e., with a lack of proficiency).	Supervisor is unfit for purpose: supervision techniques, or relationship inappropriate (e.g., boundary violations; power struggles); complications (e.g., non-compliant supervisee).
Faulty 'receipt': Supervision has the: 5. wrong effect on the supervisee (i.e., ineffective supervision plus supervisee factors prevent competence development).	Supervisee is unfit for purpose or award: fails to engage properly (e.g., avoiding experiential learning) or slow to develop competence; may be associated with adverse health conditions (physical and mental, such as burnout, impairment).
Faulty 'enactment': The supervisee provides the: 6. wrong treatment leading to the: 7. wrong clinical outcomes with the patient	Supervisee selects wrong approach, and/or uses flawed implementation (e.g., suspect techniques; under/over-treating; relationship ruptures, accidents, harm, or drop-outs). Client factors may also be influential (e.g., vulnerability; risk-taking). Ineffective treatment, achieving poor outcomes.
'Faulty workplace': 8. Faulty local management (i.e., flawed leadership)	Service managers unfit for practice (e.g., fail to monitor and detect above issues, or to apply supervision standards). May be compounded by work overload, role conflicts, and inadequate social support.
'Faulty organisational system': 9. Flawed feedback systems (i.e., faulty information) 10. Ineffective quality improvement systems (i.e., flawed attempts to improve healthcare).	Organisational systems unfit for purpose; organisation's national leaders unfit for practice (e.g., belated or inaccurate whole system feedback; under-funding of improvement efforts; governance failures; whole system violations or ineffectuality). Loss of staff morale and public trust (e.g., reduced governmental support and private donations).

or unprofessional application of supervision). Subsequent chapters deal with all the other critical issues in Table 1.1, to provide an exceptionally comprehensive coverage of the problems that supervisors face in ensuring that effective supervision is provided.

Understanding Critical Issues

So far, so good, but critical issues such as 'unprofessional supervision' are often not clear-cut or straightforward, being more often obscured by grey areas, and subjected to conflicting opinions. This highlights the significant role played by the way we cognitively appraise events: one person's critical issue is another's routine supervision. Therefore, instead of simply creating a fixed and final list of critical issues (as in Table 1.1), for a more accurate understanding we need to factor in appraisal as a characteristic of individuals, one that explains the origins of a critical issue. Cognitive appraisal is a perceptual process, one which is subjective and initially automatic (i.e., it occurs instantly, without conscious effort or awareness), serving to interpret the personal significance of the events that occur around us. It is this appraisal process that determines whether an event is judged to be a critical issue (i.e., a 'stressor') by an individual. If a supervision event (e.g., a supervisee who avoids a task) is appraised by the supervisor as something that requires a response, then the supervisor making that appraisal is by definition judging it to be a critical issue (i.e., we use 'stressor' and 'critical issue' interchangeably). This logic comes from coping theory, which helps us to understand why some things become critical issues, and which also helps us to formulate and resolve issues.

Because appraisal is such a subjective process, differences between individuals' perceptions of what happened during incidents can readily occur, including whether the incident truly merits a response. For instance, ethical issues are often unclear, and we often avoid dealing with them (e.g., dual relationships, such as a supervisor who is also a manager: see Chapter 3). An important factor during appraisal is whether the incident is perceived as a threat or a challenge. Incidents are often presented in a negative light, as a threatening or problematic event. This is indicated by the terms that are often used, including 'hassles' and 'stressful events' (Thoits, 2010). An event that is perceived as something that could overwhelm or harm us generates an automatic 'flight or fight' reaction from our nervous system (Volmer & Fritsche, 2016). If then our personal coping strategies are ineffective, we will tend to feel distressed (e.g., frustrated or angry). And if this negative coping process occurs frequently or has serious repercussions, we may become sensitised to this stressor, and cope in ways that are increasingly maladaptive (e.g., more frequent use of avoidance-based coping strategies: see Table 1.2 for examples, numbered 5–8). As this vicious cycle recurs, we are likely to experience a loss of confidence (e.g., feeling like a fraud or an imposter), and may have symptoms of personal distress (e.g., occupational burnout). Coping strategies are our ways of dealing with stressors, using all of our resources, and often also drawing on social or other resources in the process. Just like critical incidents, the range of strategies people use to cope is incredibly diverse. But Table 1.2 is an authoritative summary of the most commonly used strategies, and represents a good place to start in trying to understand critical issues.

Table 1.2 The main personal coping strategies, with examples drawn from a survey of American counsellors (Lawson, 2007). Reproduced with the permission of Pavilion books.

Personal coping strategies	Examples from a survey of counsellors
1. Logical analysis	Maintain objectivity; seek case consultation.
2. Positive appraisal	Reflect on positive experiences; gain a sense of control.
3. Seeking support	Access clinical supervision, peer support, personal therapy.
4. Problem-solving	Increasing self-awareness, Continuing Professional Development, reflection, read literature.
5. Cognitive avoidance	Put aside unwanted thoughts, avoid responsibility.
6. Acceptance/resignation	Take a vacation, turn to spiritual beliefs.
7. Seek alternative rewards	Use substances to relax, leisure activities.
8. Emotional discharge	Describe work frustrations to colleagues.

Therefore, coping theory represents a way of defining, understanding, and resolving critical issues (Brough et al., 2018; Sonnentag & Fritz, 2015). Despite a long history, it remains a cornerstone of psychological research and theory on how we function at work (Briggs et al., 2017; Volmer & Fritsche, 2016). As used here, coping theory is also consistent with a cognitive-behavioural therapy approach (CBT), our usual way of working. And like CBT, the theory represents an exceptionally practical, intuitively obvious, and evidence-based way of understanding critical issues. For these reasons, throughout this book we will use coping theory as a way of understanding and considering how to resolve critical issues in supervision. As already noted, the coping process is based on the interaction of several factors, such as an initial event appraisal (threat or opportunity), and then responding to stressors with coping strategies. There are also other factors within the theory. These processes and technical terms are illustrated in Figure 1.1, a summary of the well-established 'coping theory' (Folkman & Nathan, 2010). Critical issues that are part of the coping model (box 4 in Figure 1.1) arise from three broad sources: the general context, the specific workplace, and from the individual. Context is presented as box 1 in Figure 1.1, and refers to the wider environmental system surrounding the workplace (e.g., professional bodies' practice standards; legal considerations and national politics; pandemics). These contextual factors usually act as moderators, affecting the speed, strength, or direction of the variables within the coping cycle. 'Context is key … critical supervisory events do not occur in a vacuum' (Ladany et al., 2016, p. 35). For this reason, the context encircles the coping cycle, as indicated in Figure 1.1. The other main influencing factors are the workplace system, and personal factors. These are indicated by boxes 2 and 3 in Figure 1.1. Examples of all three factors were included in our earlier definition of normative supervision, including legal challenges, lack of peer support, or a supervisor's resilience. These examples correspond to boxes 1–3 in Figure 1.1, respectively. As a result of the way that these coping factors interact, we will tend to end up feeling good or bad about the coping episode. As per Figure 1.1, these are termed the 'well-being' or 'distress' outcomes of our coping efforts, but many other kinds of positive and negative reactions occur too. For example, in

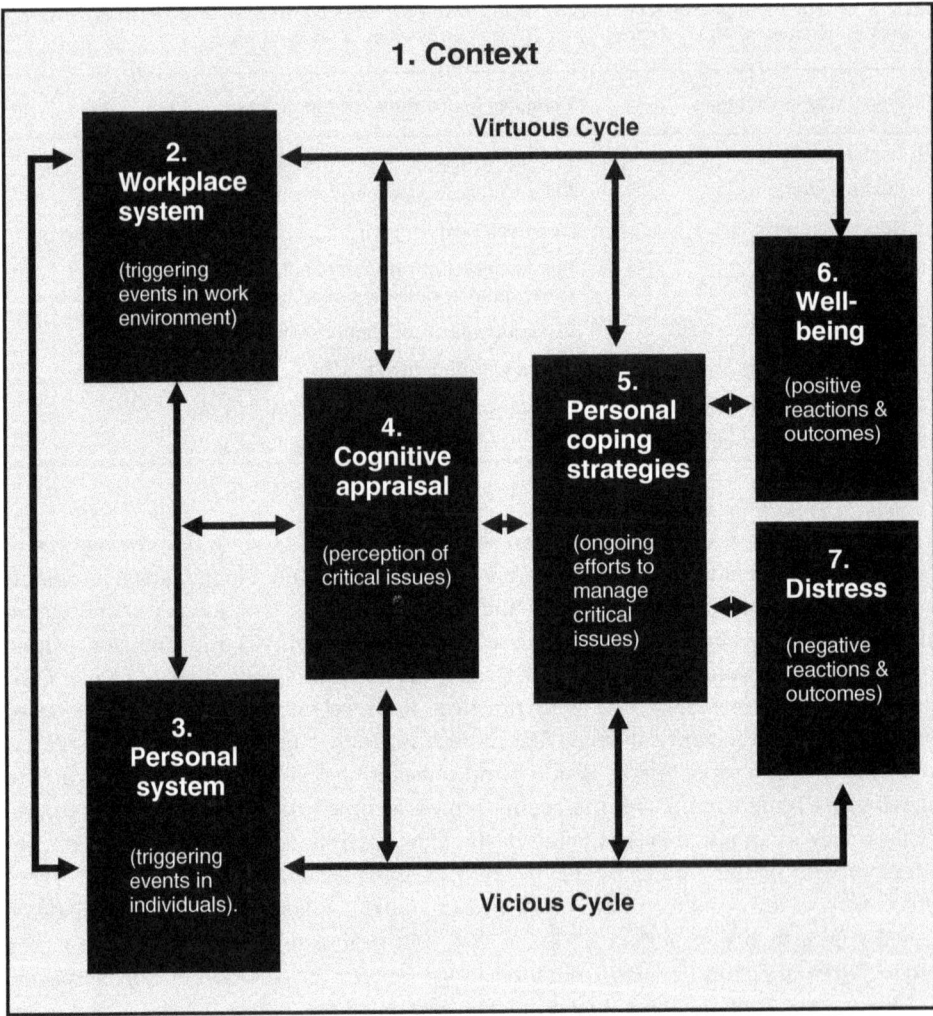

Figure 1.1 The coping cycle, a way of understanding critical issues.

the illustration below, a supervisor was asked to explain her purely didactic approach (a stressor, appraised as a threat), which she coped with by denying that there was a problem, and even arguing that her approach was actually widely accepted. The episode left her feeling angry, misunderstood, and devalued.

To explain the kind of coping process in the illustration below, the supervisor's threat appraisal triggered some emotional discharge, an emotion-focussed and typically maladaptive coping strategy (see Table 1.2). However, she was professional enough to recognise that some problem-solving work might be justified (a more adaptive coping strategy), which was done within a socially supportive if strained atmosphere. This enabled her to exit what was in danger of becoming a downward spiral towards even worse consequences than attending a supervision workshop and reading a guideline (such as being excluded from serving as a supervisor by the training programme). The downward process is called the 'vicious cycle', to reflect how several things tend to start to go wrong, and the situation worsens (e.g., our appraisals become more negative, and our coping strategies are poorly chosen and incompetently enacted).

The alternative process is when we perceive a stressor as a challenge, and enter a positive or 'virtuous' coping cycle, based on using the adaptive coping strategies (i.e., strategies 1–4 in Table 1.2). The process begins when an incident is perceived as an opportunity, rather than a threat. Our appraisal is that the event can be handled successfully, and once we start to cope with it we may even experience some positive emotions. For example, a supervisor may perceive a supervisee's display of clinical incompetence as the moment to step in and provide some training and encouragement. Consequently, the supervisor may well end up appreciating this chance to flourish, thanks to demonstrating their professional qualities (e.g., clinical expertise). But we also include as stressors those situations where there is no clear incident, but where the supervisor can see an opportunity to implement a different technique, to better help their supervisee (e.g., they sense a 'teachable moment'). This moment may occur when a supervisor notices their supervisee's curiosity over a clinical incident, and an eagerness to learn more about it. Perceiving events in this positive way, a supervisor can draw on their more adaptive (approach-based) personal coping strategies and achieve a satisfying resolution to a critical issue ('well-being' in Figure 1.1). This leads to a virtuous cycle that benefits supervisors personally and professionally (e.g., stimulating their thinking; allowing them to use their skills to the full; aiding their professional development). The sense of well-being generated by successful efforts to manage a critical issue provides a powerful positive feedback loop (the virtuous cycle), thereby further enhancing motivation to tackle critical issues in the future. The effects of the positive feelings further add to the sense of confidence that difficulties can be managed, raising motivation (Folkman & Moscowitz, 2007). Next we provide to our illustration, to bring the coping model to life.

Illustration

The following example of a vicious coping cycle concerned incompetence in the supervisor which was compounded by workload pressure and a strained working relationship with the supervisee: Due to staff shortages in her department, the supervisor had tried working faster. This led to her becoming uncharacteristically short tempered, inflexible, and confrontational. Faster working impacted the supervision that she provided, which became brief and superficial. A critical issue then arose during a routine visit to the placement by a staff member from the supervisee's training programme (a clinical tutor). Feeling under time pressure, the supervisor had got into the habit of restricting her supervision to fleeting clinical oversight, through a quick discussion of the supervisee's progress with his patients. This aggravated the supervisee's sense of being devalued, and also prevented him from developing the key competencies that had to be demonstrated to progress within the programme. When the clinical tutor pressed the supervisor to explain her purely didactic approach, she became angry, denied that there was a problem, and argued that her approach was actually widely accepted (even though she had not attended a supervision workshop for several years). The meeting became increasingly uncomfortable, but in closing the supervisor agreed to reflect on her approach, and the tutor agreed to check for and provide her with a relevant guideline. After the meeting, the supervisor felt betrayed by her supervisee's disclosures about the supervision he had received and was also angry with the clinical tutor for unsympathetically giving her more work and aggravation, at such a difficult time.

Reflections on the Illustration

This vignette illustrates the nature of critical issues, including several aspects of the coping cycle, such as the vicious cycle process. For the supervisor, the context for this vicious cycle included staff shortages, her misjudged problem-solving efforts, and a weak supervisory alliance with her supervisee. Her maladaptive coping featured avoidance of experiential learning methods, including avoiding attending training workshops in supervision, fuelled by a self-serving denial of accepted supervision guidelines. Where it was felt necessary, she justified these coping strategies in terms of the unfortunate circumstances at work. However, in practice she was actually exacerbating a stressful vicious cycle by creating yet more work, and further damaging her relationships with colleagues.

A partial resolution was achieved through the supervisor reflecting on and agreeing to review her approach, linked to her attending a supervision workshop that was designed to address some issues that she selected (anonymously). This allowed her to hear what other supervisors in her area considered to be good practice, and hence made it easier for her to adopt a more experiential and collaborative approach. She continued to act as a supervisor for this training programme, and there were no further issues. Supervisee feedback indicated that the supervisor had improved her approach, was now supervising competently, and was generally operating within a virtuous coping cycle.

How Can We 'Resolve' a Critical Issue?

As in our illustration, critical issues in supervision are resolved when there is a positive outcome or the satisfactory closure of the issue, which is attributable to the interactional process between supervisor and supervisee (or to others helping the supervisor). Intended outcomes for the host organisation include improved quality control and better staff retention. The main intended outcomes for supervisees are workplace and professional role socialisation, contributing to their effective integration with the host organisation, enabling them to work harmoniously in accordance with the relevant policies and procedures, to perform their clinical duties effectively, and to enjoy work satisfaction. By contrast, when critical issues are unresolved, this tends to engender further vicious coping cycles, often leading to greater personal and organisational concerns and potential accidents and patient harm (Milne, 2020). Specific examples of resolutions and common supervision techniques (based on Kadushin & Harkness, 2002) are:

- *discussion and education* concerning relevant organisational issues (e.g., induction to the workplace; understanding and adhering to relevant rules, conventions, and practice guidelines; awareness of policies and service priorities; leadership, coordination, and communication practices);

- *workload review and management* (e.g., identify specific duties and tasks; effective prioritisation; goal-setting; action-planning; coordination and delegation; managing clinical service logistics, such as waiting lists and caseloads);
- *joint problem-solving efforts* (including reviewing and defining clinical problems; shared decision-making over selected actions; co-working to resolve problems);
- *competence development* related to quality control and its enhancement (e.g., collecting, interpreting, and acting on audit or patient satisfaction data);
- *consideration of clinical responsibilities*, the ethical and legal context, and professional practice guidelines (e.g., discussing and guiding ethical conduct; dealing with patients' complaints or interpersonal or team strife; protecting and supporting the supervisee in response to such stressors); and
- *evaluation, monitoring, and feedback*, to ensure quality control and to facilitate quality improvements (which may include advocating for the supervisee, or jointly challenging the workplace system).

We will develop this list throughout the book (e.g., Chapter 4 identifies 12 such interventions for resolving critical issues). Various psychological and social factors are thought to be involved in such resolutions, including motivation, self-awareness, and social support. But we believe that the most powerful influence within supervision is guided experiential learning, which aids problem resolution, and drives the gradual acquisition of competence (Kolb, 2015). This view is consistent with related thinking in supervision, such as supervision 'episodes' (Ladany et al., 2016), and 'corrective experiences' (Watkins, 2018). Indeed, these reflect the general nature of human development, where challenges at an earlier developmental level, once resolved, allow movement to the next level (Stoltenberg et. al., 2014). Therefore, this book will emphasise experiential learning and human development.

What's so Special about 'Evidence-based' Supervision?

Although our approach to the resolution of critical issues is shared with others, our evidence-based clinical supervision approach is distinctive (EBCS: D.L. Milne & Reiser, 2017). This has just been indicated by our definition of the resolution process, in that we drew on the most relevant general theories of human development, rather than relying solely on the supervision literature. In addition, our classification of critical issues used the best available evidence from research (reviews of the empirical literature, surveys of supervisors), which was supplemented by expert opinion and statistical data (see Table 1.2). However, although our evidence-based approach is distinctive within the literature on supervision, it is similar to the approach taken by The National Institute for Health and Care Excellence (NICE, 2014). This Institute accepts that, in the absence of high-quality controlled research, clinical practice recommendations should be developed using the best-available scientific evidence, influenced as appropriate by other forms of evidence (expert testimony, relevant theories, views of stakeholders, service users, and practitioners).

Another feature of our EBCS approach has been to conduct supervision research, qualitative and quantitative, within a long-term, action-research programme (i.e., based on our direct involvement in supervision (Milne, 2018)). This empirical programme began by carefully discriminating between the published studies, so that we could focus our systematic reviews on a seam of interpretable and affirmative supervision research (through the 'best-evidence synthesis' method (Petticrew & Roberts, 2006)). This helped us to identify ways to improve supervision (e.g., Milne et al., 2010). This approach was unlike most other reviews, which tended to either combine other studies indiscriminately (e.g., Pollock et al., 2017), or were so exclusive that they could conclude little (e.g., Alfonsson et al., 2018). Using this best-evidence synthesis method, we next developed an empirical definition and conceptual model of supervision (Milne, 2007; Milne et al., 2008) which led to expert consensus-building efforts to develop supervision guidelines (Milne & Dunkerley, 2010) and instruments for evaluating supervision (Reiser et al., 2018). These research and development activities were guided by an evidence-based practice (EBP) cycle of problem-solving activities (Parry et al., 1996). Most recently, this EBCS approach was further developed with the creation of a supervision manual, including updated guidelines and video demonstrations of competent supervision (D.L. Milne & Reiser, 2017). Latterly we have extended the approach to the neglected 'formative' and 'normative' functions of supervision (D. Milne & Reiser, 2020; and the present book).

Is This Book for You?

This book primarily aims to help healthcare supervisors from all professions to find better ways of resolving critical issues arising in their supervision, enabling them to become better supervisors. We also consider how best to understand and resolve critical issues concerning the supervision itself, so will offer suggestions to those who support and guide supervisors (e.g., line managers and consultants). We mainly take an organisational perspective on supervision, a 'normative' perspective reflecting a manager or administrator's priorities (e.g., quality control; staff retention and well-being; adherence to service standards and guidelines; harm prevention). This normative perspective is developed to supplement the formative emphasis found within most existing texts (i.e., supervision as a way to develop competence in supervisees through education and training). The relevant branches of applied psychology, especially clinical psychology from a cognitive-behavioural angle (CBT), have been a major source of material and inspiration. But we also draw on research and expert consensus from other healthcare professions. From this multi-disciplinary perspective, our objectives are to classify and clarify the nature of the most common critical issues (by describing and formulating the situation in an objective but empowering manner); enable readers to better judge whether the issues described in the book affect them (by raising awareness and understanding); and to provide evidence-based options and guidelines for resolving critical issues. Written in a constructive manner, the book is practical, firmly grounded in current healthcare challenges internationally, and so is intended to be relevant and useful to a wide range of healthcare professions. However, although supervision is now an integral part of mental health services, it is not yet as well-utilised in healthcare generally (Hession & Habernicht, 2020). Also, because our background is in clinical psychology, we will draw extensively from the literature within the mental health professions. But we will pursue the same goals identified by these authors: to develop detailed models of effective supervision and thereby inform practice. We also include social work within the mental health professions, as social workers often work within mental health teams, and because there is a strong tradition of valuable research from within that profession.

Style and Structure

We will provide a resource that is exceptionally accessible, so that you can quickly locate the information that you may find helpful when seeking to resolve your critical issues. A standard chapter structure is part of making it as straightforward as possible for readers to access what they need. Aside from this first chapter and the final one, we will provide a descriptive and succinct title, define key terms, and describe the main critical issues. Drawing on the best-available evidence, we will then aim to pinpoint the nature of this problem, and its seriousness (in terms of data on its prevalence or significance). This leads into a formulation section, where we will explain how such issues arise, and the factors that maintain or exacerbate them. We will then flag the key implications, both for individuals and for healthcare systems. The main section in the chapters will be the action options, including specific evidence-based techniques to consider. This will follow the style of a professional guideline or instructional manual, so that readers can clearly understand how to tackle a critical issue of concern to them. In these action sections and elsewhere we will use summary tables and diagrams to articulate and portray the nature of the issues. And as far as possible we will infuse the chapters with clear links to research and relevant theory, while recognising that there has been little empirical research directed to the topic of critical issues in supervision. To compensate, we will place greater emphasis on relevant theory and the guidance of experts. We will also extrapolate from the clinical supervision and related literatures, where there are clear parallels. Further boosting our practical bent, we will provide a suitable illustration in each chapter, being a relevant case study or vignette, a real supervision scenario drawn from our own experience, or from that of colleagues, to ensure relevance by drawing on the experiences of a range of healthcare professionals. These illustrations will show how this material can come together in clinical practice, and how resolutions can be obtained across the different healthcare disciplines. At the close of chapters, we will draw out the most important conclusions and action implications.

Based on the summary of critical issues that we presented earlier (Table 1.1), the chapters will cover these areas: ethical and legal issues (e.g., vicarious liability); personal impairments (adverse health and personality issues); relationship problems (boundary violations; failures of due process); concerns over competence (supervisors and supervisees); challenges in evaluation and feedback; diversity dilemmas; supervision muddles and mistakes (flawed supervision methods, such as peer supervision); supervisor training; and organisational disorganisation (role blurring, weak leadership, and other system failures at a local and national level). Reflecting the scale and frequency of some critical issues, some of these topics will be covered in more than one chapter (e.g., unethical conduct issues). We will end the book with a chapter that crystallises the main challenges and outlines the way towards more successful resolutions in your supervision.

By following this style and structure, we aim to facilitate all aspects of your experiential learning cycle, enabling you to resolve your own critical issues as effectively as possible.

This means that we will present the key research studies and theories in ways that will encourage improved understanding. We will also try to foster your reflections on your own experiences, and your grasp of the issues. If practical resolutions are to be achieved, these cognitive outcomes need to lead to behavioural action, and this is why guidelines are so important. Accompanying action are various emotions, positive and negative, which also merit our attention. Additionally, we will help readers to better notice and channel such feelings (e.g., bewilderment, frustration, and anxiety). Completing this experiential learning cycle, we will encourage readers to consider our suggestions and guidelines, so that real progress can be made.

Readership

In addition to those involved in pre-licensure supervision (i.e., supervision as part of initial professional training), we assume that many of our readers will also receive or provide career-long supervision, being an accepted practice in healthcare systems in countries such as the UK and Australia, and an informative model of possible best-practice arrangements. Although primarily addressed to supervisors, this book is highly relevant to supervisees, healthcare leaders (managers, executives, administrators), those who support and guide supervisors (e.g., consultants), and the associated professional bodies and organisations (e.g., university training programmes). There are also points of interest for supervision researchers and trainers. We will consider supervision in relation to healthcare in general, including mental health and social work, and will present material that we trust will be relevant and helpful to all those involved in healthcare.

Summary

Supervision is a uniquely valuable procedure for improving the way that healthcare staff function, helping to ensure that workplace arrangements are effective, smooth, and satisfactory (D. Milne & Reiser, 2020). However, many critical issues threaten supervision, such as work incidents which are unplanned, unwanted, and often feel like an overwhelming threat. Such issues include challenges arising within supervision itself, alongside work factors that are judged by supervisors as being critical to the successful provision of supervision. To help to clarify the main critical issues, we scanned staff surveys, statistics, research reviews and expert opinion. This triangulation effort indicated that the most common critical issues, cited in all four of these sources, concerned the supervisor's personal misconduct (e.g., unethical behaviour); addressing incompetence (mostly in supervisees, but also in supervisors); and relationship problems (e.g., supervisees' 'games', supervisors' harassment). Next most common, cited in 2–3 of these sources, were communication breakdowns (e.g., misunderstandings over evaluation) and workplace stressors (e.g., high workloads). Cited only once were problematic supervisee behaviours, and low staff morale/social support. However, as this breakdown indicates, these lists of common critical issues are inconsistently reported, and there is no definitive list or classification of critical incidents. Therefore, we integrated concepts and findings from neighbouring literatures with the triangulation data, and created a preliminary classification scheme, based on the patient harm framework (Milne, 2020). This provided a practical and logical foundation for classifying critical issues, and created the basis for organising this book.

We believe that our preliminary classification scheme is a valuable general statement of critical issues, an effective way to summarise and make sense of the often disparate literature. But we also knew that critical issues are not as clear-cut or neatly defined as this scheme suggests. To develop our thinking, we next turned to coping theory to better understand why critical issues arise, starting with the initial process of cognitive appraisal. We then linked this to the other factors in the theory (see Figure 1.1), to provide an evidence-based and powerful way of understanding and resolving critical issues. As shown through the illustration, these factors transact in complex ways to define the critical issues in supervision. In this sense, our graphical depiction of the complex coping process in Figure 1.1 is a practical simplification of what is in reality a far more dynamic coping process, an ongoing effort at adapting to situations. Although we fear that some readers will find this emphasis on theory off-putting, or even misplaced in a primarily practical book, we urge you to consider just how practical a good theory can be. In the chapters that follow we will aim to show the huge value of coping theory, when linked to the best-available supervision methods and techniques.

The resolution of a critical issue in supervision is a positive outcome that is primarily attributable to the interactional process between supervisor and supervisee. Resolutions include clarifying perspectives, aiding understanding, redefining difficulties, ventilating feelings, and gaining fresh insights. These outcomes are driven by the general processes in human development, especially the kind of guided experiential learning that good supervision offers (Kolb, 2015). Given this psychological and developmental emphasis, we feel well-placed to write this book, using our distinctive approach to evidence-based supervision (D.L. Milne & Reiser, 2017). Although we are aware that there are important differences in the ways that the different professional groups in healthcare tackle supervision, we aim to capture the widely shared and most user-friendly methods, enabling readers from all healthcare backgrounds to resolve their own critical issues as effectively as possible.

References

Alfonsson, S., Parling, T., Spännargård, Å., Andersson, G., & Lundgren, T. (2018). The effects of clinical supervision on supervisees and patients in cognitive behavioral therapy: a systematic review. *Cognitive Behaviour Therapy, 47*(3), 206–228. https://doi.org/10.1080/16506073.2017.1369559

Association of State and Provincial Psychology Boards (ASPPB) (2019). *ASPPB Disciplinary Data System: Historical Discipline Report Reported Disciplinary Actions for Psychologists: 1974–2019*. https://cdn.ymaws.com/www.asppb.net/resource/resmgr/dds/dds_historical_report_2019.pdf. Accessed on 20 November 2020.

Barnett, J. E., & Molzon, C. H. (2014). Clinical supervision of psychotherapy: Essential ethics issues for supervisors and supervisees. *Journal of Clinical Psychology, 70*(11), 1051–1061. https://doi.org/10.1002/jclp.22126

Basa, V. (2018). 'Self-supervision' in the therapeutic profession. *European Journal of Counselling Theory, Research and Practice, 2*(6), 1–7. Retrieved from http://www.europeancounselling.eu/volumes/volume-2-2018/volume-2-article-6

Beddoe, L., & Davys, A. (2016). *Challenges in professional supervision.* Jessica Kingsley Publishers.

Beidas, R. S., & Kendall, P. C. (2010). Training therapists in evidence-based practice: A critical review of studies from a systems-contextual perspective. *Clinical Psychology: Science & Practice, 17*(1), 1–30.

Bellg, A. J., Borrelli, B., Resnick, B., Hecht, J., Minicucci, D. S., Ory, M., Ogedegbe, G., Orwig, D., Ernst, D., Czajkowski, S., & Treatment Fidelity Workgroup of the NIH Behavior Change Consortium (2004). Enhancing treatment fidelity in health behavior change studies: best practices and recommendations from the NIH Behavior Change Consortium. *Health Psychology : Official Journal of the Division of Health Psychology, American Psychological Association, 23*(5), 443–451. https://doi.org/10.1037/0278-6133.23.5.443

Bernard, J. M., & Goodyear, R. K. (2014). *Fundamentals of clinical supervision.* Pearson.

Bhatt K, & Raman R (2016) Job burnout: A literature review. *Indian Journal of Research, 5*(9), 203–205.

Briggs, A., Brough, P., & Drummond, S. (2017). Lazarus and Folkman psychological stress and coping theory. In C. L. Cooper & J. C. Quick (Eds.), *The Handbook of stress and health.* Chichester.

Brough, P., Drummond, S., & Biggs, A. (2018). Job support, coping, and control: Assessment of simultaneous impacts within the occupational stress process. *Journal of Occupational Health Psychology, 23*(2), 188–197. https://doi.org/10.1037/ocp0000074

Chang, A., Schyve, P. M., Croteau, R. J., O'Leary, D. S., & Loeb, J. M. (2005, December 8). The JCAHO patient safety event taxonomy: A standardized terminology and classification schema for near misses and adverse events. *International Journal for Quality in Health Care, 17*(2), 95–105. https://doi.org/10.1093/intqhc/mzi021

Chatburn, E., Macrae, C., Carthey, J., & Vincent, C. (2018). Measurement and monitoring of safety: Impact and challenges of putting a conceptual framework into practice. *BMJ Quality & Safety, 27*(10), 818–826. https://doi.org/10.1136/bmjqs-2017-007175

Curran, J., Parry, G. D., Hardy, G. E., Darling, J., Mason, A. M., & Chambers, E. (2019). How does therapy harm? A model of adverse process using task analysis in the meta-synthesis of service users' experience. *Frontiers in Psychology, 10*, 347.https://doi.org/10.3389/fpsyg.2019.00347

Dawson, J. B. (1926). The case supervisor in a family agency without district offices. *The Family, 6*(10), 293–295. https://doi.org/10.1177/104438942600601004

Department of Health. (1993). A vision for the future: The nursing, midwifery and health visiting contribution to health and health care. NHS Management Executive: Stationery Office, London.

Ellis, M. V., Berger, L., Hanus, A. E., Ayala, E. E., Swords, B. A., & Siembor, M. (2014). Inadequate and harmful clinical supervision: Testing a revised framework and assessing occurrence. *The Counseling Psychologist, 42*(2), 434–472. https://doi.org/10.1177/0011000013508656

Falender, C. A., & Shafranske, E. P. (Eds.). (2008). *Casebook for clinical supervision: A competency-based approach.* American Psychological Association. https://doi.org/10.1037/11792-000

References

Folkman, S. & Nathan, P. E. (Eds., 2010). *The Oxford handbook of stress, health, and coping.* Oxford University Press.

Folkman, S., & Moskowitz, J. T. (2007). Positive affect and meaning-focused coping during significant psychological stress. In M. Hewstone, H. A. W. Schut, J. B. F. De Wit, K. Van Den Bos, & M. S. Stroebe (Eds.), *The scope of social psychology: Theory and applications* (pp. 193–208). Psychology Press.

Gonge, H., & Buus, N. (2010). Individual and workplace factors that influence psychiatric nursing staff's participation in clinical supervision: A survey study and prospective longitudinal registration. *Issues in Mental Health Nursing, 31*(5), 345–354.https://doi.org/10.3109/01612840903427849

Griffiths, A., Harper, W., Desrosiers, P., Murphy, A., & Royse, D. (2019). "The stress is indescribable": Self-reported health implications from child welfare supervisors. *The Clinical Supervisor, 38*(2), 183–201. https://doi.org/10.1080/07325223.2019.1643433

Haarman, G. B. (2013). *Clinical supervision: Legal, ethical and risk management issues.* Foundations: Education & Consultation.

Hardy, G. E. Bishop-Edwards, L. Chambers, E., Connell, J. Dent-Brown, K. Kothari, G. Rachel O'hara R. & Parry, G.D. (2019) Risk factors for negative experiences during psychotherapy. *Psychotherapy Research, 29*(3), 403–414, https://doi.org/10.1080/10503307.2017.1393575

Hession, N., & Habenicht, A. (2020). Clinical supervision in oncology: A narrative review. *Health Psychology Research, 8*(1), 8651. https://doi.org/10.4081/hpr.2020.8651

Hattie, J., & Timperley, H. (2007). The power of feedback. *Review of Educational Research, 77*, 81–112.https://doi.org/10.3102/0034654302984

Kadushin, A. (1968). *Supervision in Social Work.* Columbia University Press.

Kadushin, A., & Harkness, D. (2002). *Supervision in social work* (4th ed.). Columbia University Press.

Klatte, R., Strauss, B., Flückiger, C., & Rosendahl, J. (2018). Adverse effects of psychotherapy: protocol for a systematic review and meta-analysis. *Systematic Reviews, 7*(1), 1–7. https://systematicreviewsjournal.biomedcentral.com/articles/10.1186/s13643-018-0802-x

Kolb, D. A. (2015). *Experiential learning: Experience as the source of learning and development.* New Jersey: FT Press.

Ladany, N., Friedlander, M. L., & Nelson, M. L. (2016). *Supervision essentials for the critical events in psychotherapy supervision model.* American Psychological Association.

Ladany, N., Hill, C. E., Corbett, M. M., & Nutt, E. A. (1996). Nature, extent, and importance of what psychotherapy trainees do not disclose to their supervisors. *Journal of Counselling Psychology, 43*(1), 10 24.https://doi.org/10.1037/0022-0167.43.1.10

Lawson, G. (2007). Counsellor wellness and impairment: A national survey. *Journal of Humanistic Counselling, Education and Development, 46*(1), 20–34.

Martin, P., Milne, D. L., & Reiser, R. P. (2018). Peer supervision: International problems and prospects [Editorial]. *Journal of Advanced Nursing, 74*(5), 998–999. https://doi.org/10.1111/jan.13413

McMahon, A., & Errity, D. (2014). From new vistas to life lines: Psychologists' satisfaction with supervision and confidence in supervising. *Clinical Psychology and Psychotherapy, 21*(3), 264–275. https://doi.org/10.1002/cpp.1835

Milne, D., Reiser, R., Aylott, H., Dunkerley, C., Fitzpatrick, H., & Wharton, S. (2010). The systematic review as an empirical approach to improving CBT supervision. *International*

Journal of Cognitive Therapy, 3(3), 278–294. https://psycnet.apa.org/doi/10.1521/ijct.2010.3.3.278

Milne, D., & Reiser, R. P. (2020). *Supportive clinical supervision: From burnout to well-being, through restorative leadership.* Pavilion.

Milne, D. L. (1983). Some paradoxes & findings in the training of clinical psychologists. *Bulletin of the British Psychological Society, 36*, 281–282.

Milne, D. L. (2007). Developing clinical supervision through reasoned analogies with therapy. *Clinical Psychology and Psychotherapy, 13*, 215–222.

Milne, D. L. (2018). *Evidence-based CBT supervision.* Wiley-Blackwell.

Milne, D. L. (2020). Preventing harm related to CBT supervision: A theoretical review and preliminary framework. *The Cognitive Behaviour Therapist, 13.* https://doi.org/10.1017/S1754470X20000550

Milne, D. L., Aylott, H., Fitzpatrick, H., & Ellis, M. V. (2008). How does clinical supervision work? Using a best evidence synthesis approach to construct a basic model of supervision. *The Clinical Supervisor, 27*, 170–190.

Milne, D., & Dunkerley, C. (2010). Towards evidence-based clinical supervision: The development and evaluation of four CBT guidelines. *The Cognitive Behaviour Therapist, 3*(2), 43–57. https://doi.org/10.1017/S1754470X10000048

Milne, D. L., & Reiser, R. P. (2017). *A manual for evidence-based CBT supervision.* Wiley-Blackwell.

Michie, S., & Williams, S. (2003). Reducing work related psychological ill health and sickness absence: A systematic literature review. *Occupational and Environmental Medicine, 60*(1), 3–9. https://doi.org/10.1136/oem.60.1.3

National Institute for Health and Care Excellence. (2014) Nice Guidelines. https://www.nice.org.uk/about/what-we-do/our-programmes/nice-guidance/nice-guidelines.

Parry, G., Roth, A. & Fonagy, P. (1996). Psychotherapy research, funding & evidence-based practice. In A. Roth & P. Fonagy (Eds.), *What works for whom?* (pp. 37–56). New York: Guilford Press.

Mark, Petticrew, Helen, Roberts. (2006) Systematic reviews in the social sciences: a practical guide. (pp. 164–214) Oxford: Blackwell. https://doi.org/10.1002/9780470754887.ch6

Pollock, A., Campbell, P., Deery, R., Fleming, M., Rankin, J., Sloan, G., & Cheyne, H. (2017). A systematic review of evidence relating to clinical supervision for nurses, midwives and allied health professionals. *Journal of Advanced Nursing, 73*(8), 1825–1837. https://doi.org/10.1111/jan.13253

Reiser, R. P., Cliffe, T., & Milne, D. L. (2018). An improved competence rating scale for CBT supervision: Short-SAGE. *The Cognitive Behaviour Therapist, 11*, e7. https://doi.org/10.1017/S1754470X18000065

Sonnentag, S., & Fritz, C. (2015). Recovery from job stress: The stressor-detachment model as an integrative framework. *Journal of Organizational Behavior, 36*(S1), S72–S103. https://doi.org/10.1002/job.1924

Stoltenberg, C. D., Bailey, K. C., Cruzan, C. B., Hart, J. T., & Ukuku, U. (2014). The integrative developmental model of supervision. In C. E. Watkins, Jr. & D. L. Milne (Eds.), *The Wiley international handbook of clinical supervision* (pp. 576–597). Wiley-Blackwell. https://doi.org/10.1002/9781118846360.ch28

Thoits, P. A. (2010). Stress and health: Major findings and policy implications. *Journal of Health and Social Behavior, 51*(1), S41–S53. https://doi.org/10.1177/0022146510383499

Thomas, J. T. (2014). Disciplinary supervision following ethics complaints: Goals, tasks, and ethical dimensions. *Journal of Clinical Supervision: In Session, 70*, 1–11. https://doi.org/10.1002/jclp.22131

Vandette, M.-P., & Gosselin, J. (2019). Conceptual models of clinical supervision across professions: A scoping review of the professional psychology, social work, nursing, and medicine literature in Canada. *Canadian Psychology, 60*, 302–314.

Volmer, J., & Fritsche, A. (2016). Daily negative work events and employees' physiological and psychological reactions. *Frontiers in Psychology, 7*, 1–10. https://doi.org/10.3389/fpsyg.2016.01711

Watkins Jr, C. E. (2018). Educationally corrective experiences as a common factor in psychotherapy supervision. *Journal of Psychotherapy Integration, 28*(2), 242–252. https://psycnet.apa.org/doi/10.1037/int0000103

Watkins, C. E., & Milne, D. L. (Eds.). (2014). *The Wiley international handbook of clinical supervision.* Wiley-Blackwell.

White, E. (2017). Clinical supervision: Invisibility on the contemporary nursing and midwifery policy agenda. *Journal of Advanced Nursing, 73*, 1251–125. https://doi.org/10.1111/jan.12970

White, E., & Winstanley, J. (2014). Clinical supervision and the helping professions: An interpretation of history. *The Clinical Supervisor, 33*, 3–25. http://dx.doi.org/10.1080/07325223.2014.905226

2

What Is the Appropriate Supervisory Relationship?

Introduction

Supervision is not immune from the general human tendency to avoid dealing with critical but difficult interpersonal issues. As a result, relationships can become distorted and problematic. Examples include cancelling supervision (Buus et al., 2016), providing pseudo-supervision (Shapiro & Smith, 2011), engaging in peer supervision (Martin et al., 2017), and collusion (Milne et al., 2009). Even experienced supervisors who 'viewed giving negative feedback to their supervisees as important ... felt it to be difficult and tended to avoid it' (Norberg et al., 2016, p. 279). The most probable explanation for avoidance behaviours in supervision is anxiety over exercising the necessary authority over supervisees, when for many healthcare staff the dominant professional ethos is one of supportive professional collegiality (sometimes called 'the cult of niceness'). Social workers, for instance, have been described as 'resorting to power and authority self-consciously, hesitantly, and apologetically. It evokes a sense of shame and guilt' (Kadushin & Harkness, 2002, p. 98).

Being clear about the fundamental nature of professional supervisory relationships can reduce anxieties all round, even though acting with due authority may continue to feel uncomfortable for many healthcare professionals (Copeland et al., 2011). This common reaction was borne out in interviews with 15 experienced psychodynamic supervisors (Norberg et al., 2016, p. 281), in that these supervisors acknowledged that they 'experienced difficulties when they had to take the role of an expert and become an authority figure' (e.g., when evaluating competence). But they accepted that exercising authority was an obligation that went with the role. Part of the difficulty was striking a balance between encouraging supervisees to have the freedom to find their own way of working, while still ensuring that the therapy was conducted correctly. These supervisors reported being intolerant of any divergences, a balancing act that they labelled 'freedom within limits'. Psychodynamic supervision is much less prescriptive than most other therapy approaches (particularly CBT), so these firm boundaries and decisive actions underline the general importance of exercising authority when necessary.

In this chapter we discuss the inherent power imbalance within supervision, presenting the critical issue as a tension between freedom and control (i.e., between the supervisee's autonomy and the supervisor's authority). Following this formulation, we will move on to

---

Resolving Critical Issues in Clinical Supervision: A Practical, Evidence-based Approach, First Edition.
Derek L. Milne and Robert P. Reiser.
© 2023 John Wiley & Sons Ltd. Published 2023 by John Wiley & Sons Ltd.

summarise some suitable professional coping strategies, in the form of practical action implications and an illustration. We will indicate an appropriate, evidence-based response that can resolve the critical issues associated with forming the appropriate supervisory relationship. We start by clarifying the key terms and functions, as relationship problems start with misunderstandings.

Authority and Accountability

Authority is a major foundation for Western organisational bureaucracies, where individuals are delegated the power or right to give orders by a higher authority (e.g., a chief executive), including permission to make decisions and enforce compliance. This right is usually based on an individual's duties, status, or role, and is designed to increase organisational efficiency: 'If groups of individuals are to work together to accomplish desired ends, their efforts must be integrated. Some administrative officer, in this case the supervisor, has to be given authority to direct and coordinate individual activities toward the achievement of a common purpose, to review and evaluate work, and to hold workers accountable' (Kadushin & Harkness, 2002, p. 83).

It is tempting to use the terms 'power' and 'authority' interchangeably, but there are some important differences and scope for misunderstandings (Hawkins & McMahon, 2020). Authority is formally delegated power ('legitimate' or 'role power'), as when hierarchical organisations give an individual the right to supervise (e.g., an employer, a training programme, and a professional regulatory body permit someone to supervise). But effective supervision also depends on the functional capacity to exercise that right. This is not always straightforward, as there are other types of interpersonal power at play within a supervision relationship (e.g., 'reward', 'personal', 'cultural', and 'coercive' power). There are also other stakeholders, such as the employing organisation, and the various professional bodies involved. As a result, authorised supervisors may sometimes find it surprisingly difficult to exercise their role power, especially if they lack some of these other types of power (e.g., because they are new to the role of supervisor), or because the supervisee is relatively interpersonally powerful, effectively exercising counter-control. Another complication can arise from the lack of explicit authorisation by an organisation, leaving the right to supervise to be assumed (e.g., from one's seniority, status, or role), when it should provide 'express' authority, as clarified in a job description.

This overview highlights how supervision is exercised within a transactional relationship, where organisational and personal forms of power interact and can create critical issues, such as collusive or pseudo-supervision. Kadushin and Harkness (2002) have provided examples, such as the supervisee who exercises control over her supervisor by deciding what clinical information to share, partly based on judging what the supervisor wants to hear: 'I tell her what I want her to hear. I decide what to talk about and where I want advice, so in a sense it's not really supervision. If you like, I'm supervising her by what I say. I sort of control it' (p. 109). In this sense, supervisees may have personal qualities, such as assertiveness or self-confidence, which represent the 'personal' power to make the decisions and direct the work. But supervisors will also tend to have personal qualities, such as clinical wisdom (expert power). Consequently, the use of the different forms of power in supervision can be understood as a personal transaction between the parties, operating within an organisational and social context (Kadushin & Harkness, 2002): in exchange for one thing, the other person provides another. In this sense, supervision relies on mutual dependency and professional reciprocity, which can be complex and challenging, requiring careful management on both sides if critical issues are to be avoided. This is illustrated when legitimate power needs to be used (e.g., the authority to sanction or control supervisees).

In clinical practice, authority is frequently delegated to another individual, such as a supervisee. This delegation makes the supervisee responsible for carrying out a duty, an authorisation that should be clear and specific (e.g., empowering the supervisee to carry out explicit procedures with an identified patient at a specific time and place, on behalf of the supervisor). In turn, accountability means holding supervisees responsible for ensuring that proper procedures are followed, and that results are achieved (e.g., requiring them to explain their work). In this sense, both supervisor and supervisee are accountable, in their hierarchical turn, to their organisational seniors (i.e., answerable to a specified individual, such as a clinical manager), in relation to the duties for which they are responsible. Therefore, responsibility differs from accountability in that responsibilities are our professional duties (the ongoing care processes, often shared by several professionals working as a team), whereas accountability specifies a reporting arrangement and emphasises the care outcomes that are achieved by these duties, where typically one person owns the outcomes (e.g., is promoted or awarded a bonus). Another difference, at least in legal respects, is that responsibility implies remediation (i.e., that a responsible person will rectify problems or pay damages). The supervisor's job description should make clear the employer's expectations on these points, and a supervision contract should do likewise for the supervisee.

From this summary, it follows that even during their initial professional training supervisees are responsible for playing their part, within their sphere of competence (e.g., interacting in a professional manner with patients; complying with their supervision contracts). This logic also extends to other areas of working life, such as ethical, legal, and professional accountability. For example, registered nurses and midwives are professionally accountable to the Nursing and Midwifery Council for upholding professional standards, set out in a code of practice (NMC, 2018). To return to the issue of delegation, an example from this code is that nurses should only delegate duties that are within the other person's competence, while ensuring that they fully understand the instructions; that they are adequately supervised and supported; and checking that the result meets the required standard.

As this example of delegation indicates, giving someone the formal authority to undertake a task, such as supervision, should logically follow from giving them responsibility (Beddoe & Davys, 2016). Expressed in everyday language, if we expect a supervisor to be held accountable for the work outcomes of a supervisee, then we must ensure that they have the formal power to discharge this responsibility (e.g., the necessary authority, resources, and time to supervise effectively, such as ensuring that the supervisee behaves responsibly). This includes having the right to monitor and direct the work of their supervisees, an example of the legitimate power bestowed on supervisors by their employing organisations (Haarman, 2013). In turn, this 'clinical oversight' arrangement means that the supervisor is rightly held accountable by their employing organisation (and by other interested parties, such as a professional regulator). For the employing organisation, this arrangement helps to enhance the quality of care, and to decrease the risk of harm to patients, alongside several other important benefits (Milne & Reiser, 2020). Other stakeholders also invest in this hierarchical relationship because it manages other risks (such as harm to patients: Kirkup, 2015), for instance, by encouraging adherence to the policies of employee/labour unions and those of relevant professional bodies (e.g., The NMC).

Although this line of reasoning should be made clear to all involved, practical organisational arrangements may still raise some critical issues. These can pit the traditional autonomy of fully qualified professional clinicians against the necessity for external control, as when a supervisor asks a senior clinician to discontinue a favoured approach because it causes them concern. This is not such an issue in countries where supervision stops once an initial professional qualification is obtained (i.e., once registered as an independent practitioner). But in countries such as Australia and the UK, supervision is an essential aspect of the career-long 'continuing professional development' (CPD) for all staff, even the most senior clinicians. This introduces an extra degree of tension, because qualified and experienced professionals naturally expect greater clinical freedom. On the other hand, employers, managers, and others equally naturally expect more from a qualified clinician, and so will create pressures intended to help the organisation (e.g., carrying a larger caseload; being more clinically efficient). This situation can make supervision particularly helpful.

In summary, 'Supervision is not a collegial relationship, not a relationship with peers, and not a relationship of equals' (Haarman, 2013, p. 14). Rather, the supervisee is legally an agent acting on behalf of the supervisor, who in turn is acting on behalf of their employer (Knapp & VandeCreek, 2006), unless self-employed. This is how we should understand authority and accountability, ensuring that the supervision arrangements follow on accordingly (e.g., organisational policies that make this understanding explicit; guidelines and supervisor training that embeds this understanding in practice). As Kadushin and Harkness (2002) have summarised it, 'The supervisor needs to come to terms with the delegation of authority (which) should be used only when necessary to help achieve the objectives of the organization in a flexible, impartial manner and with a sensitive regard for (the supervisee's) response' (p. 127). However, this advice can still be problematic, as the illustration shown next indicates. A related critical issue is often that the supervisor's responsibilities are unclear, making accountability fraught with uncertainty. We next suggest how this should be resolved.

The Terms and Scope of Supervision

Accountability starts with the employer's authorisation of an employee, a mandate that formally asks them to become a clinical supervisor. This should be based on a specification of the associated supervision duties and responsibilities. These activities are consistent with the job description, and foreseeable by the employer (see examples below, such as 'providing consistent and timely supervision'). Known formally as the 'terms of appointment' or 'scope of responsibility', this specification defines the range of a supervisor's duties and is essential in an increasingly litigious world. The information is also helpful in setting some practical boundaries and should be stated in considerable detail. This detail matters because liability in law will rest on the facts of any allegation of negligence, considered within the context of the terms of appointment agreed between the employer, the supervisor, and the supervisee, taking account of the scope of the supervision.

However, in practice, statements regarding the terms and scope of supervision appear to be somewhat minimal, at least within the UK's National Health Service (NHS). This also seems to be consistent with the situation in Australia, where 'beyond listing supervisor responsibilities and assessment parameters, little direct guidance is provided about the process and structure of supervision sessions' (Lu et al., 2019, p. 225). Similarly, from New Zealand, Beddoe and Davys (2016) cited the example of what they termed 'supervision on a desert island': a contract for external supervision that only specified that supervision should occur monthly, at a venue to be provided by the supervisor. There was no information concerning methods or objectives, nor the links with the employing organisation (e.g., arrangements for communication and feedback). Thankfully, there are some helpful examples for ensuring more complete information, such as the three-way agreements established within medical supervision (Webb et al., 2017). These agreements are supervision contracts between the supervisors (physicians), the placement providers (NHS sites), and the training body (the university), 'designed to be an explicit demonstration of the three parties' responsibilities and is intended to enhance communication and accountability between those responsible for delivering and supporting ... supervision' (p. 2). Survey data and interviews indicated that the participants viewed this contract as maintaining high standards in training physicians by making arrangements more professional and accountable, while also increasing supervisors' power to negotiate for supportive resources (Webb et al., 2017).

Another helpful example comes from a job description, sourced by the authors from the internet. This was an advertisement from Scotland's State Hospital (sourced on 11 August 2020), which indicated that the successful applicant would be expected to actively participate in the clinical supervision process by directly and regularly supervising staff in the delivery of therapies on the ward, including clinical psychologists and nurses (this example is drawn from the job description for a senior clinical psychologist). Additionally, the responsibilities included work allocation, appraisals, and personal development plans for those staff members that were also line-managed by the supervisor. Helpfully, the same job description listed some 'key results areas', such as ensuring the effective, efficient, and economic utilisation of staff resources, in order to help improve the patients' functioning. In the case of trainees, the supervisor was also held responsible for ensuring that they acquired the necessary clinical and research competencies to contribute to good psychological practice, in conjunction with contributing to the assessment and evaluation of these competencies. This example provides a broad outline of the supervision duties and responsibilities, with a valuable emphasis on the objectives. A supervisor's duties and responsibilities are also influenced by contextual factors, such as the standards for professional practice (including supervision) that need to be met to maintain professional registration; and by any collaboration with universities, especially when this concerns initial professional training (i.e., pre-registration education programmes). Taken together, these influences help to ensure that supervision is organised in a suitably professional way.

At times, different countries and states have distinct guidance on the relevant content or standards governing supervision (Thomas, 2014). But based on the summary within Falender and Shafranske (2004), common responsibilities or duties are to:

- Facilitate the professional development of the supervisee, providing consistent and timely supervision, but only within one's own sphere of competence.
- Inform clients in writing that treatment will be provided by a trainee (and/or qualified individual, in the UK), under the supervision of a suitably qualified and identified person (contact details provided).
- Inform the supervisee in writing (commonly through the learning contract) about the content and methods of supervision, particularly how appropriate monitoring and evaluation will occur.
- Personally assess clients from time to time, in order to monitor treatment; and
- Document supervision (maintaining some kind of log or record, and requiring trainees to document what they are doing, with both parties signing off these records).

A specification of the scope of supervision may also usefully clarify who else is involved (e.g., holiday/vacation cover for the supervisor), how supervision will be conducted (e.g., the approach to be used), the format (e.g., 1:1 or in a group), where and when sessions will be held, alongside other helpful details (e.g., the duration of supervision sessions). A full list of the general contents of a suitably detailed clinical supervision contract has been set out by The American Psychological Association (American Psychological Association, 2015), and Haarman (2013) lists 14 topics (p. 90). Within the supervision contract, the aims and objectives would normally be specified individually, to reflect the supervisee's learning and support needs. As this indicates, supervisees should also shoulder their own related responsibilities, and the contract can include these too. For instance, they should prepare thoroughly for supervision, prioritise their agenda items, reflect carefully on supervision, invite opportunities for experiential learning, be willing to discuss difficulties, and be open to feedback (Milne & Reiser, 2017).

As already noted, the supervision role outline will tend to have greater detail, in order to satisfy the standards of relevant professional bodies and training programmes (such as the required total number of hours, frequency, and nature of supervision). For example, in the profession of psychiatry in Australia and New Zealand, the minimum supervisory requirement for trainees is 4 hours per week over at least 20 weeks, per 6-month rotation (Lu et al., 2019). Other important details include the personalised objectives of supervision (i.e., reflecting the individual strengths and learning needs of each specific supervisee, usually linked to an established competence framework), the methods to be used in supervision, the nature of assessments and evaluations, and other general goals (e.g., duties and responsibilities; fall-back supervision arrangements). Further details on supervision contracts are provided in Chapter 4, and there is an evidence-based guideline on goal-setting available in Milne and Reiser (2017), together with video demonstrations of competent supervisory practice.

Such written material is usually supplemented by a few days of training in supervision, usually provided by the university programmes which are organisationally linked to the supervisor's employing body (Watkins & Wang, 2014). This typically includes initial training in how to supervise, accompanied by formal documentation (e.g., training handbooks; competence statements for supervisors and supervisees; written standards or best-practice guidelines). These sources of guidance will require that a supervision contract is negotiated and signed by the supervisor and supervisee, as outlined above. In legal terms, this represents their joint written and informed consent, one of the important pre-conditions for liability. In agreeing to this contract, supervisees should be aware of the scope and terms of supervision, as this information improves clarity on the supervisor's role. This organisational context also helps to indicate a suitable level of clinical responsibility for the supervisee.

Illustration: Consultancy Versus Supervision

An experienced psychologist regularly provided a consultancy service to a small group of third-year psychiatric residents (i.e., trainees). Consistent with the definition of consultancy, this service consisted of training the residents to use cognitive-behaviour therapy (CBT), including expert advice to them on how they might apply this training with their individual patients. But as a consultant, the expert had no authority over the residents' clinical work. This training was part of a national CBT competency requirement in psychiatric training programmes in the USA, designed to meet the minimum competency requirements for psychiatrists who were completing their initial professional training. In addition, senior psychiatrists who were members of staff within the host clinic were responsible for supervising the residents' practice (i.e., they were the authorised clinical supervisors). These senior supervising psychiatrists were mainly psychodynamic in their theoretical orientation, and spent typically 10–20 minutes directly observing the residents' therapy sessions in order to qualify for insurance reimbursement (In the USA, it is customary for patients' insurance companies to pay the therapists' fees).

These senior psychiatrists were viewed as the authorised supervisors in that they 'signed off' on the medical record and on the associated paperwork required for insurance billing purposes. As far as the consulting psychologist knew, this direct observation was not necessarily accompanied by consistent formal feedback, as would be expected in routine supervision. Also, it appeared to the consulting psychologist that there may not be a formally designated, regular supervision session with residents, and in some cases supervision only seemed to take place 'in the hallways', as needed. In addition, during the same training period there were other advising groups with a psychoanalytic focus that residents attended.

This situation made the psychologist feel accountable for the quality of the CBT that these residents were providing to their patients, but relatively powerless to intervene. A case in point concerned one trainee in the CBT group with a strong psychodynamic orientation. He had difficulties identifying a patient suitable for CBT, and several patients that he had considered were already being seen in long-term psychodynamic therapy. The solution was the referral of a patient in long-term psychodynamic therapy for concurrent CBT treatment, in relation to some specific treatment issues (e.g., insomnia, emotion regulation). As this patient was also on a waiting list for a group practice specialising in dialectical behaviour therapy (DBT), there was a confusing array of consultations and therapy approaches for this trainee to assimilate. Specifically, in addition to the DBT group staff, this trainee also had to liaise with the colleague who was providing the selected patient's psychodynamic therapy, the senior psychiatrist (the psychoanalytically oriented clinical supervisor), another DBT expert within the staff group, and the consulting psychologist responsible for the CBT training.

The consulting psychologist found this mix of people who were advising, consulting, and supervising the same resident confusing and difficult to navigate. Furthermore, the potential lack of clarity created by the extreme differences in theoretical orientation and the varied roles of various consultants and supervisors was compounded by the lack of a formal agreement between the clinic and the consulting psychologist. To develop some clarity at the start of his involvement, the psychologist introduced a Consulting Contract with the residents. This document attempted to clarify his role (i.e., consulting only in relation to CBT-focused competency development), distinguishing it from the roles and responsibilities of the other participants. In particular, the contract stated that it would be the clinical psychiatrist-supervisor who would shoulder the medico-legal responsibility for the clinical care of the residents' patients. Hence if any conflict arose between the psychologist's CBT suggestions, then the supervising senior psychiatrist would retain the primary responsibility for clinical decision-making and patient care. This is illustrated by part of the contract with the resident:

> *As a consultant I depend solely upon the information provided by you, the treating clinician. I may not have all of the facts and implicitly I will rely on your good-faith and clinical judgment in incorporating any of my suggestions into the larger clinical picture. My consultative role is delimited in the sense that I may make instructional or educational recommendations, but your clinical supervisor is ultimately responsible for the care you deliver, and your clinical judgment must be used to make any direct decisions about patient care in the light of that supervision. Therefore, I have no direct medical or clinical responsibility for the patients we discuss, and I am not acting as your clinical supervisor. Hence, we agree that I have no direct treatment relationship with your patient, hence no duty of care, and that your clinical supervisor is solely responsible for the course and quality of treatment.*

The consultant reviewed this agreement with the resident concerned, as a way of clarifying roles and responsibilities. While this process helped to address some of the consultant's concerns about the multiple participants, it also underlined the limitations of his consulting position. It seemed clear to him that, even if he wanted to, he did not have the authority to tell the trainee to limit his consultations with the other clinic staff, or the power to instruct the trainee to ignore their advice (if that was ever considered necessary). But at least it was clear all round that the responsibility for patient care rested solely with the senior psychiatrist, as the clinical supervisor. By signing this contract, the resident also gave his informed consent to the arrangement for consultancy.

This shared understanding over the balance between power and responsibility was reassuring for the consultant. However, he still struggled with the irritating sense that the trainee had undermined his authority in some way (as if the resident was playing one of the transactional 'games' in supervision). Therefore, the consultant had a direct discussion with the trainee requesting that (unless there was an emergency or a directive from the senior psychiatrist providing clinical supervision) he preferred to get advance notice of any planned discussions of the selected patient with any of the other staff involved. He was also frustrated that his options were limited by the clinic's complex administrative system, which seemed at times to work at cross-purposes with his consulting activities. While there was no final resolution of these relational difficulties and organisational dilemmas, the consultant did achieve satisfactory closure through helping clarify the authority and power dynamics inherent in this training context.

Reflections on This Illustration

a. Roles and responsibilities: *The consultant was wise to view the number of advisors involved with these trainees/residents as a reason to establish very clear lines of authority, responsibility, and accountability. This need for clarity regarding the respective roles and responsibilities was further emphasised by the lack of a formal agreement between the clinic and the consultant, covering the terms of appointment or the scope of his responsibility. However, one clarifying aspect was that the consultant understood that he was not expected to see the trainee's patients, which also helped to distinguish his role from that of the supervisor. This lack of an agreement was why the consultant established a contract with the residents. With hindsight, and consistent with the material in this chapter, we believe that the clinic should have informed the consultant of the terms and scope of his role on appointment (including his authority; the responsibilities of those involved; and accountability arrangements). This background information should then have dictated the contents of the contract, including noting and differentiating the roles of the other advisors and the supervisor. It would also be good practice for the contract to contain clauses absolving the consultant of inappropriate responsibilities (e.g., seeing the residents' patients). In turn, the consultant should only be advising the trainee within the scope of the overall supervision arrangements. Once there is suitable clarity about such terms, scope and roles, the contract should have been signed off by a senior administrator on behalf of the university that operated the clinic, and then by the consultant and the trainees. To try to ensure the clarity of roles, the supervisor and other advisors should have then been sent a copy of the contract, for information.*

Another point of reflection includes the honorary status of the consultant, as he contributed his time as a volunteer, partly in consideration of various reciprocal benefits (e.g., an honorary university title; access to the library). Not being an employee could sometimes decrease authority and increase the risk of vicarious liability, but in this instance the consultant was formally appointed, and these reciprocal considerations indicated membership of the organisation. As a result, the consultant's vicarious liability can be regarded as similar to that of an employee (i.e., where ultimately the liability tends to fall on the organisation). On the other hand, had the consultant been employed directly by the trainee psychiatrists, then he rather than the host organisation would have become the 'principal party', the subject of any claims of vicarious liability.

b. Experiential learning: *Sometimes perspective-taking requires additional time and experience. In this case, the consultant was subsequently able to reflect more fully on his experiences by comparing this frustrating experience with two really motivated residents in the next training cycle. They had selected training cases quickly, had readily begun showing the consultant their work, and eagerly accepted his feedback. Further illustrating their personal engagement in the learning process, one of these residents also admitted to a disturbing deskilling moment: in the middle of one of her therapy sessions, she suddenly felt that she had no idea what she was doing. While completing a thought record, she felt that she was 'waffling' and completely off course. When the consultant reviewed this bit of the recording with her, they had* *a really deep and engaging discussion of uncertainty and doubt, reframing them as quite central elements in training and often showing up even in senior clinicians. The consultant aimed to collaboratively conceptualise this as a positive transitional experience, linked to ongoing learning and adapting to new schemas/understandings (i.e., the CBT approach). Furthermore, this type of doubt and ongoing reflection on one's work was viewed as an important and highly valuable driver for pursuing higher levels of expertise and competence while working independently. This led to an interesting set of reflections by this resident about the culture of medicine and psychiatry, which did not really allow for such moments of confusion and uncertainty.*

Reflecting on this more positive second training cycle, the consultant came to the view that this 'deskilling' experience with his current set of trainees highlighted the extent to which the resident in the prior training cycle had effectively blocked him from really engaging in a learning process. It also had the effect of making the consultant feel more confident about his final evaluation of the prior resident. This was an evaluation in which the consultant had indicated 'low confidence' in his ability to make an assessment of this resident's competence, because of the very limited observation opportunities. That is, in the light of these current, highly cooperative trainees, the consultant was now sure that the previous resident had used his coercive interpersonal power to avoid engaging fully in the learning opportunity.

Formulation

This illustration indicates how hierarchical power relationships can be complicated by multiple training roles within the host organisation and may even be exploited unhelpfully by a supervisee. As already noted, the rationale for maintaining an authoritative, hierarchical relationship generally sits uncomfortably alongside the more democratic, collegial, and empowering spirit of professional life. We realise that this spirit is inherent in the definition of 'professional', which indicates a large degree of autonomy: the freedom to exercise choice and to make decisions based on an extended training, and on accumulated clinical expertise. Indeed, an ethical obligation within supervision is to promote autonomy, in terms of encouraging supervisees' self-determination and empowerment. Adding to the inherent tension between autonomy and authority, clinicians may experience a growing sense that organisations are exercising ever-increasing control over their activities (e.g., outcome monitoring, efficiency initiatives, clinical guidelines, practice standards and audits, annual performance reviews, and evidence based practice). This may seem to some to be rampant 'managerialism', creating growing resentment towards organisational control, and setting the scene for responses that create difficult interpersonal issues. A common example is the arrangement where the service manager is also the clinical supervisor, a dual relationship where the potential for strife is clearly significant. For example, supervisees may hesitate to disclose any of their clinical mishaps to their manager, for fear of undermining their career prospects. Indeed, 'non-disclosure' by supervisees is known to be frequent and clinically significant, even in supervision relationships that do not involve a manager (Ladany et al., 1996). For instance, trainees may seek to present a favourable picture of their competence and so omit to mention their errors, omissions, or 'near-misses', hoping to create a favourable impression and evaluation. In Table 2.1 we summarise these

Table 2.1 A summary of factors that may heighten a supervisor's anxiety, or limit the implementation and effectiveness of supervision (based on Kadushin & Harkness, 2002).

Barriers to supervision	Concerns and considerations, to aid the supervisor's reflections	Examples
State of the art	How advanced are the clinical interventions? Are the techniques clear enough to permit confidence in their application? If rather basic and rather unclear, this increases the barrier.	Supervisees may resist advanced techniques (e.g., high technologies).
Competing approaches	Is there anything about the supervision approach that influences collaboration? Are there diversity aspects, such as different views of treatment, or of the patients' role? Do ideologies conflict (e.g., role of supervisor seen as peer or equal; organisational hierarchy seen as old fashioned or irrelevant).	In therapy, the different theoretical orientations can create divisions or low motivation (e.g., between CBT & psychodynamic psychotherapy). Supervisees may quietly undermine or subtly challenge approaches that suggest that they are power-down (e.g., unfavourable comparisons drawn with other supervisors).
Competence	Are you sure that your supervision skills are up-to-date and appropriate? Would your peers agree? Do you follow authoritative guidelines or attend refresher training events? Lack of self-confidence or competence may also jeopardise success, or limit use of latest techniques. Difficult to measure or prove appropriateness of supervision, which may encourage rather cautious and basic approach. Can you be sure that you are more expert clinically?	Too much or too little supervisory competence risks the supervisees' collaboration. For example, challenging experiential techniques used by highly able supervisors may scare supervisees (e.g., irrationally fearing being found out as an imposter). Supervisees may use their 'countervailing' power to undermine supervisors' authority or effectiveness.
Lack of information	Do you know what your supervisee is actually doing? Have you a clear picture of their patients' needs, and does your supervisee have the necessary competencies? How much discretion is the supervisee exercising, and are you comfortable with the associated risks?	Complexity of clinical work and the healthcare environment (including patients) makes it hard to judge the difficulty of the work, and hard to assess progress. Supervisee may exacerbate matters, by ensuring that you have insufficient information (difficult to know what supervisee is doing if they avoid sharing hard data or co-working; also hard to infer effects of supervision/get feedback).

(Continued)

Formulation | 33

Table 2.1 (Continued)

Barriers to supervision	Concerns and considerations, to aid the supervisor's reflections	Examples
Unsupportive context	Has your employer provided you with clear objectives, so that you are sure you are working towards shared goals? Are there policies, guidelines, support, and training? Does your employing organisation share your idea of supervision?	Organisations may be vague about the kind of supervision you should be doing, including a lack of endorsed methods, published objectives, or a system for ensuring that there is corrective feedback. As a result, you may be at cross-purposes, and encounter a lack of support or even counter-control (e.g., public criticism).
Supervisees' power	You may have the authority to supervise, but do you have the power? Both parties have access to different kinds of power: are these balanced sufficiently to enable collaboration?	Supervisees may use their 'countervailing' power to undermine supervisors' authority or effectiveness. Transactional 'games' may be played (e.g., 'treat me, don't beat me')

and other barriers to effective supervision, taking into account contextual, organisational and interpersonal issues.

Supervisors are human too and have themselves been known to 'play games' that avoid anxiety (Kadushin, 1968; McIntosh et al., 2006). These games are interpersonal manoeuvres or transactions which have the ulterior motive of easing any tensions and avoiding critical issues. An example is 'Two against the agency', in which the supervisor minimises their status to play the role of supportive colleague, playing the role of an ally of the supervisee in relation to a tyrannical employer. Supervisees have been known to be fine game players themselves. An example is 'BBC-manship', in which the supervisee employs technical wizardry to ward-off the threat of being proved an imposter, as in procrastinating over supplying a recording of their work to the supervisor (e.g., by tinkering with state-of-the-art recording equipment, to ensure that the eventual recording is of sufficiently high fidelity to merit the supervisor's attention). In turn, those who manage the supervisors and supervisees may choose 'quick-fix' organisational arrangements, such as regularly cancelling supervision (Gonge & Buus, 2010), or substituting 'peer supervision' for authentic supervision (Martin et al., 2017). Peer supervision is a popular way of avoiding proper supervision, at least in the UK's National Health Service (NHS), although these kinds of denials also appear to occur internationally (Beddoe & Davys, 2016). Unfortunately, peer supervision is an illogical, risky, and educationally flawed arrangement (Martin et al., 2017). Nonetheless, it has become popular, partly as it enables supervisees to avoid the anxiety associated with more formal supervision arrangements. Due to the lack of oversight of the supervisees' work, and the absence of authority (e.g., there is typically no observation or corrective feedback), the supervisee basically has the freedom to do as they please: the arrangement lacks accountability relationships. Another common contributor to this form of pseudo-supervision is the mutual avoidance, by supervisor and supervisee, of the kind of experiential learning which might provide vital information on ways to improve supervision, or reveal either party as a fraud or imposter (e.g., educational role-plays; modelling competent practice; recordings of representative clinical work: Milne et al., 2009). The managers and other stakeholders are also colluding with peer supervision, perhaps because this arrangement is convenient, cheap, and popular. This is as there is no need to employ a proper supervisor, as anyone can assume the role of supervisor, and everyone is relieved that the usual threats and tensions associated with authority are replaced by the comforting warmth of peer support. While such social support undoubtedly has a vital role to play in professional life, including supervision (Milne & Reiser, 2020), they are examples of 'sham' or 'phantom' supervision (Shapiro & Smith, 2011), and no substitute for authentic supervision.

Conclusions

Supervision should be a profoundly satisfying activity, enabling young professionals to flourish, and encouraging more senior colleagues to contribute to the future of their profession. But as we have seen, supervision is also fraught with challenges, such as the critical issue of balancing responsibility with authority. There are powerful motivations, such as anxiety, that can often encourage supervisors to avoid dealing effectively with the inherent power imbalance between supervisee and supervisor. Avoidance may well escalate problems, and risk harming patients. By contrast, we have argued that adaptive coping strategies better characterise a professional orientation to supervision, and one that can resolve critical issues. Clinical supervision that is implemented and practiced in a professional manner is necessarily founded on a hierarchical relationship, with explicit terms of appointment and a specified scope of responsibility, as clarified by the employing organisation. This does not imply an authoritarian stance, nor that supervisees should be disempowered, but rather that supervisors and supervisees need to be encouraged and supported in establishing an appropriate collaborative alliance. This uses authority and personal power minimally and sensitively, as appropriate to the context, in pursuit of patient well-being. We believe that this is the appropriate supervisory relationship. The supervision contract helpfully addresses many of these issues, providing a firm foundation for a satisfying experience of supervision. In the next chapter we highlight the importance of supervisory authority within the legal context, including the vexed matter of vicarious liability.

Action Implications

What are the main action implications for proactively addressing the authority–autonomy tension? The following suggestions are based on Copeland et al. (2011), Haarman (2013), and on Polychronis and Brown (2016), with elaboration and detail drawn from our own experience.

- **Face up to critical issues:** Collusion and similar behaviours represent a collective form of maladaptive coping, one that is based on avoiding difficult issues. This is maladaptive due to the likelihood that problems will mount (e.g., client harm; expensive lawsuits for malpractice). A clear illustration that involved pseudo-supervision as an organisational avoidance strategy can be found in the report on the Morecambe Bay disaster (Kirkup, 2015). Find ways to strike the right balance between authority and responsibility, such that supervisees feel free to flourish, within the proper limits.

- **Think before you act:** A related implication is to adjust and refine the adaptive coping strategies of participating individuals, and the associated organisational arrangements, through the process of problem formulation. Although there are many different ways to conduct formulations of the issues and dilemmas that commonly emerge in supervision, hopefully this chapter serves to indicate the significant kinds of psychological and systemic forces that help us to understand what is happening, and why problems arise. Such formulations represent the best guide to corrective action, although of course a formulation should be developed for the specific critical issue in a particular context.
- **Clarify authority and accountability:** An example that might well emerge from a specific formulation is to ensure initial clarity of purpose, including clear lines of accountability. A direct discussion and review of the supervision contract and related policy statements formalises relevant aspects of authority and responsibility, as per the above illustration (consultancy versus supervision). Supervisors must be given the formal authority to play their role, while the respective responsibilities and accountability arrangements should be clear to all parties. From the start of a supervisory relationship, discuss the legal and clinical requirements indicated by this hierarchical context, including the the need for ongoing documentation.
- **Clarify the role:** Ensure that supervision is specified as a duty by the employing body (the 'principal party' in law), and that it is consistent with any policy statements or other formal guidance on the terms, scope and responsibilities of supervision (within the employing organisation, and consistent with guidance from relevant professional associations and registration bodies). Supervision should be organised so that the supervisor and employer have given their informed consent, according to the publicly agreed terms and scope of supervision.
- **Communicate:** It is of course vitally important to also inform patients of the supervisory arrangements that are in place, to avoid any misunderstandings and to safeguard the clinician–patient relationship (e.g., regarding working relationships, confidentiality, and complaints). If the terms and scope of supervision are addressed at the outset, then misunderstandings and acts of negligence can be more easily addressed during supervision, and tackled within the supervisee's provision of treatment. Equally, it will be more apparent to all parties when a clinician–patient relationship is floundering. This may actually be because the patient is fully informed of the supervisory arrangement that is in place (to safeguard their treatment), so enhancing communication; or because the procedure for raising concerns or making complaints is straightforward.

Supervisees must be informed about the mutual duties and responsibilities, with key points supplied in writing (e.g., within the supervision contract). This should include an understanding that supervision is fundamentally a hierarchical relationship, and therefore that supervisees must accept certain responsibilities (e.g., to keep their supervisor

fully informed, including the provision of work samples, compliance with the supervisor's directives). The bottom line is that supervisees are legally the 'hands and legs' of the supervisor (Haarman, 2013, p. 139).
- **Monitor:** Supervisors should monitor the clinical work of their supervisees, which may include screening patients in terms of their suitability, in order to match suitable patients to their supervisee's training needs and experience, the regular review of clinical outcome data, convening meetings with the supervisees' patients, or directly providing treatment to these patients. Monitoring should include ongoing discussions and evaluation of the supervision itself. We need to be wary of adopting a dogmatic stance in which seniority or expertise bestow automatic correctness of judgement, and try to consider what is right or acceptable from different perspectives, including of course that of the supervisee. Supervisors should teach from their understanding and expertise, while being sensitive to power dynamics, so that they end up empowering the supervisees to collaborate and co-construct (in supervision and clinical practice).
- **Organise:** Managers, clinical leaders, and administrators shoulder responsibility for ensuring that there are detailed written policies governing supervision. For example, there should be explicit performance standards that include the supervisee, together with best-practice guidelines. According to Recupero and Rainey (2007) 'A well-run programme with structured supervision guidelines is likely to carry less risk than one characterised by unclear or poorly communicated standards. To minimise risk, policies should be well documented and agreed on by all who enter into supervisory relationships' (p. 191).

Acknowledgements

We are grateful for feedback on a draft version of this chapter from lawyer Ken Hunt, and a second legal advisor, who prefers to remain anonymous.

References

American Psychological Association. (2015). Guidelines for clinical supervision in health service psychology. *The American Psychologist, 70*(1), 33–46. https://doi.org/10.1037/a0038112

Beddoe, L., & Davys, A. (2016). *Challenges in professional supervision*. Jessica Kingsley Publishers.

Buus, N., Lisa Lynch, L., & Gonge, H. (2016). Developing and implementing 'meta-supervision' for mental health nursing staff supervisees: Opportunities and challenges. *The Cognitive Behaviour Therapist, 9*, e22. https://doi.org/10.1017/S1754470X15000434

Copeland, P., Dean, R. G., & Wladkowski, S. P. (2011). The power dynamics of supervision: Ethical dilemmas. *Smith College Studies in Social Work, 81*(1), 26–40. https://doi.org/10.1080/00377317.2011.543041

References

Falender, C. A., & Shafranske, E. (2004). *Clinical Supervision: A competency-based approach*. APA.

Gonge, H., & Buus, N. (2010). Individual and workplace factors that influence psychiatric nursing staff's participation in clinical supervision: A survey study and prospective longitudinal registration. *Issues in Mental Health Nursing, 31*(5), 345–354.https://doi.org/10.3109/01612840903427849

Haarman, G. B. (2013). *Clinical Supervision: Legal, ethical and risk management issues*. Foundations: Education & Consultation.

Hawkins, P., & McMahon, A. (2020). *Supervision in the Helping Professions*. Open University Press.

Kadushin, A. (1968). *Supervision in Social Work*. Columbia University Press.

Kadushin, A., & Harkness, D. (2002). *Supervision in Social Work* (4th ed.). Columbia University Press.

Kirkup, B. (2015). *Morecambe Bay Investigation*. This publication is available at https://www.gov.uk/government/publications. ISBN 9780108561306

Knapp, S. J., & VandeCreek, L. (2006). Practical ethics for psychologists. In *A positive Approach*. American Psychological Association.

Ladany, N., Hill, C. E., Corbett, M. M., & Nutt, E. A. (1996). Nature, extent, and importance of what psychotherapy trainees do not disclose to their supervisors. *Journal of Counselling Psychology, 43*(1), 10–24. https://doi.org/10.1037/0022-0167.43.1.10

Lu, D., Suetani, S., Cutbush, J., & Parker, S. (2019). Supervision contracts for mental health professionals: A systematic review and exploration of the potential relevance to psychiatry training in Australia and New Zealand. *Australasian Psychiatry, 27*(3), 225–229. https://doi.org/10.1177/103985621984548

Martin, P., Reiser, R., & Milne, D. (2017). Peer supervision: International problems and prospects. *Journal of Advanced Nursing, 74*(5), 998–999. https://doi.org/10.1111/jan.13413

McIntosh, N., Dircks, A., Fitzpatrick, J., & Shuman, C. (2006). Games in clinical genetic counselling supervision. *Journal of Genetic Counselling, 15*(4), 225–243. https://doi.org/10.1007/s10897-006-9029-4

Milne, D., & Reiser, R. P. (2020). *Supportive Clinical Supervision: Enhancing Well-Being and Reducing Burnout Through Restorative Leadership*. Pavilion.

Milne, D. L., Leck, C., & Choudhri, N. Z. (2009). Collusion in clinical supervision: Literature review and case study in self-reflection. *The Cognitive Behaviour Therapist, 2*(2), 106–114. https://doi.org/10.1017/S1754470X0900018X

Milne, D. L., & Reiser, R. P. (2017). *A Manual for Evidence based CBT Supervision*. Wiley-Blackwell.

Norberg, J., Axelsson, H., Barkman, N., Hamrin, M., & Carlsson, J. (2016). What psychodynamic supervisors say about supervision: Freedom within limits. *The Clinical Supervisor, 35*(2), 268–286. https://doi.org/10.1080/07325223.2016.1219896

Nursing and Midwifery Council (NMC). (2018). *The Code: Professional standards of practice and behaviour for nurses, midwives and nursing associates*. NMC.

Polychronis, P. D., & Brown, S. G. (2016). The strict liability standard and clinical supervision. *Professional Psychology: Research and Practice, 47*(2), 139–146.https://doi.org/10.1037/pro0000073

Recupero, P. R., & Rainey, S. E. (2007). Liability and risk management in outpatient psychotherapy supervision. *Journal of the American Academy of Psychiatry and the Law, 35*(2), 188–195.

Shapiro, D. L., & Smith, S. R. (2011). *Malpractice in psychology: A practical resource for clinicians.* American Psychological Association. http://dx.doi.org/10.1037/12320-000

Thomas, J. T. (2014). Disciplinary supervision following ethics complaints: Goals, tasks, and ethical dimensions. *Journal of Clinical Supervision: In Session, 70*(11), 1104–1114.

Watkins, C. E., & Wang, C. D. C. (2014). On the education of clinical supervisors. In C. E. Watkins & D. L. Milne (Eds.), *The Wiley International Handbook of Clinical Supervision* (pp. 177–203). Wiley-Blackwell.

Webb, K. L., Bullock, A., Groves, C., Saayman, A. G. (2017). A mixed methods evaluation of the educational supervision agreement for Wales. *BMJ Open, 7*(7), e015541. https://doi.org/10.1136/bmjopen-2016-015541.

3

Who Is Ultimately Responsible for Patient Care?

Introduction

In Chapter 2 we concentrated on the supervisory relationship and the fundamental power imbalance between supervisor and supervisee. As a critical issue, this essentially pits freedom against control: the clinical autonomy of the supervisee creates a tension with the authority of the supervisor. In the present chapter we build on that foundation to consider the vexed matter of clinical responsibility. We will next explain the legal context, so that readers can clearly understand the need to strike a suitable balance between freedom and control. Following this formulation, we will then summarise some professional coping strategies, in the form of risk management actions and specific recommendations of relevance to all targeted readership groups (especially supervisors). In this way, we will explain who is responsible for patient care, provide illustrations drawn from professional practice, and indicate a suitable, evidence-based response that can help us to resolve this critical issue.

Illustration

This anecdotal illustration concerns the long-standing confusion over who shoulders clinical responsibility. In our experience, supervisors will tend to minimise or even deny clinical responsibility for the work of their supervisees. One of us (DM) knows this from having played the role of 'clinical tutor' for a decade, a consultant to supervisors on behalf of a university-based training programme. For instance, at supervision workshops DM typically asked for a show of hands in response to the question: 'Who accepts that they are responsible for the clinical work of their supervisee?' In the very many workshops that he led over the years, attended by over 1,000 supervisors, DM cannot recall ever seeing a majority of hands going up among a group of supervisors. Instead, supervisors would often become anxious about their responsibilities, as if in denial. A difficult discussion usually ensued, which allowed DM to emphasise this reality: supervisors are likely to be held clinically responsible. His goal was to encourage a thoroughly professional approach. By contrast, supervisees were more than comfortable with the concept of the supervisor carrying ultimate responsibility, consistent with the perspectives adopted by training organisations, managers, and others in universities in the UK.

Resolving Critical Issues in Clinical Supervision: A Practical, Evidence-based Approach, First Edition.
Derek L. Milne and Robert P. Reiser.
© 2023 John Wiley & Sons Ltd. Published 2023 by John Wiley & Sons Ltd.

Staying on the Right Side of the Law

But are supervisors always responsible? Do supervisees not also shoulder some responsibility? In any case, surely if employees, they will be protected from personal litigation? We will now set about addressing these legal questions. The need for supervisors to assume the hierarchical, authoritative role noted in Chapter 2 has been illuminated through an exacting examination by the legal system. For example, the failure to monitor and control the behaviour of a supervisee has been underscored by a Delaware case, Masterson v. Board of Examiners of Psychologists (1995). The supervisor Masterson lost her licence because she allowed the supervisee to exploit social relationships (counselling a friend). Ethical supervision is similar to ethical practice in other areas of professional life, and there are detailed guidelines that govern the conduct of supervisors (e.g., American Psychological Association, 2015; Association of State and Provincial Psychology Boards, 2020; British Psychological Society, 2018) and detailed texts (e.g., Knapp et al., 2017; Thomas, 2014). In addition, supervisors will hopefully have access to colleagues, consultants, managers, and others who can reflect with them on difficulties, drawing on the above principles to tackle ethical or relationship issues appropriately. However, there are bottom-line legal parameters that must be recognised, even though they might conflict with the dominant professional culture (i.e., the increasing democratisation of supervision, and general collegial 'niceness'). The law provides exceptionally clear and well-reasoned principles and precedents, representing a vital point of reference when dealing with critical issues inherent to clinical supervision. A particularly anxiety-provoking example is the situation where a supervisor or employer may be held directly liable for the clinical negligence of a supervisee.

Vicarious Liability

Liability means being responsible or answerable in law. According to this definition, a supervisor may be the subject of a legal challenge, charged with direct responsibility for their own negligence (e.g., as a result of unethical acts, like relationship boundary violations; or through providing flawed advice on treatment techniques). In Andrews v. United States (1984), a supervisor failed to investigate an allegation of a supervisee's sexual relationship with a patient and was found liable in negligently failing to handle the complaint appropriately. Haarman (2013) gives the example of a supervisor who repeatedly cancelled supervision sessions, which resulted in harm to the supervisee's patients, because the supervisee had not exercised the necessary clinical competence. This example meets the definition of liability, in that a successful claimant (the supervisee and/or the patient) could show that they have suffered foreseeable loss or harm as a direct result of such negligence (i.e., a breach of the supervisor's professional duty of care, the responsibilities owed to the supervisee and the patient). Consequently, the supervisor may have to pay damages to a supervisee and/or a patient. In turn, vicarious responsibility means being answerable in law for the actions of others. Vicarious responsibility follows from the legal theory of *respondeat superior* (let the master answer), in which an employer or employee is held responsible for the malpractice of its staff. Similarly, if self-employed, the supervisor may be held vicariously liable for the work of their supervisee. This liability depends primarily on the demonstration of clinical negligence.

Negligence is defined as carelessness (e.g., omissions) and/or a failure to perform one's professional duties properly (e.g., incompetence), directly causing foreseeable harm. Failure to adequately supervise is among the top ten forms of negligence in the USA leading to malpractice lawsuits, with inadequate or improper supervision ranked fifth among violations considered by State Psychology Licencing Boards in the USA (Haarman, 2013). One precondition that may increase vicarious liability is when the supervisee formally agrees to work under the direction and control of the supervisor (i.e., gives informed consent, usually through signing a supervision contract). This makes it a formal, professional relationship. Liability is increased if the supervisor deviates from the appropriate standards of care, entailing a breach of their responsibilities; and if that breach directly causes foreseeable harm (Harrar et al., 1990). This is re-stated by Haarman (2013): a successful malpractice suit, one that proves professional negligence, has to demonstrate the 'four D's': *dereliction of duty directly causing damages*. But as we shall see, there are significant qualifications to these statements, especially in the USA.

In addition to negligence, vicarious liability depends on the nature of the employment relationship. This is not simply a matter of whether or not one is an employee or is self-employed (private practice): generally, the employment status of the supervisor is not relevant in law. Rather, to incur vicarious responsibility, the working relationship must be such that the supervisor (or supervisee) is acting within the limits of the ordinary course of the employer's business (i.e., there is a close connection to that business, or other employer-authorised activities). That is, it is the supervisor's responsibilities and working practices that are the proper focus in considering liability. For example, an employing body may be held vicariously liable if it makes a contract with a supervisor in private practice, one in which the supervisory tasks and methods to be used are specified, and where they clearly represent doing the authorised and closely connected business of the employer. The legal reasoning is that these kinds of similarities to employment make it right for the employer to be held liable.

By contrast, the phrase used in the UK for not acting in a manner that is akin to the employer's business is that an individual is 'on a frolic of their own', engaging in actions that are not 'fairly or properly' connected with the employer's business (e.g., embezzling the employer; causing malicious damage; having sex with patients). In this instance, the employer will not normally be held vicariously liable. To illustrate, Polychronis and Brown (2016) cite an example from the USA where a psychologist had repeated sexual interactions with a current patient, often within the clinic during their psychotherapy appointments. The psychologist's employer (not his clinical supervisor) was also named in the lawsuit as vicariously liable for the psychologist's misconduct, under the theory of *respondeat superior*. The court ultimately found that the employer was not liable for the damages to the client, reasoning that the offending psychologist's behaviour was clearly a 'frolic', outside of the scope and course of his employment. In other instances, supervisors have been found negligent in cases of inappropriate sexual relationships between supervisees and patients, because they should monitor therapy and should know what is taking place, through closely supervising the supervisee's work (Simmons v. United States, 1986).

This legal distinction between doing the work of the employer and engaging in personal 'frolics' has been reaffirmed in a recent Supreme Court judgement in the UK (Morrison Supermarkets v. Various Claimants, 2020). A second Supreme Court judgement dealt with the associated issue of whether the relationship between the parties is 'akin to employment' (Barclays Bank v. Various Claimants, 2020). In other words, at least in the UK, vicarious liability provides for a two-stage test, and these 2020 cases deal with each in turn. As a consequence of passing these two tests (i.e., a relationship akin to employment, and a close connection between the employer's business and the malpractice), supervisors and supervisees in employment (or in a relationship akin to employment) appear only likely to be held directly liable when engaged in deviant actions serving their own private purposes (i.e., having 'frolics' that depart significantly from the employer's business). Consequently, there have been very few direct liability actions against clinical supervisors. Furthermore, these actions appear to be non-existent outside the USA (Hawkins & McMahon, 2020), and even within the USA only a minority of cases lead to successful prosecutions. For example, in social work only 12 of 634 lawsuits resulted in the supervisor being sued (Kadushin & Harkness, 2002). Also, there has apparently not yet been a single test case of strict liability decided by a jury or a trial court. To date, it appears that such cases have been resolved through an out-of-court settlement for damages (Polychronis & Brown, 2016).

Implications

But before taking an unduly relaxed perspective, it is important to realise that these legal precedents and principles that govern the evaluative judgements of vicarious or direct liability are not set in stone: ultimately, every instance is arguable in court, and judgements can be highly fact-specific (i.e., taking due account of the details of the situation). The implication one might draw as a supervisor is to practice in a vigilant and demonstrably professional manner (i.e., consistent with best-practice guidelines), and entirely consistent with the employer's business (e.g., where authorisation and responsibilities are specified in writing: Polychronis & Brown, 2016).

Strict Liability

Another reason to stay vigilant and professional about supervision is the advent of 'strict liability', at least if you work in the USA, where 'the concept of strict liability makes supervisors responsible for supervisees' actions, without having to establish that a given supervisor was negligent or careless. Consequently, in jurisdictions where the strict liability standard is used, it is virtually inevitable that clinical supervisors will be named in civil suits over a supervisee's actions, regardless of whether a supervisor has been appropriately conscientious' (Polychronis & Brown, 2016, p. 139). To make matters worse, this does not preclude attempts by lawyers to discredit supervisors and their supervisory approaches, to strengthen their argument. This has led to the view that clinical supervision is a risky business, at least in the USA, best conducted within the confines of employment (i.e., where the supervisor may be indemnified against the attendant risks by their employer).

Illustration

Supervision of Practicum Students in a University Training Clinic

The director of a University training clinic was responsible for managing 12 supervisors who provided the direct supervision for psychology students in a second-year practicum (placement). Clinic supervisors were a mix of faculty employed by the University and others were who were part-time independent contractors hired by the clinic exclusively to provide supervision (i.e., self-employed supervisors). In practice, the great majority of supervisors were independently contracted and very few faculty supervised in the clinic. All 12 supervisors were independently licensed clinicians operating under their own psychology license (professional registration). Contracted supervisors were selected for their commitment to utilising evidence-based practices in psychotherapy and their theoretical orientation and consistency to the CBT orientation espoused in the clinic.

With the advent of the new clinic director, the clinic had also instituted a standard written supervision agreement, and each supervisor was required to review this agreement with their supervisees. Latterly, the clinic director brought in a supervision expert who provided a two-day training on the fundamentals of supervision. While this training was not mandatory for clinic supervisors, it was attended by most of them. Clinic supervisors (with the exception of a handful of advanced graduate students who provided supervision) did not receive direct individual supervision of their supervision. Instead, they were asked to participate in a monthly administrative meeting designed to address any supervision problems with students, and to assure that there was a consistent application of clinic policies and guidelines within supervision. While most of the clinic supervisors routinely attended this monthly meeting, the bulk of time was taken up with questions about clinic policies and guidelines, and supervisors were very reluctant to bring up specific problems with individual supervisees. This reticence seemed to stem from the fact that most supervisors were reluctant to share their supervisory work in a general meeting. Hence, in practice, very little specific oversight of student trainee problems occurred in this potentially valuable forum.

Another area of concern was that while the individual supervision agreement was quite specific and detailed as to supervisory roles, responsibilities, and expectations, the employment contract with the University was extremely generic, and did not have any clear or specific language specifying the contractual obligations for supervisors beyond simply elaborating on the fixed number of supervision hours that would be required during a term, and the responsibility for attending the administrative monthly meeting.

Hence, based on the loose provisions of this employment agreement, clinic supervisors had a good deal of freedom to operate with a wide degree of latitude. Furthermore, as they were all independently licensed clinicians, they were reluctant to accept close supervision of their supervisory practices. In practice, clinic supervisors had quite different supervisory styles, some adhering to a more formal approach to supervision, but many supervisors tended to take a more collaborative and relaxed approach, in some cases being willing to sign therapy notes with very little review, and not insisting on the direct observation of the student (despite a clinic requirement that all student therapy sessions would be videotaped). Furthermore, lines of authority were blurred by the fact that senior tenured faculty supervised in the clinic, but the clinic director was a relatively junior, non-tenured faculty member.

Reflections on This Illustration

This case illustrates many of the problems discussed in this chapter, including the difficulties supervisors experience taking responsibility, the problems employers face in coping with strict and vicarious liability, and the challenges of managing multiple supervisors within a clinic setting who have different employment and status relationships. How good a job did this organisation do overall in managing its legal liability in supervising students? This is a complex question and deserves attention at several levels. At the first level, having a formal supervision agreement between supervisors and students provides a framework for informed consent (see Chapter 2). If that supervision contract also spells out roles, rules, responsibilities, obligations, and clinic policy, then it can provide a potentially very effective means of clarifying the legal and professional context for supervision. It likely encourages supervisors to adopt an appropriately formal relationship with their supervisee, as opposed to falling into the trap of simply being 'nice' colleagues. Unfortunately, at the second level, the value of this supervision agreement was eroded by the fact that in practice, supervisors were themselves only loosely supervised. They received no routine supervision of supervision where their work was observed, and discussion of student training cases in the administrative meeting was quite limited. Also, because many supervisors were independent contractors who worked part-time for the clinic, extended periods of observation or discussion were often impractical. Similarly, as the clinic director wanted more senior faculty supervisors involved, he tended to give them sufficient autonomy to operate independently. This was compounded by status, in that the senior tenured faculty in the clinic were hardly disposed to report to the clinic director, a non-tenured junior faculty member.

In this context, it was not surprising that there was a good deal of variability in the standards which supervisors applied to their practice: some being quite formal and structured, and others being loose and informal, and hence less likely to adhere to best practices in supervision (standards such as directly observing supervisees). A potentially complicating factor was the fact that the lines of responsibility between the clinic director and senior tenured faculty were at times ambiguous and not well defined. For example, when a senior faculty member indicated in an aside that he rarely read students' progress notes, the clinic director felt conflicted about challenging him on this important lack of oversight. In short, the clinic director did not consistently ensure adherence to the clinic's policy on supervision standards, by neglecting to provide proper oversight of supervision. In turn, this undermined any standards that might have been judiciously specified in the supervision agreement between supervisor and supervisee.

Finally, at a third level a significant weakness in this system was the fact that the employment contract with the University for independent contractors (i.e., self-employed supervisors) was quite generic, and vague as to specific expectations of a clinical supervisor. Specifically, it did not reference the supervision agreement, clinic policy, or best practice guidelines for supervision, nor state explicit terms of appointment, or specify the scope of responsibility. This of course leaves a great deal of room for variations in supervision practice, limiting accountability to the employing organisation (see Chapter 2 for more). Consequently, if there had been a legal complaint filed about a student trainee by a patient, this contractual gap and limited oversight of supervisors might suggest unwanted additional liability for the University.

This real-world example of a supervision system was intended to illustrate the inherent complexity and challenges of operating within a complex, multilevel organisational system. These reflections should be viewed in their historical context, given that these events occurred before the advent of many best practice guidelines for supervisors. For example, American Psychological Association guidelines on supervision were published in 2015, several years after these events recorded above took place. Unfortunately, based on current standards, we must conclude that the lack of close monitoring and oversight of supervisors potentially represents a failure of the professional duty of care to supervisees, and consequently that any legal action taken against a negligent faculty supervisor by a supervisee could presumably hold the University directly responsible for the negligence of the supervisor, in seemingly not ensuring that its policies were clearly stated within the contract, and duly implemented (i.e., accountable, in accord with respondeat superior). In essence, this illustration portrays a real-world clinic that was striving towards meeting a higher standard of supervision but fell short in adopting the appropriate formal and legal relationships that might have provided additional protection and more rigorous risk management.

Conclusions

Clinical supervision that is implemented and practiced in a professional manner is based on a hierarchical relationship with explicit terms of appointment and a specified scope of responsibility. Managers, clinical leaders, and administrators shoulder responsibility for ensuring that there are detailed written policies governing these and other aspects of supervision. For example, there should be explicit performance standards that include the supervisee, together with best-practice guidelines. According to Recupero and Rainey (2007) 'A well-run programme with structured supervision guidelines is likely to carry less risk than one characterised by unclear or poorly communicated standards. To minimise risk, policies should be well documented and agreed on by all who enter into supervisory relationships' (p. 191). As noted in the preceding section on risk-management strategies, supervisors, supervisees, and other stakeholders also shoulder their fair share of the responsibilities for a professional approach. In this way, we can reduce the likelihood of facing many of the critical issues that may arise in supervision.

To provide clarity and to encourage vigilance, this chapter has taken a legal perspective to such vexatious issues as authority and responsibility. This carries the added benefit of providing exceptionally well-reasoned principles and precedents, representing a vital point of reference when dealing with the many issues and dilemmas inherent within clinical supervision. The rarity of legal proceedings in relation to clinical supervision, at least outside the USA, should not be taken as evidence that all is well, nor that supervisors have nothing to fear. In the previous chapter we highlighted how a range of avoidance behaviours involving supervisors, supervisees, and clinical service managers, among others (e.g., training programme staff), can undermine the quality of supervision, increasing the risk of litigation. These behaviours are worryingly common (Martin et al., 2017), and include major concerns, such as engaging in pseudo-supervision (Shapiro & Smith, 2011) or peer supervision. These behaviours undermine the effectiveness of supervision, hamper treatment success, carry the risk of causing harm, and may trigger litigation leading in turn to hugely significant costs to healthcare organisations (Milne & Reiser, 2020). Even when supervision is addressed in a professional manner, there often remain worrying weaknesses, such as the brief, inadequate, or non-existent training of supervisors (Watkins & Wang, 2014), or the absence of regular supervision within organisations (Gonge & Buus, 2010). These increase the risk of professional negligence, with the associated consequences.

Two critical tests influence liability in law: whether there is a relationship akin to employment, and whether a close connection exists between the employer's business and the malpractice. Supervisors who pass these two tests appear only likely to be held directly liable when engaged in private 'frolics'. But it is important to understand that the legal precedents and principles that govern the evaluative judgements of vicarious or direct liability are all potentially arguable in court, and prior judgements can be highly fact-specific. The conclusion one might draw as a supervisor is to assume that you are 'liable to be held liable', and therefore to practice in a demonstrably professional manner (i.e., consistent with best-practice guidelines), entirely congruent with the employer's business (e.g., where responsibilities are specified in writing).

We should close with a disclaimer: we have no legal background or expertise. Although we have taken reasonable steps to confirm the accuracy of the chapter's legal contents, those readers who are faced with legal action will no doubt wish to take independent legal advice from a suitably experienced practitioner, with sufficient expertise in the relevant field and jurisdiction.

Action Implications: Risk Management

We believe that 'being conscientious' (i.e., vigilant and professional) remains vital, regardless of the strict liability standard. This is because a professional approach minimises the risk of harm in the first place, and because a test case might well take such professionalism into account. The 'risk management' suggestions that follow operationalise what we recommend as a professional approach to supervision. In the USA, supervisors have been held legally accountable for the malpractice (professional negligence) of their supervisees. According to Hawkins and McMahon (2020), a supervisor has not yet been held legally accountable outside the USA. However, there is a growing risk of legal action, as litigation is also generally on the increase, at least in the UK and the USA (Kadushin & Harkness, 2002). Therefore, we recommend the working assumption that supervisors are 'liable to be liable'. As a precaution, Hawkins and McMahon (2020) emphasised the importance of supervisors and others taking out professional liability insurance. In addition, we should note the associated threat that practice licenses or other credentials may be suspended or revoked, alongside the employment and disciplinary threats associated with complaints or malpractice. In this increasingly litigious context, clinical supervisors and other interested parties would be wise to consider some risk-management strategies. There now follow the main action implications arising from this chapter. They are based on Copeland et al. (2011), Haarman (2013), Kadushin and Harkness (2002), and Polychronis and Brown (2016). We have added some elaboration and detail, drawn from our own experience. As a result, we identify the 'top ten' risk management strategies as follows:

Conclusions | 47

- Supervisors should receive initial and continuing evidence-based training in supervision (CPD), including support materials such as supervision guidelines; video-presented demonstrations of competent supervision. As stated in the ASPPB (2020) guidelines: 'It is equally vital that the supervisor is competent in supervision that is to have the appropriate education, training, and experience in methods of effective supervision .... Having supervised without specific training in supervision for some period of time does not guarantee supervisor competence.' (p. 6) Supervisors should also consult regularly with suitably experienced and specialised colleagues, especially regarding any critical issues. In essence, supervisors should be able to routinely review their approach with a peer or a consultant, obtaining expert guidance and emotional support.
- In settings where independent private practitioners provide the clinical supervision for an employing body, a thorough screening process should be used for supervisor selection, one that includes background, training, and criminal history checks. Supervisors should also 'screen' their potential supervisees and have the right to decline to supervise unsuitable individuals.
- Supervisees must be informed about their duties and responsibilities, with key points supplied in writing within a supervision contract. This should include an understanding that supervision is fundamentally a hierarchical relationship, and therefore that supervisees must keep their supervisor fully informed, including the provision of work samples, and must ultimately comply with supervisors' directives. Specific recommendations as to the content of a supervision contract are available in The Association of State and Provincial Psychology Boards (ASPPB) Supervision Guidelines (ASPPB, 2020, p. 17).
- Supervisors should employ the same level of professionalism during supervision as in their clinical work. This includes maintaining appropriate relationship boundaries, and being accessible to their supervisees (including regular formal meetings, brief interim advice, and in emergencies). In conducting clinical supervision, the input of more than one supervisor is optimal for providing enhanced clinical oversight in relation to the supervisee's work.
- Supervisees should routinely provide written feedback on their supervision, shared with key stakeholders (e.g., managers; training programmes). Supervisees (and supervisors) should have ready access to a system for raising concerns, or for making complaints. In essence, there should be adequate information available within a supervision system to identify negligence as quickly as possible, and to promote excellence.
- Document, document, document! Keep written notes of all supervision sessions (or other key discussions, such as with managers), and encourage the supervisee to do the same. Polychronis and Brown (2016) note: 'The more thorough, detailed, and the greater the variety of content in clinical supervision documentation, the better. The more questions asked of supervisees, the better. The more sessions viewed while they are conducted, the better. The more video-recordings viewed after the sessions have been conducted, the better. The more of each individual video-recording that is viewed, the better.' (p. 149). Thomas (2010) suggests that supervision or consultation records include a case monitoring log on each individual client, summarising information briefly and recording dates the case was discussed in supervision; a progress note on the content of each session; and, if appropriate, work samples that have been reviewed for training

- purposes such as case notes and reports. So, in summary, while professional standards vary and may be quite non-specific as to how records are kept, there is a significant requirement for record keeping and, specifically for legal purposes 'more is better'.
- Through being fully informed, supervisors should monitor the clinical work of their supervisees, which may include screening patients in terms of their suitability, matching suitable patients to their supervisee's training needs and experience. It should also include the regular review of clinical outcome data, and, if indicated, assessing or treating the supervisees' patients.
- When such monitoring or evaluation indicates difficulties, problems should be thoroughly addressed according to the appropriate professional practice standards, such as an agreed and written plan for improvement (including fresh objectives and review plans). Through careful communication and documentation, it should be clear to eveyone what is required to resolve the problem, and how resolution will be pursued and demonstrated. Competence frameworks and similar public clarifications of competence are a valuable benchmark (e.g., supervision standards, guidelines, and video-presented demonstrations).
- Understand the law in relation to supervision, especially as it applies in your region; discuss ethical codes, and be aware of administrative regulations.

Finally, as there is clearly a threat of litigation in providing supervision, supervisors should consider professional liability insurance.

Acknowledgements

We are grateful for feedback on a draft version of this chapter from lawyer Ken Hunt and a second legal advisor, who prefers to remain anonymous.

References

Andrews v. United States. (1984). 732 F.2d 366 (4th Cir. 1984).
American Psychological Association. (2015). Guidelines for clinical supervision in health service psychology. *American Psychologist*, *70*(1), 33–46. https://doi.org/10.1037/a0038112
Association of State and Provincial Psychology Boards. (2020). Supervision Guidelines. Retrieved September 30, 2022 from https://cdn.ymaws.com/www.asppb.net/resource/resmgr/guidelines/asppb_supervision_guidelines.pdf
Barclays Bank v. Various Claimants. (2020). Case ID: UKSC 2018/0164.
British Psychological Society. (2018). *Code of ethics and conduct*. BPS.
Copeland, P., Dean, R. G., & Wladkowski, S. P. (2011). The power dynamics of supervision: Ethical dilemmas. *Smith College Studies in Social Work*, *81*(1), 26–40. https://doi.org/10.1080/00377317.2011.543041
Gonge, H., & Buus, N. (2010). Individual and workplace factors that influence psychiatric nursing staff's participation in clinical supervision: A survey study and prospective longitudinal registration. *Issues in Mental Health Nursing*, *31*(5), 345–354. https://doi.org/10.3109/01612840903427849

Haarman, G. B. (2013). *Clinical supervision: Legal, ethical and risk management issues.* Foundations: Education & Consultation.

Harrar, W. R., VandeCreek, L., & Knapp, S. (1990). Ethical and legal aspects of clinical supervision. *Professional Psychology, 21*(1), 37–41. https://doi.org/10.1037/0735-7028.21.1.37

Hawkins, P., & McMahon, A. (2020). *Supervision in the helping professions.* Open University Press.

Kadushin, A., & Harkness, D. (2002). *Supervision in social work* (4th ed.). Columbia University Press.

Knapp, S. J., VandeCreek, L., & Fingerhut, R. (2017). Practical ethics for psychologists. In *A positive approach.* American Psychological Association. http://dx.doi.org/10.1037/0000036-001

Martin, P., Reiser, R., & Milne, D. (2017). Peer supervision: International problems and prospects. *Journal of Advanced Nursing, 74*(5), 998–999. https://doi.org/10.1111/jan.13413

Masterson v. Board of Examiners of Psychologists. (1995). Del.Super. LEXIS 589, 1995 WL 790949 (Del. Super. Ct. 1995).

Milne, D., & Reiser, R. P. (2020). *Supportive clinical supervision: From burnout to well-being, through restorative leadership.* Pavilion.

Morrison Supermarkets v. Various Claimants. (2020). UKSC 12 On appeal from: [2018] EWCA Civ 2339.

Polychronis, P. D., & Brown, S. G. (2016). The strict liability standard and clinical supervision. *Professional Psychology: Research and Practice, 47*(2), 139–146. https://doi.org/10.1037/pro0000073

Recupero, P. R., & Rainey, S. E. (2007). Liability and risk management in outpatient psychotherapy supervision. *Journal of the American Academy of Psychiatry and the Law, 35*(2), 188–195.

Shapiro, D. L., & Smith, S. R. (2011). *Malpractice in psychology: A practical resource for clinicians.* American Psychological Association. http://dx.doi.org/10.1037/12320-000

Simmons v. United States. (1986). 805 F.2d 1363 (9th Cir. 1986).

Thomas, J. T. (2010). The ethics of supervision and consultation: Practical guidance for mental health professionals. American Psychological Association. https://doi.org/10.1037/12078-000

Thomas, J. T. (2014). Disciplinary supervision following ethics complaints: Goals, tasks, and ethical dimensions. *Journal of Clinical Supervision: In Session, 70*(11), 1–11. https://doi.org/10.1002/jclp.22131

Watkins, C. E., & Wang, C. D. C. (2014). On the education of clinical supervisors. In C. E. Watkins & D. L. Milne (Eds.), *The Wiley international handbook of clinical supervision* (pp. 177–203). Wiley-Blackwell.

4

Understanding Unethical Issues in Clinical Supervision

Introduction

Critical issues in supervision are dominated by ethical challenges. In the first chapter we surveyed textbooks, research, and relevant statistics to try to summarise the most common critical issues. We found that they concerned the problematic provision of supervision, including malpractice (a lack of due process in supervision); unethical behaviour towards the supervisee (e.g., bullying and relationship boundary violations); and misconduct (e.g., fraud and dishonesty). Part of the explanation for these three categories of unethical conduct may be the personal incapacity of the supervisor, namely physical or mental health problems that impair their conduct. Although less frequently mentioned, supervisees may also enact these unethical behaviours (e.g., manipulating the supervisor), and suffer from related problematic health status, attitudes, or behaviours (e.g., personality issues). This chapter focusses on these intertwined ethical issues, referred to under the heading of 'fitness to practise'. Based on an analysis of the ethics codes from 24 countries, it appears that there is considerable international agreement over these ethical challenges in supervision. For example, ten specific standards repeatedly occurred in more than 75% of these national codes of practice (e.g., respecting relationship boundaries: Leach & Harbin, 1997).

Chapter 1 also included an orientation to ethical conduct, noting that ethics runs through all areas of our work, representing the accepted conventions guiding how we ought to behave in professional life, 'helping to regulate, educate and guide us (e.g., with respect to doing no harm, doing what is beneficial, and doing justice'; Watkins & Milne, 2014, p. 684). These moral principles are founded on the value systems of individuals, and the ethical standards of their professional colleagues and organisations (other common principles are integrity, respect, and dignity). These values, principles, and conventions are sometimes simply referred to as 'professional values', or as personal 'character', such as integrity, fairness, and caring. Character is then formalised in professional codes of ethics. For example, *the standards of conduct, performance, and ethics* of The Health and Care Professions Council (HCPC, 2016), a body that registers 15 healthcare professional groups, contains a list of 10 standards embodying ethical conduct. The first of these standards is to 'Promote and protect the interests of service users and carers'. This includes 'Maintain

---

Resolving Critical Issues in Clinical Supervision: A Practical, Evidence-based Approach, First Edition.
Derek L. Milne and Robert P. Reiser.
© 2023 John Wiley & Sons Ltd. Published 2023 by John Wiley & Sons Ltd.

appropriate boundaries: You must keep your relationships with service users and carers professional' (p. 5). There follows a standard with a specific link to supervision: 'Delegate appropriately. You must only delegate work to someone who has the knowledge, skills and experience needed to carry it out safely and effectively. You must continue to provide appropriate supervision and support to those you delegate work to' (p. 7). These standards are infused with terms relevant to ethical conduct, including honesty, openness, acting responsibly, and helpfulness. Such standards inform registrants about how they are expected to behave as healthcare professionals, what patients are entitled to expect, and so form the basis for dealing with any complaints.

These standards therefore define character and include it as a criterion for 'fitness to practise': 'When we say someone is "fit to practise", we mean that they have the skills, knowledge, character and health they need to practise their profession safely and effectively' (HCPC, 2016, p. 11). Fitness to practise includes any unethical conduct which undermines trust or confidence in a practitioner, or which increases the risk of causing harm to patients. This can, therefore, include issues arising in a registrant's personal life (e.g., drug addiction, a criminal conviction), as well as in their professional life. These external standards are very similar to the list of 10 ethical supervision behaviours for professionals working in the USA (Haarman, 2013). In applying these standards to supervision, some specific recommendations emerge, such as orientating supervisees, and receiving regular supervision-of-supervision. However, these differences of detail, not principle, suggest agreement between these UK and US ethical standards, and considerable overlap with the ethical issues we identified in Chapter 1. But supervision multiplies the number of times ethical standards arise and increases the complexity of the associated critical issues. For example, as a supervisor, the principle of not causing harm (non-maleficence) extends to all of the supervisee's patients in addition to one's own, and the associated complications also multiply (e.g., overcoming practical obstacles to clinical oversight).

In Chapter 2 we clarified the most relevant legal context for supervision. For instance, in the risk management strategies we noted that legally appropriate behaviour sometimes explicitly assumed ethical conduct. Examples from these strategies included 'Supervisors should be as professional about supervision as they are about their clinical work. This concerns maintaining appropriate relationship boundaries, and being accessible to their supervisee', and 'When ... monitoring or evaluation indicates difficulties, these should be thoroughly addressed according to the appropriate professional practice standards, such as an agreed and written plan for improvement'. Conversely, it is also true that ethical conduct assumes obeying the law. For instance, the HCPC (2016) states that registrants 'must keep up to date with and follow the law ...' (p. 7). But there are important differences between legal and ethical systems. For instance, it is possible to obey the law while behaving unethically. For example, it is legal for someone who works as a supervisor to have sex with a consenting adult, but unethical to do so if that adult is their supervisee. It is also theoretically possible to break the law while behaving ethically. A hypothetical example is where a supervisor exceeds the legal speed limit while driving to a supervision meeting, travelling quickly to ensure that they have as much time as possible to address their concerns about the supervisee's safety or well-being. But it is less likely that a supervisor is behaving illegally and ethically, as ethical codes of practise tend to follow the HCPC (2016) example of requiring legal behaviour of registrants. Such differences between legal and ethical systems are inevitable because ethical behaviour includes every aspect of our lives, and with much less specificity than the law. This makes our ethical conduct more open to interpretation than our adherence to the law (Haarman, 2013). It is because legal and ethical guidelines differ in these ways that we need separate chapters to do them justice in this book.

So far, we have suggested that these complementary and intertwined ethical and legal systems are based on personal, interpersonal, and societal factors. These include moral principles, personal character, attitudes, personal impairment, shared value systems (such as service standards), and social conventions. These personal standards usually complement external standards, but again there is not a perfect overlap. An example is whistleblowing, where a professional may feel so strongly that clinical practice is wrong (i.e., that practice violates their moral principles) that they disregard external standards or other constraints (i.e., their conscience requires them to expose the faulty practice). There are many wonderfully uplifting instances through history where a guilty conscience has made someone feel that they must try to correct a wrong, come what may. In healthcare, whistleblowing has flagged disastrous care practices such as the poor quality of children's heart surgery at Bristol Royal Infirmary in England in the 1980s, which was identified by an anaesthetist, Stephen Bolsin. When his colleagues and the Infirmary managers failed to address the problem, Bolsin drew public attention to the problem, knowingly sacrificing his job in defence of his conscience (i.e., feeling he had to do what he knew was morally right). Bolsin's actions led to a major government inquiry, and ultimately to major reforms in medicine and healthcare, designed to prevent a repeat (e.g., clinical governance: Smith, 1998).

While identifying ethical issues is most likely to cause distress to supervisors and supervisees, it is also likely that resolving such issues will ultimately result in well-being (e.g., enhanced resilience, improved effectiveness). In the case of Stephen Bolsin, this not only included national reforms of likely benefit to thousands of patients; but also, a fresh and successful career in Australia, where he continued his efforts at improving healthcare quality. It is touching to read of the numerous awards and recognition that he received there, even including one from lawyers (the Civil Justice Award, Australian Plaintiff Lawyers Association, 1998).

Bolsin is an inspiration whose coping efforts boosted international healthcare systems. In the next chapter, we will describe the more modest but nonetheless important coping strategies that can be used to resolve ethical issues successfully at the individual level, in keeping with the coping process (see Figure 1.1 and Chapter 1). But in this present chapter we set the scene for those coping guidelines, by defining the main ethical issues involved in fitness to practise, noting their importance and implications. This will lead us into a description and formulation of these issues, again drawing on the coping model. As before, we will also provide an illustration. This carefully constructed understanding enables us to conclude with some general action implications, and we will supplement these with some more specific guidelines in the next chapter, with the aim of helping readers to be fit for practise and better able to resolve the ethical issues that they experience.

Types of Unethical Conduct

In Chapter 1 we introduced ethical concerns as a major category of the various critical issues arising within supervision. We also noted that these concerns were complex and ubiquitous, making it difficult to reduce workplace ethics to a small number of discrete critical issues. We summarised one helpful approach to classifying the issues affecting supervision (Thomas, 2014), which combined the most common issues appearing in the codes of ethics and guidelines that have been developed within regulatory bodies and professions internationally. This approach enabled Thomas (2014) to define the most common ethical transgressions as relationship boundary violations, lack of due process, and incompetence in supervisors and supervisees. For the purposes of our classification scheme (Table 4.1), we have updated her summary by reference to more recent guidance documents also based on expert consensus, namely the General Medical Council (GMC, 2013, 2019), and the Health and Care Professions Council (HCPC, 2016, 2019). We have also drawn on other kinds of data, to seek a more thorough evidence-based classification of ethical transgressions. Taken together, we refer to these as transgressions that render a clinician 'unfit to practice', following the broad definition used by the HCPC (2016).

Another source of information on ethical concerns are surveys of the participants in supervision. Ladany (2014) reviewed studies in psychotherapy dating back to the 1990s and concluded that supervisees report that their supervisors' adherence to ethical guidelines is improving modestly over time (i.e., 49% in 1999, up to 67% in 2011). The most common

Table 4.1 A classification of unethical issues in supervision.

Type of unethical issue	Definition of supervisor's unethical conduct
Character failings	Moral weakness (e.g., dishonesty, indecency, and theft). Lack of humility/integrity/responsibility/moral courage.
Ill-health	Physical or mental incapacity (e.g., personality disorder, drug addiction) affecting performance or judgement, or putting others at risk.
Misconduct	Unprofessional behaviour (e.g., unacceptable supervision); misconduct (e.g., improper relationships and sexual impropriety); abuse of power or trust (e.g., racial and other forms of discrimination). Ignoring duties (e.g., cyber-loafing; chronic lateness; no CPD).
Rule-breaking	Due process failings: not respecting or protecting the rights and welfare of patients and supervisees (e.g., breaches of confidentiality); ignoring established rules and principles (unfair); condoning unethical conduct of others; not fostering ethical behaviour (moral coward/no conscience). Criminal convictions.
Incompetence	Malpractice in relation to ethical issues, including irresponsibility, negligence and ineffectiveness; lack of ethical training, proficiency, or engagement (e.g., self-centred, instead of helping others).
Destructiveness	Counter-productive, uncivil, malign, deviant, or dysfunctional behaviour towards organisation/colleagues/patients (e.g., bullying, sabotage, property destruction, absenteeism, extreme apathy, vindictiveness, ostracism).

aspect of non-adherence was in relation to evaluating supervisees (e.g., evaluations being made without ever observing the supervisee, or providing no evaluation at all). Although the situation may be improving, surveys of therapists indicate alarmingly high levels of unethical supervision (e.g., Ellis et al., 2014, 2017), including incompetent supervision; lack of recognition of the importance of power, privilege, and cultural differences; poor supervisory boundaries; accounts of unresolved and unrecognised difficulties in the supervisory alliance; lack of consistent formative feedback; and inadequate, inconsistent documentation of problems in supervision.

Similar ethical issues have been reported for other healthcare professions, and this appears to be an international problem (Frank et al., 2006; Qian et al., 2015). For example, a survey of 309 nursing and medical students at a British medical school indicated that approximately 20% of these students reported bullying or harassment by their teachers and supervisors within the first year of starting their clinical placements, with a higher prevalence amongst nurses (Timm, 2014). Bullying or harassment was defined as behaviour within the clinical environment which was unwelcome, unwarranted, and caused a detrimental effect. For nurses there was a wide range of 'perpetrators', including peers, senior clinicians, and patients; whereas for medical students the source was usually a consultant physician. There was no explicit mention of supervisors, though they may have been included as clinical teachers. Examples of bullying or harassment included these responses from students: 'talking down, incredibly condescending, and derogatory comments; being rude and obtuse; expectations were very unrealistic; ridiculed during placement; felt unwanted, not part of the team; intimidated and hindered; sexual innuendos' (p. 3). Regarding their coping strategies, the nurses appeared to be more reflective than the medical students, and more likely to address the problem, though both groups coped by reporting the matter (e.g., on feedback forms), supporting affected peers, confrontation, and reflecting on resolving problems with a mentor. But avoidance was also a common reaction (e.g., ignoring issues or trying not to offend individuals). Timm (2014) concluded that these unethical behaviours were no less frequent than reported in a survey 10 years earlier, a 'shocking' situation, including highly problematic role-modelling. This worrying picture was confirmed in a theoretical review of unethical behaviour related to supervision (Falender, 2020), that summarised surveys of supervisees. In one study of 151 early-career supervisees (Ladany et al., 1999), 51% reported at least one ethical violation by their supervisors (e.g., breaking confidentiality, disregarding boundaries, and disrespectful behaviour).

Other sources of information include statistical data on the most common ethical and related concerns about a healthcare professional's fitness to practice (i.e., the skills, knowledge, character, and health they need to practise their profession safely and effectively: HCPC, 2019). An example is the complaints made to professional registration bodies by patients and others. For instance, in the USA The Association of State and Provincial Psychology Boards (ASPPB, 2019) reports annual statistics for its registrants/licensees (i.e., professional psychologists on their register, from more than 12 different areas of specialisation, such as counselling and industrial–organisational psychology). For the period 1974–2019, the most common complaints were 'unprofessional conduct' and 'sexual misconduct', each representing 10% of all disciplinary actions during this 45-year period. These reasons were followed by 'negligence' (7%) and 'dual relationships' (not sexual: 6%). Making up the remaining top 10 reasons were: criminal convictions; failure to maintain adequate records; failure to comply with continuing education or competency requirements; incompetence; improper or inadequate supervision; and substandard or inadequate care. The total number of disciplinary actions has slightly decreased over the past five years. The ASPPB (2019) also reported the main types of sanctions that were applied to the affected registrants. From least to most frequent were: revocations (i.e., cancelling practice licences); suspensions (i.e., temporary interruptions to licences); probations (i.e., a period of supervised practice, while still licensed); and the most frequent sanction, reprimands (i.e., formal expressions of disapproval, including specific criticisms of practice, with related requirements for improved practice, such as CPD).

Similar statistical data have been reported for other disciplines. In the UK, fitness to practise complaints are handled by the General Medical Council (GMC), which regulates the medical profession and protects the public by ensuring that only those doctors who meet the relevant standards are allowed to work in the UK. Complaints to the GMC have increased considerably in recent years, from just over 5000 in 2007, to more than 10,000 in 2012 (GMC, 2013). In order of frequency, complaints most commonly concerned dubious clinical practice, dishonesty, fraud, improper relationships, and sexual impropriety. Other professional groups, including dietitians, occupational therapists, social workers, paramedics, and radiographers are regulated by the Health and Care Professions Council (HCPC, 2019). Complaints and concerns raised about these healthcare professionals were related to such issues as: dishonesty (e.g., exploiting a vulnerable person); not managing their own health problems appropriately, affecting the safety of service users (e.g., having a substance abuse or misuse problem); having an improper relationship with a service user; seriously or persistently failing to meet professional standards; and violent or threatening behaviour.

Conclusions

In summary, unethical conduct that compromises a clinician's fitness to practise has been reported across all the indicators we have used: expert opinion, surveys of supervisees, patients' complaints, colleagues' concerns, and the disciplinary actions of regulatory bodies. This triangulation of data sources strengthens our confidence in two conclusions: unethical conduct is common, and it is wide-ranging. That it is common is also borne out in data on the resulting harm to patients, which is so frequent in healthcare that it has been described as 'normal' (Jha et al., 2013).

Implications

The main implication is that we need robust systems in place across healthcare provision to monitor and combat unethical conduct. The above data indicates a pressing need for an evidence-based approach to supervision that can contribute to more potent surveillance systems. A secondary conclusion might be the need for standardising taxonomies of unethical conduct, a challenge most dramatically indicated by the 86 different reasons for disciplinary action reported by the ASPPB (2019). The diversity of unethical behaviours cited above bears out this heterogeneity, in that no two data sources employed a similar classification scheme. Generally, these classification frameworks also lack any kind of validation, although a welcome exception was the consensus-building work undertaken by Ellis et al. (2014), concerning inadequate and harmful supervision. Therefore, we next integrate the various sources cited above to create an illustrative classification framework for ethical issues in supervision.

Classifying Ethical Issues in Supervision

In this section we aim to define and describe the most relevant ethical issues, partly to aid understanding, and partly to guide our suggestions on resolving these issues. Table 4.1 provides our classification scheme, using everyday terms wherever possible. Although this scheme integrates the above material with relevant frameworks (Brown et al., 2009; Chang et al., 2005; Lasakova & Remisova, 2015; Wiernik & Ones, 2018), we present it as an illustration of the main ethical issues related to supervision, rather than attempting to provide an exhaustive list. Unethical supervision can be defined as an unwillingness or inability to integrate professional standards into one's professional practice (Haarman, 2013). It can be intentional or unintentional, may be active or passive, and it tends to cause harm to others, as well as to employing healthcare organisations or society (adapted from: Lasakova & Remisova, 2015).

Table 4.1 starts with the category 'character failings'. This refers to a supervisor's moral weaknesses, or absent personal attributes including a lack of humility, integrity, or moral courage. This description is drawn from a taxonomy of professional behaviour (character domain: Brown et al., 2009). The second category in Table 4.1 is 'ill-health', meaning physical or mental health problems that create an incapacity, such as a transient fever or a negative life event, as well as more enduring concerns (e.g., chronic illness, drug addiction, and personality disorder). It may seem strange to include health status in a list of unethical behaviours, but the reason is that poor management of our health affects our behaviour and creates additional risks. To quote the relevant standard of conduct from the HCPC (2016): 'You must make changes to how you practise, or stop practising, if your physical or mental health may affect your performance or judgement, or put others at risk for any other reason' (p. 8). These health-related conditions or circumstances may affect our self-awareness or insight, so we may need to be guided by colleagues to avoid placing supervisees or their patients at risk. In turn, we should note that a major responsibility for supervisors is monitoring the well-being of their supervisees, including clinical oversight to ensure that patients are receiving a safe and suitable treatment, and 'gatekeeping' to ensure that adverse health informs decision-making about career interruption, remediation, or progression (Haarman, 2013). At this point we should note that adverse health may itself be an explanation for other types of unethical behaviour, as in the example of an illness reducing a supervisor's motivation or competence. We will consider this causal aspect in the formulation section in the following paragraphs.

The third type of unethical behaviour in Table 4.1 is 'misconduct', involving unacceptable or improper professional behaviour, including relationship boundary violations, harassment, or bullying the supervisee for personal gain. This can range widely, from ignoring one's duties or refusing reasonable instructions from a manager to racial discrimination and sexual impropriety. Like many other ethical examples, sometimes the judgement about what is and is not ethical is far from clear. For instance, not every multiple relationship is improper or even avoidable: one could have a clinical relationship with someone who also shared a recreational activity in your community, or who was a neighbour. Such links may be particularly unavoidable in small rural communities, and in a suitable context such a dual relationship would be ethical, provided both parties judged this relationship acceptable. Falender (2020) has noted that some ethical codes explicitly state that not all multiple relationships are unethical, placing the emphasis on the consequences. For instance, The American Psychological Association regards ethical dual relationships as ones that would not reasonably be expected to cause impairment, or risk exploitation or harm (APA, 2017). Thomas (2010) adds that, in some cultural contexts, avoiding dual relationships may be considered disrespectful and insensitive. Similarly, in certain professional contexts multiple relationships may be beneficial to the supervisee, such as a supervisor who collaborates with a supervisee over a research project (if this is helpful and not exploitative (Thomas, 2010)). By contrast, some other dual relationships are deemed boundary violations, such as providing a clinical service to a supervisee.

Deciding what is acceptable is not always straightforward, and may entail a subjective judgement, at least initially. We can start to address the uncertainty by considering the consequences (e.g., would this action risk harming the supervisee?). Here are the main ethical principles, presented as criteria against which to judge the acceptability of your intended actions. Could this action (e.g., starting a multiple relationship) reasonably be expected to have this effect on you, or the person concerned:

- impair your competence or effectiveness (uncaring: infidelity)?
- risk exploiting or harming them (dishonest: maleficence)?
- lead to criticism from an esteemed peer (unhelpful or immoral: non-beneficence)?
- reduce or jeopardise their independence and freedom (create dependence on you: impairing autonomy)?
- unfairly limit access to your clinical service (discriminatory or otherwise inequitable: unjust)?
- undermine your self-care (damage your ability to adhere to ethical principles)?

If the answer to any one of these questions is 'yes', then the action might well be judged unethical by others and should at least be discussed with a colleague before proceeding. In addition to consultation, it is wise and ethical to document actions that may fall into grey or borderline ethical areas. This documentation should include specifying the action, the circumstances, the nature of the relationship, and the reasoning behind the action. In this kind of reflective process, supervisees and others can develop and apply thoughtful ethical decision making strategies, rather than avoiding the issue, or simply looking for 'the right answer' (Barnett & Molzon, 2014).

Another type of challenge is where a supervisee behaves unethically towards their supervisor (e.g., manipulating the supervisor, as a result of personality issues). The same applies in relation to patients, some of whom can be highly manipulative, including seeking sexual contact with their clinician. Healthcare professionals also have their own personal issues, and may at times feel attracted to patients sexually. However, the onus is on the clinician to behave ethically, and sexual contact with a patient is a clear-cut boundary violation. Nonetheless, it is one of the most common kinds of unprofessional conduct, a very likely source of disciplinary action, and in some jurisdictions also a crime (Knapp et al., 2013, p. 79). Even though clinicians are aware of this boundary, some still engage in sexual relationships with their patients ('2% to 3% of psychologists, will have a sexual relationship with at least one patient sometime during their careers': Knapp et al., 2013, p. 89). These authors suggest supervision as a way of managing romantic feelings for patients, and recommend transferring the patient to another professional. Given these considerations, before commencing a dual relationship it is good practice to discuss any specific consideration of harm or benefit with a colleague, to seek an independent view and to get an objective opinion (e.g., from a clinical service manager).

'Rule-breaking' is the fourth type of unethical behaviour in Table 4.1, involving a failure to adhere to what is formally termed due process, or procedural justice. These phrases refer to protecting the rights and welfare of patients and supervisees, especially ensuring that established rules, principles, and procedures are followed correctly. The aim is to ensure 'fair play', especially when more powerful adversaries are involved. For example, it is difficult for a supervisee to allege sub-standard supervision when their supervisor has greater formal power and is probably backed by the employing organisation or training body. In such situations the system needs to ensure that the supervisee is given support and guidance in raising legitimate concerns (e.g., misunderstandings over evaluation criteria, breaches of confidentiality, and poor record-keeping). Informed consent from the outset of supervision is an important example of due process, where a supervision contract is agreed and signed off by both parties, covering these kinds of concerns. From the review by Lasakova and Remisova (2015), we also note that rule-breaking can also include colluding with the absence of rules: failing to enforce or encourage rule-adherence among colleagues (e.g., modelling self-interest at the expense of the team; ignoring unethical behaviour in others; discouraging peers from considering ethical issues).

We use the term ethical 'incompetence' to refer to skill or knowledge deficits, amounting to negligence (Category 5 in Table 4.1). As a result of such incompetence, supervisors may fail to meet the standards of care that are expected, directly resulting in harm, loss, or damage to the supervisee or their patients (i.e., malpractice: see Chapter 2). Incompetence is the failure to exercise the customary degree of professional skill within supervision (termed 'unfit for practice' in Chapter 1). Examples include: failing to establish a supervision contract; failing to develop ethical competence in supervisees; a lack of clinical oversight; inappropriate delegation of responsibilities to the supervisee; lack of supervisor training or consultation; and multicultural incompetence. According to Knapp et al. (2013), the most common reasons for malpractice complaints from patients were, in order of frequency, ineffective treatment or failure to consult or refer; failure to diagnose or improper diagnosis; child custody disputes; sexual intimacy; harassment or misconduct; breach of confidentiality; suicide; and supervisory issues.

Table 4.1 closes with 'destructiveness', a category that includes a range of anti-social activities technically termed 'counter-productive work behaviours'. This category of unethical conduct is defined as deviant and dysfunctional employee behaviours that undermine the employing organisation, harming property, employees, and patients. The behaviours and activities deemed as counter-productive in the literature are again very wide-ranging, including employee theft, sabotage, drug abuse, aggression, and employee withdrawal (e.g., absenteeism and lateness: Bowling et al., 2010). As this list indicates, some of these counter-productive behaviours have already been included in Table 4.1 under other headings. This overlap seems unavoidable given the range of cited behaviours, and the absence of an agreed or definitive classification framework. In Table 4.1 we have therefore clustered descriptions and examples on what we believe is the most logically coherent basis.

Bowling et al. (2010) indicated that employee theft alone costs US companies several billion dollars annually, and has been cited as a major cause of business failures. The combined costs of all forms of counter-productive behaviours are assumed to be 'staggering' (p. 54). To make matters worse, there are also indirect costs, including lost productivity, damage to the organisation's reputation, and of course harming the well-being of individual employees. A related category of destructive workplace behaviours is incivility, which appears to be ubiquitous and on the increase. Recent studies with samples again drawn from the USA have reported that between 43% and 95% of respondents reported experiencing incivility at work, and 38% believed that their workplace is becoming more uncivil and disrespectful over time (studies cited in Clark et al., 2013). As a result, it is thought that many workers become unethical through being disengaged, less productive, and intentionally undermining their organisation and their co-workers. To restore some perspective, we should note that the opposite also occurs, where staff engage in mutually civil behaviours. Sometimes termed 'employee prosocial behaviours' or 'organizational citizenship behaviours', these behaviours include truthfulness, confidentiality, fairness, and respect (part of a taxonomy of 10 ethical staff behaviours: Russell et al., 2017). Supervisors should of course take every opportunity to develop civil behaviour in their supervisees.

Illustration

Several of the types of unethical conduct took place within a clinical psychology department, featuring the lead psychologist. Quite appropriately, she had asked a junior member of the department to summarise her part-time PhD, which was in the very early stages. This PhD was funded by the department and involved collecting data from within the service. In this context, it would have been remiss of the manager not to take an interest. However, during the meeting the manager started to challenge the staff member, asserting that the proposed study had already been done, and citing several references to confirm the pointlessness of continuing with that study plan. This pattern was repeated in relation to other PhD plans, with the staff member becoming increasingly baffled by her manager's behaviour. She then felt that she had to say that, from her reading so far, she was unaware of any of these prior studies, authors, or references, so was a bit confused. The manager responded by becoming even more insistent, even slightly aggressive, implying that this questioning was improper. She also began to undermine the whole idea of this staff member undertaking a part-time PhD. However, at the end of a difficult meeting she promised to furnish the references that she had mentioned.

Not only were those mysterious references never provided, but there were no more such meetings, nor any further sign of interest in this project from the lead psychologist. Thankfully, a senior manager in the department became the field supervisor (providing academic supervision), and he took an appropriate interest in the PhD, which was concluded successfully as per the original plan (it transpired that no prior studies had been done). This senior manager soon dismissed the lead psychologist for unethical behaviour at work. It turned out that this lead psychologist was also a negligent supervisor, regularly failing to provide at least one trainee with sufficient supervision to guide her clinical work. Not surprisingly, this supervisory incompetence had a negative impact on the supervisee, who in one instance was panicking ahead of an appointment. Furthermore, a fellow supervisee tried to provide some last-minute supervision, to help to calm her down, and to enable the appointment to proceed (as described in the vignette on page 43 of Milne & Reiser, 2020). Although the appointment went smoothly, and no harm appeared to be caused to the patient, this illustration indicates several instances of unethical behaviour, directly affecting at least two colleagues in this example.

Reflections

In relation to Table 4.1, there are indications of 'character failings', 'misconduct', and 'incompetence' in the lead psychologist, including lying about the references, a lack of integrity in discouraging the staff member from pursuing the PhD, and a failure to offer any further support or encouragement (lack of engagement). In turn, her supervisee and her peer could be said to have behaved unethically, in going beyond their competence or duties (e.g., 'Rule-breaking'). Also, the senior manager had previously been aware of related problems with this lead psychologist, but had not addressed the matter (to the extent that at one stage some staff members walked out of her department). In this general sense, initially the organisational system was unsupportive, exposing staff and patients to the risk of incompetent supervision, therapy, and personal harm. Thankfully, once sufficient evidence had been collated, the lead psychologist was soon dismissed, struck off the professional register, and faced criminal charges for her unprofessional behaviour. In sum, although there was a successful resolution, this was altogether a most unfortunate business, which at least seemed to cause no direct harm to patients. But this example illustrates a pattern of negligent supervision that surely carried risks for other supervisees and their patients.

Formulating Unethical Issues

Having defined and described the main unethical issues, we now utilise a 'problem formulation' approach that provides a sound and helpful basis for resolving the issues. We have already hinted at some ways of understanding unethical conduct, such as the reported link just mentioned between incivility and disengagement at work. Table 4.1 suggests other reasons, including character failings, adverse health, and incompetence. Although we indicated some more specific explanations for unethical conduct in that table (e.g., a lack of knowledge or training), we now want to outline how a deeper understanding can be achieved. We propose to use the coping cycle as the basis for the formulations we make in this book (see Figure 1.1). The formulation answers the question 'how did this happen?' and does so at the personal level. This is the intra-personal equivalent of what is termed the 'root cause' within the patient safety literature, where the cause is located in the healthcare system and wider environmental context (i.e., beyond the individual level of problem analysis). This literature also emphasises the need to identify what exactly happened (including the consequences, such as the nature of any patient harm), and any contributory factors (human or system problems: NHS, 2015). We share this functional analysis approach to developing a problem formulation, but use different terms, to emphasise the personal rather than the system-level explanations for unethical behavior and harm.

In summary, although the causes of unethical behavior are often complex (Thomas, 2014), we assume that personal problems such a incivility or disengagement can usually be understood adequately by applying the coping model (including any consequences for others, or for the healthcare system). In clinical work this would normally be done by assessing the unethical behavior in some detail, also defining the triggers or antecedent events, together with the consequences (i.e., an antecedent-behaviour-consequence approach to functional analysis). The assessment would include the use of interview, observation, and other assessment techniques (e.g., self-report questionnaires, such as the counter-productive work behavior scale: Zahid, 2019). In this book we have used hypothetical examples to sketch out how supervisors (or supervisors-of-supervisors) in particular can do this kind of assessment themselves, but others may also find this approach helpful (e.g., training programmes seeking to tackle unethical conduct). This process will increase understanding of what happened, enable formulation of the problem, and hence provide the proper basis for knowing how best to resolve matters. A bonus is that this collaborative assessment process can itself begin to resolve some problems, since the perpetrator may also gain an improved understanding, developing their insight and improving their coping.

Figure 4.1 provides a hypothetical formulation of an incident where a supervisor has provided an evaluation of the supervisee's work, which the supervisee becomes aware of through the workplace system (box 2). This could be an email from the supervisor, attaching a completed competence rating form that indicates areas of concern. The Figure summarises how this evaluation impacts on the supervisee, an individual whose high emotional intelligence (box 3) exaggerates the perception that this rating form is not a fair assessment (box 4). The supervisee attempts to cope with this perceived procedural injustice by replying angrily that the evaluation is unfair (box 5), on the grounds that the supervisor has never observed the supervisee's work. Unfortunately, this strategy is not successful, getting no positive reaction from the supervisor and so giving no satisfaction to the supervisee (box 6). Not surprisingly, the supervisee is left feeling distressed (box 7). In frustration, and with growing anger and resentment (the vicious cycle), the supervisee engages in some counter-productive behaviour by spreading the message (among the peer group), that this supervisor breaks the rules (by not observing) and is excessively critical (giving a negative evaluation), in a workplace context where organisational injustice is common (box 1: allegations are known to be managed unfairly).

This scenario is actually one we have encountered repeatedly in real life, so some aspects of this formulation are not hypothetical. For instance, this scenario occurred in a majority of instances when visiting supervisees half-way through their placements as a clinical tutor/placement supervisor, on behalf of their training programme. At these visits, conducted jointly with the supervisor/s and the supervisee, we often discovered that observation had not happened at all (but was planned); and more frequently finding that no evaluation of progress had been shared with the supervisee. These kinds of unethical

4 Understanding Unethical Issues in Clinical Supervision

1. Context

2. Workplace system
(disputed evaluation)

Desensitisation feedback loop

4. Cognitive appraisal
(supervisee's perception: no procedural justice)

5. Personal coping strategies
(supervisee disputing allegations)

6. Well-being
(no positive reactions or outcomes)

7. Distress
(counter-productive supervisee behaviour)

3. Personal system
(emotional intelligence)

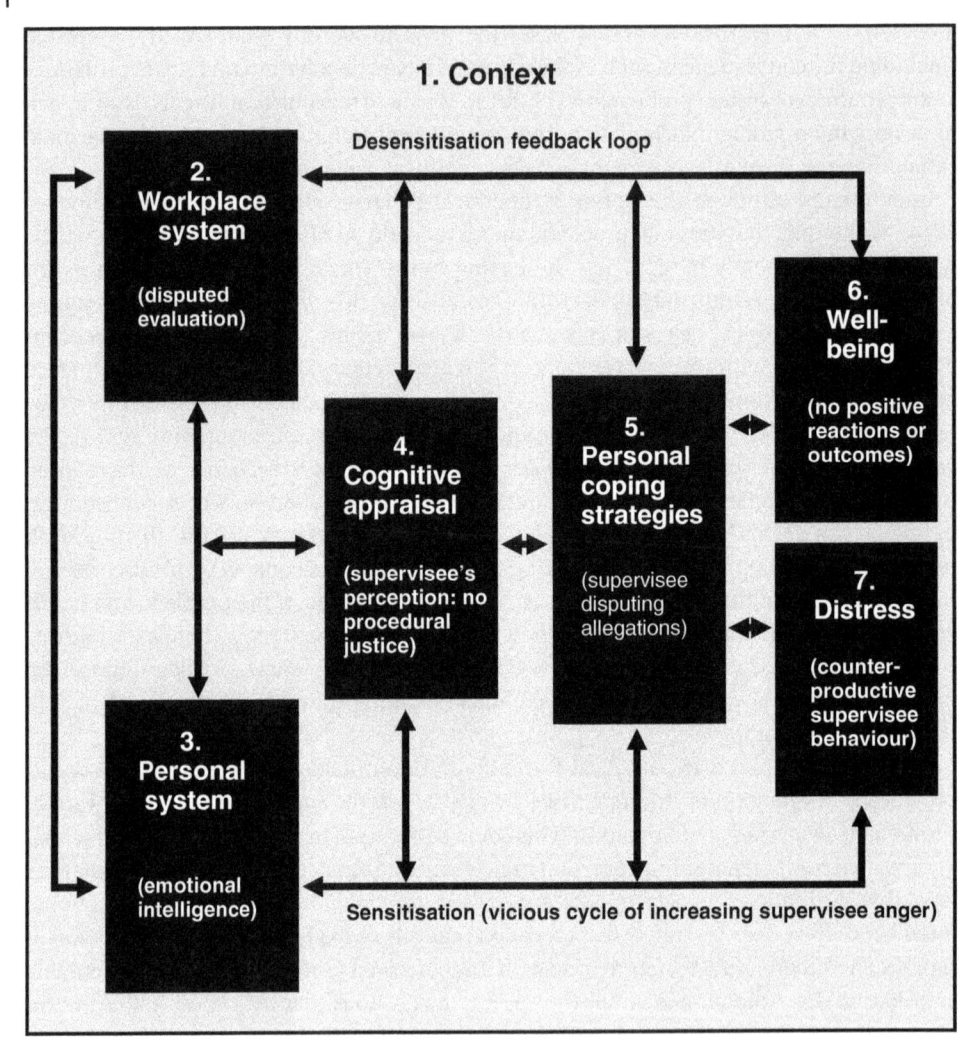

Sensitisation (vicious cycle of increasing supervisee anger)

Figure 4.1 A hypothetical formulation based on the coping cycle, explaining a supervisee's unethical conduct.

supervisor behaviours can be expected to fuel a sense of injustice in supervisees. But we also based this formulation (i.e., Figure 4.1) on a study of organisational justice and emotional intelligence by Devonish and Greenidge (2010). They reported a direct link between injustice and counter-productive work behavior, which was moderated by emotional intelligence (EI). Consistent with prior research, they found that those individuals who were high in EI were better able to perceive and appraise their own emotions (as well as the emotions of others) and coped with their emotions more constructively. As a result, high EI workers were more likely than those with low EI to react positively (i.e., to respond adaptively and to experience well-being). Devonish and Greenidge (2010, p. 84) drew out some practical implications, stating that 'Managers must ensure that the procedures and interactions involved in various systems of organisational governance, including human resource management practices and industrial relations systems, are applied in a fair and unbiased manner ... supervisors must be vigilant and cautious in ensuring that fairness is administered at all times in all practices employed at their organisation to safeguard overall organisational efficiency and effectiveness'.

Emotional intelligence is a factor within the personal system of the coping cycle, an individual's characteristics (box 3 in Figure 4.1). Such characteristics are typically less important than an individual's self-regulation behaviour. This is part of their coping repertoire, and can be thought of as a metacognitive activity, in which an individual monitors and adjusts their own coping behavior. This has been described as a negative feedback loop, beginning with attending to information (input) from the environment, and comparing this against the desired state (the standard: Iliescu et al., 2014). When there is a discrepancy, the individual is usually motivated by negative emotions to take corrective action (the output). As these authors note, a discrepancy can be reduced by intervening at different points in this self-regulation process. For example, the behavioural standard set by an individual may be unrealistically high, or their emotional reaction may be excessive. It may also be possible to alter the input from the environment (e.g., improving procedural justice). Below we illustrate these theoretical possibilities with practical methods.

We should also clarify that we are considering self-regulation by the individual, as an internal psychological process of self-management. The term also has a significant history in terms of the tradition of self-regulation by some professional groups (e.g., nurses). Because this has ultimately proved ineffective in preventing unethical conduct, governments are increasingly insisting that all healthcare professionals are externally regulated, requiring national bodies such as the HCPC to require that certain standards for supervision (etc.) are achieved by individual members (e.g., Kirkup, 2015). In this sense, national systems should reinforce individual efforts to behave ethically. Here, we are dealing with these individual psychological efforts at self-regulation.

We introduce personal self-regulation as it is essential to understanding and resolving critical issues in supervision, especially unethical conduct. It expands our thinking from a list of coping strategies (see Chapter 1, Table 1.1) to include a corrective system that coordinates the coping cycle to prevent or resolve ethical problems. Self-regulation is especially relevant because our goals (ends), and our efforts to achieve them (means), are understood to occur in relation to our moral identity and ethical ideals (Bandura, 2006). This includes trying to alter the workplace system, to better regulate ourselves (i.e., self-control). According to this theory, workplaces contain multiple and conflicting ends and means, at times entailing complex moral choices, frustration tolerance, and imperfect trade-offs between the costs and benefits of decisions. Related to supervision, specific aspects of an individual's self-regulation that may be amenable to intervention include cognitive appraisal; self-awareness; task analysis, goal-setting and planning; interpretation (perception); thinking and action processes (e.g., how a problem is understood, coping strategies, feeling reactions); monitoring and performance feedback; reflection; and the overall strategic management (regulation) of all these aspects (Panadero, 2017). We now consider how exactly key aspects of individual self-regulation can be beneficially changed in relation to unethical conduct.

Conclusions and Action Implications

This chapter has developed an understanding of unethical conduct related to supervision that is based on a classification of the main critical issues (see, Table 4.1), and a formulation strategy (the coping cycle: see, Figure 4.1). These can help us to explain why these critical issues occur and inform our attempts to resolve them. From drawing on various data sources, we must conclude that unethical conduct is diverse and common. This conduct renders a clinician unfit to practise, a term that encompasses the six types of unethical conduct in Table 4.1, and which undermines trust or confidence in a practitioner, or which increases the risk of their causing harm to patients. Our classification system helps to specify the nature of any unethical conduct. This kind of clarification is badly needed, since much of the literature 'is clogged by ... ambiguous notions and related confusion of terms and overlapping constructs ...' (Lasakova & Remisova, 2015, p. 320). The summary in Table 4.1 is consistent with international standards for ethical supervision (e.g., Haarman, 2013; Leach & Harbin, 1997). There is one more key term that we should note here, namely our personal conscience. This 'inner voice' helpfully integrates the diverse and common aspects of unethical conduct, reminding us of our own moral standards, and helping us to regulate our own behaviour. Although introducing conscience may appear to complicate the reasons behind unethical conduct, there is a sense in which our conscience helpfully integrates the other factors, flagging awareness of a possible issue, and so regulating, educating, and guiding us.

Action Implications

- **Define the problem**: Use Table 4.1 to help to specify the nature of any unethical conduct. This kind of clarification should remove ambiguity and confusion.
- **Formulate the problem**: We used the coping cycle to formulate a hypothetical example of unethical conduct (counter-productive work behaviours). But we should acknowledge that this is not by any means the only way to formulate critical issues in supervision. Indeed, we have ourselves used alternative approaches, one based on the CBT model, and a second on patient safety logic (Milne, 2020; Reiser & Milne, 2017). In the same way, we encourage you to consider which approach is most appropriate in your situation. Whichever approach you choose, use it to pinpoint the specific nature of the ethical transgression, and to understand why it is happening. This is the proper basis for intervening to try and resolve the problem (see Chapter 5 for relevant guidelines).
- **Manage the problem**: Supervisors should strive to model ethical standards for their supervisees, encouraging organisational citisenship (prosocial behaviours), and other virtuous behaviours. Part of this professional development includes the supervisee (or supervisor) exercising continual self-regulation, a form of meta-cognitive coping that can become more salient and effective with regular discussion within supervision (e.g., by reviewing how an ethical issue was handled).

References

American Psychological Association. (2017). *Ethical principles of psychologists and code of conduct*. Retrieved from http://www.apa.org/ethics/code/ethics-code-2017.pdf

Association of State and Provincial Psychology Boards (ASPPB). (2019). *ASPPB disciplinary data system: Historical discipline report reported disciplinary actions for psychologists: 1974–2019*. https://cdn.ymaws.com/www.asppb.net/resource/resmgr/dds/dds_historical_report_2019.pdf. Accessed on 20 November 2020.

Bandura, A. (2006). Toward a psychology of human agency. *Perspectives on Psychological Science*, *1*(2), 164–180. https://doi.org/10.1111/j.1745-6916.2006.00011.x

Barnett, J. E., & Molzon, C. H. (2014). Clinical supervision of psychotherapy: Essential ethics issues for supervisors and supervisees. *Journal of Clinical Psychology*, *70*(11), 1051–1061. https://doi.org/10.1002/jclp.22126

Bowling, N., Eschleman, K., & Wang, Q. (2010). A meta-analytic examination of the relationship between job satisfaction and subjective well-being. *Journal of Occupational and Organizational Psychology*, *83*(4):915 –934. https://doi.org/10.1348/096317909X478557

Brown, D., Ferrill, M. J., & Gregory, L. L. (2009). The taxonomy of professionalism: Reframing the academic pursuit of professional development. *American Journal of Pharmaceutical Education*, *73*(4), 1–10. https://doi.org/10.5688/aj730468.

Chang, A., Schyve, P. M., Croteau, R. J., O'Leary, D. S., & Loeb, J. M. (2005). The JCAHO patient safety event taxonomy: A standardized terminology and classification schema for near misses and adverse events. *International Journal for Quality in Health Care*, *17*(2), 95–105. https://doi.org/10.1093/intqhc/mzi021

Clark, C. M., Olender, L., Kenski, D., & Cardoni, C. (2013). Exploring and addressing faculty-to-faculty incivility: A national perspective and literature review. *Journal of Nursing Education*, *52*(4),211-218. https://doi.org/10.3928/01484834-20130319-01

Devonish, D., & Greenidge, D. (2010). The effect of organizational justice on contextual performance, counterproductive work behaviours, and task performance: Investigating the moderating role of ability-based emotional intelligence. *International Journal of Selection and Assessment*, *18*(1), 75–86. https://doi.org/10.1111/j.1468-2389.2010.00490.x

Ellis, M. V., Berger, L., Hanus, A. E., Ayala, E. E., Swords, B. A., & Siembor, M. (2014). Inadequate and harmful clinical supervision: Testing a revised framework and assessing occurrence. *The Counseling Psychologist*, *42*(2), 434–472. https://doi.org/10.1177/0011000013508656

Ellis, M. V., Taylor, E. J., Corp, D. A., Hutman, H., & Kangos, K. A. (2017). Narratives of harmful clinical supervision: Introduction to the special issue. *The Clinical Supervisor*, *36*(1), 4–19. https://doi.org/10.1080/07325223.2017.1297753

Falender, C. (2020). Ethics of clinical supervision: An international lens. *Psychology in Russia: State of the Art*, *13*(1), 43–54. https://doi.org/10.11621/pir.2020.0104

Frank, E., Carrera, J. S., Stratton, T., Bickel, J., & Nora, L. M. (2006). Experiences of belittlement and harassment and their correlates among medical students in the United States: Longitudinal survey. *British Medical Journal*, *333*(7570), 682–688. https://doi.org/10.1136/bmj.38924.722037.7C

General Medical Council (GMC). (2013). *2012 annual statistics: Fitness to practise.* General Medical Council. http://www.gmc-uk.org/2012_Annual_Statistics.pdf_53844772.pdf

General Medical Council (GMC). (2019). *Guidance for doctors: Requirements for revalidation and maintaining your licence.* General Medical Council.

Haarman, G. B. (2013). *Clinical supervision: Legal, ethical and risk management issues.* Foundations: Education & Consultation.

Health and Care Professions Council (HCPC). (2016). *The standards of conduct, performance, and ethics.* The Health and Care Professions Council.

Health and Care Professions Council (HCPC). (2019). *Protecting the public promoting professionalism; Fitness to practise annual report.* The Health and Care Professions Council (Publication code: 20191031F2PPUB).

Iliescu, D., Ispas, D., Sulea, C., & Ilie, A. (2014). Vocational fit and counterproductive work behaviours: A self-regulation perspective. *Journal of Applied Psychology, 100(1).* Advance online publication. http://dx.doi.org/10.1037/a0036652

Jha, A. K., Larizgoitia, I., Audera-Lopez, C., Prasopa-Plaizier, N., Waters, H., & Bates, D. W. (2013). The global burden of unsafe medical care: Analytic modelling of observational studies. *British Medical Journal, Quality & Safety, 22*(10), 809–815. https://doi.org/10.1136/bmjqs-2012-001748

Kirkup, B. (2015). *Morecambe bay investigation.* This publication is available at https://www.gov.uk/government/publications.

Knapp, S., Younggren, J. N., VandeCreek, L., Harris, E., & Martin, J. N. (2013). *Assessing and managing risk in psychological practice* (2nd ed.). American Psychological Association.

Ladany, N. (2014). The ingredients of supervisor failure. *Journal of Clinical Psychology: In Session, 70*(11), 1–10. https://doi.org/10.1002/jclp.22130

Ladany, N., Lehrman-Waterman, D., Molinaro, M., & Wolgast, B. (1999). Psychotherapy supervisor ethical practices: Adherence to guidelines, the supervisory working alliance, and supervisee satisfaction. *The Counseling Psychologist, 27*(3), 443–475. https://doi.org/10.1177/0011000099273008

Lasakova, A, & Remisova, A. (2015). Unethical leadership: Current theoretical trends and conceptualization. *Procedia Economics and Finance 34* (2015), 319-328. https://doi.org/10.1016/S2212-5671(15)01636-6

Leach, M., & Harbin, J. (1997). Psychological ethics codes: A comparison of 24 countries. *International Journal of Psychology, 32*(3), 181–192. https://www.google.com/search?rlz=1C1CHBF_enUS909US909&q=Leach,+M.,+%26+Harbin,+J.+(1997).+Psychological+ethics+codes:+A+comparison+of+24+countries.+International+Journal+of+Psychology,+32(3),+181%E2%80%93192.+https://doi.org/10.1080/002075997400854&spell=1&sa=X&ved=2ahUKEwi50pyog736AhVuLkQIHf8aBWUQBSgAegQIARA3&biw=1472&bih=827&dpr=1

Milne, D. L. (2020). Preventing harm related to CBT supervision: A theoretical review and preliminary framework. *The Cognitive Behaviour Therapist, 13.* https://doi.org/10.1017/S1754470X20000550

Milne, D., & Reiser, R. P. (2020). *Supportive clinical supervision: From burnout to well-being, through restorative leadership.* Pavilion.

National Health Service (NHS). (2015). *Serious incident framework.* NHS.

Panadero, E. (2017). A review of self-regulated learning: Six models and four directions for research. *Frontiers in Psychology*, *8*, 1–28. https://doi.org/10.3389/fpsyg.2017.00422

Qian, J., Wang, H., Han, Z. R., Wang, J., & Wang, H. (2015). Mental health risks among nurses under abusive supervision: The moderating roles of job role ambiguity and patients' lack of reciprocity. *International Journal of Mental Health Systems*, *9*, 22–28. https://doi.org/10.1186/s13033-015-0014-x

Reiser, R. P., & Milne, D. L. (2017). A CBT formulation of supervisees' narratives about unethical and harmful supervision. *The Clinical Supervisor*, *36*(1), 102–115. https://doi.org/10.1080/07325223.2017.1295895

Russell, T.L., Sparks, T.E., Campbell, J.P., et al. (2017). Situating ethical behavior in the nomological network of job performance. *Journal of Business Psychology*, *32*(2017), 253–271. https://doi.org/10.1007/s10869-016-9454-9

Smith, R. (1998). All changed, changed utterly. *British Medical Journal*, *316*(7149), 1917–1918. https://doi.org/10.1136/bmj.316.7149.1917

Thomas, J. T. (2010). The ethics of supervision and consultation: Practical guidance for mental health professionals. American Psychological Association. https://doi.org/10.1037/12078-000

Thomas, J. T. (2014). Disciplinary supervision following ethics complaints: Goals, tasks, and ethical dimensions. *Journal of Clinical Supervision: In Session*, *70*(11), 1–11. https://doi.org/10.1002/jclp.22131

Timm, A. (2014). 'It would not be tolerated in any other profession except medicine': Survey reporting on undergraduates' exposure to bullying and harassment in their first placement year. *British Medical Journal, Open Access*, *4*(1–7), e005140. https://doi.org/10.1136/bmjopen-2014-005140

Watkins, C. E., & Milne, D. L. (Eds.). (2014). *The Wiley International Handbook of Clinical Supervision*.

Wiernik, B. M., & Ones, D. S. (2018). Ethical employee behaviors in the consensus taxonomy of counterproductive work behaviors. *International Journal of Selection and Assessment*, *26*(1), 36–48. https://doi.org/10.1111/ijsa.12199

Zahid, F. (2019). Self-serving counterproductive work behaviours: The development and validation of a scale. *Pakistan Journal of Commerce and Social Sciences*, *13*(2), 257–282. http://hdl.handle.net/10419/200992

5

Resolving Unethical Issues in Clinical Supervision

Introduction

In Chapter 4, we developed a classification system for understanding unethical conduct in supervision, suggesting interventions based upon an individualised formulation of the problem. We now describe the 12 best techniques, in the form of practical guidelines for resolving unethical issues. Our evidence-based guidelines were developed based on the advice of experts (e.g., Barnett & Molzon, 2014; Falender, 2020; Knapp et al., 2013; Thomas, 2014), general supervision theories, research (e.g., Kolb, 1984; Watkins & Milne, 2014), and from supervision competence frameworks (e.g., Reiser et al., 2018). For example, where we found it necessary to supplement the meagre research literature on the supervision of unethical conduct, we have drawn significantly on SAGE, an instrument that outlines a general range of evidence-based supervision techniques (Milne & Reiser, 2014). We have also drawn on the relevant guidelines from our supervision manual (e.g., feedback: Milne & Reiser, 2017). This manual includes video demonstrations of competent supervision in many of the interventions that we will now describe.

While our primary focus remains on supervisors and what they can do to support and guide their supervisees, these techniques are also applicable to supervisors themselves, in relation to critical issues that can arise in supervision (e.g., relationship boundary violations, as discussed in Chapter 1). It follows that, where necessary, supervisors should in turn be supported and guided, if we are to enhance the effectiveness of supervision. This guidance is most commonly provided by consultants, managers, tutors, peer groups, or through supervision-of-supervision (meta-supervision: Newman & Kaplan, 2016). To reflect this broad potential use of the 12 techniques, whenever possible we will phrase them in suitably general terms (e.g., 'leader'). When this is difficult we will refer to 'supervisor' and 'supervisee', but we wish to encourage the reader to recognise that this guidance may equally apply to other dyads involving a leader (e.g., consultant and supervisor).

Techniques for Resolving Unethical Conduct

We start with the need to manage the supervision session, as the proper structuring of supervision is fundamental. We offer guidelines on best practices, then provide an example related to unethical conduct. We follow this structure for all remaining techniques,

Resolving Critical Issues in Clinical Supervision: A Practical, Evidence-based Approach, First Edition.
Derek L. Milne and Robert P. Reiser.
© 2023 John Wiley & Sons Ltd. Published 2023 by John Wiley & Sons Ltd.

incorporating possible explanations and formulations. An illustration will then indicate how these different strategies might be applied, before we close with the chapter conclusions and remaining action implications.

- **Manage the session**: Support and guidance in relation to critical issues occurs within a formal session (1:1, group, or other format) that is authorised by the employer, and where there is clear and effective leadership. The management of supervision starts with ensuring that there is an appropriate structure governing how the time is to be used, related to the main objectives and intended outcomes. This includes agreeing to and prioritising the agenda, noting the session duration, and being explicit about the supervision methods to be used. A contract should formalise these details, listing any relevant competencies to be addressed, where applicable, how evaluation will happen, and emergency coverage arrangements. Managing also includes time-keeping through prompts on progress, using 'signposting' about the pace and direction of the session, ensuring a smooth progression by limiting digressions or avoidance behaviours, and generally 'chairing' the session to ensure that the agenda is covered efficiently.

    An example of the importance of effective session management involves addressing boundary violations within the supervisee's practice. In this instance the supervisor takes special care to establish and maintain clear boundaries in supervision, and be alert to the possibility that the past boundary violations involving patients may repeat themselves within the supervision relationship (i.e., a 'parallel process' may occur: Thomas, 2014). This may take subtle forms, such as the boundary-violating transactional games played by supervisees, such as 'two against the agency' (Kadushin & Harkness, 2002). In turn, such problematic interactions may be inadvertently encouraged by the supervisor's beliefs. A common problem is the misattribution of responsibility, a cognitive process of inferring the causes of critical events through our own common-sense explanations, in order to attach blame to others for negative events, and to ensure credit to ourselves for positive events. This is an example of a common self-serving bias where responsibility and credit is allocated in ways that boost our self-esteem.

    In the example of 'two against the agency', the supervisor may collude with the supervisee in not complying fully with requirements due to attributing responsibility for some injustice to the host organisation (e.g., 'boundaries have been badly managed here for years, so we can be relaxed about them in supervision too – why should my supervisee suffer?'). The problematic attribution in this instance is 'self-justification', namely that the workplace environment is to blame, and this justifies having relaxed boundaries ('My line manager never bothers with structuring our meetings, so why should I structure supervision?'). Other possible problematic attributions are to 'discount' or minimise the consequences, by accepting some responsibility, but discounting the significance, by believing that in practice things like structure 'do not really matter that much'. This can be coupled with a sense that 'I'm the expert' and consequent inattention to or disregard of the evidence-base that might suggest otherwise.

    In the above discussion, we could just as readily have highlighted the attributions of the supervisee, as we all utilise biased attributions designed to help us to feel better about ourselves. The same applies to organisations, which will often seek to escape blame by attributing responsibility elsewhere ('passing the buck'), such as the political context of underfunding (Gailey & Lee, 2005).

- **Build an alliance:** This second technique involves creating a supportive and trusting environment, featuring an emotional bond, shared objectives, and task collaboration. The sense of bond is strengthened when leaders such as supervisors or consultants provide warmth, genuineness, empathy, and understanding in a confident, genuine manner. Effective leaders are attentive to emergent personal issues as they relate to work (e.g., performance anxiety), but are careful not to enter into a therapeutic or clinical relationship. The focus needs to remain firmly on work-related tasks, not the supervisee's personal issues. If therapy or treatment is indicated, then referral should be discussed. In order to highlight the importance of attending to the emotional climate of the workplace, sessions can start with a personal 'check-in' (such as: 'How are you coping with your work today?'). This can flag problematic events or feelings, which may become agenda items. Therefore, this relationship aspect of the session should remain 'normative', rather than therapeutic or educational, by emphasising social support, coping strategy enhancement, and similar supportive methods (including self-disclosure and emotional support). A nurturing mode of relating fosters a safe relationship, including non-specific reassuring, agreeing and encouraging, and building rapport including empathy, motivational messages, and validating or praising the supervisee.

  Thomas (2014) describes how a supervision alliance that lacks such qualities runs the risk that supervisees censor or do not fully disclose critical incidents to the supervisor, for fear of criticism or rebuke. The most serious adverse consequences are that supervision becomes superficial and disengaged, with resulting compromises of patient safety. Conversely, an empowering alliance is engaging and emotionally supportive, helping the supervisee to identify and process distressing feelings. In this context, the supervisor validates and responds to distress by encouraging the supervisee to describe the distressing experience or critical event. This progresses through to problem clarification, improving understanding, then 'working-through' the problem (by developing and applying problem-solving actions, despite emotional discomfort). If this technique is successful, the distress is replaced by well-being, such as a sense of mastery over such experiences (Stiles et al., 1990). A useful heuristic that can be extrapolated to supervision is the process by which any problematic or distressing experiences are assimilated/integrated as described by Gabalda et al. (2016). This process often follows a saw-toothed pattern in which advances alternate with setbacks, such as alliance ruptures. (ZPD). The alliance repair procedure (Safran et al., 2007) and the 'resolution' method (Greenberg & Malcolm, 2002) also share similar techniques. All three techniques have their origins in therapy, so another task in maintaining the alliance is to ensure that they do not cross over into therapy, which constitutes a boundary violation. Key pointers are to be explicit about the reason for using such techniques (i.e., to facilitate the supervisee's work behaviour, not their personal growth), to monitor the supervisee's experience (does it feel like therapy?), and to study the effect that any techniques have on their behaviour (is the outcome helpful?). These considerations echo the ethical decision-making criteria, suggesting that we can best manage supervision sessions when we behave ethically (e.g., by ensuring that we can use such techniques competently, without causing harm or limiting autonomy).

- **Facilitate discussion:** A third valuable technique is to help the supervisee reflect on work-related ethical issues routinely, as 'part and parcel' of the job. This should normalise ethics as an appropriate topic for regular discussion, and help the supervisee to develop ethical awareness and competencies. Ask questions to help clarify how issues are perceived or interpreted (e.g., 'What would make that response unethical?'). Pose scenarios to encourage the supervisee to apply the relevant rules, standards or procedures to relevant events (e.g., 'How should we respond, bearing in mind the profession's guidance?'). Discussion is fundamentally an educational activity, to be used to aid the exploration of ideas, including the application of theory to practice, and the making sense of events (e.g., causal reasoning). Discussion was the third most frequently used method (employed in 75% of studies) in a review of 52 successful manipulations of supervision (Milne et al., 2008; Milne & James, 2000). In these studies, it included explaining, question and answer episodes, goal-setting, and challenging through different kinds of questioning (e.g., awareness-raising; critical). The aim was to develop the follower's current thinking. In this sense, discussing is intended to skilfully and constructively destabilise and so shift the follower's understanding of issues, opening up fresh possibilities and more appropriate ways of thinking (e.g., by creating some perplexity, then suggesting a possible solution). In an analogue study of therapy supervision (Bearman et al., 2017), the condition that resulted in significant increases in therapist competence included discussion for 22% of the session time. These authors referred to their discussion as 'cognitive restructuring discussion', which they defined as disputing dysfunctional or irrational thoughts that might lead to unhelpful emotions or actions. Other approaches to discussion include the less confrontational use of 'guided discovery', also known as 'Socratic dialogue'. This has been defined as helping the follower recognise their own assumptions and internal contradictions, to encourage new perspectives, and to acquire new skills in reflecting on situations (Prasko et al., 2020). These authors suggest that leaders can facilitate this through inductive questioning, drawing out the supervisee's understanding, while sharing truly in the process of discovery (i.e., not assuming the answer is known). Illustrative questions suggested by Prasko et al. (2020) might lead a leader to ask: 'Can you see how your relationship boundary might be similar to ours?'; 'How would what you just said alter this boundary? What do you think about the ethical aspect?', 'How does your view on clinical ethics relate to your view on professional relationships?'. These questions should change as the supervisee proceeds to reconsider something. The initial questions seek information about the issue, accompanied by empathic listening that leads to a summary by the supervisor. This sets the scene for analytical synthesis questions that invite the follower to apply this summary to their understanding (e.g., 'Do you still believe so strongly in your conclusions about our relationship boundary?' 'How does this affect the way you now think about your clinical relationships?'). Guided discovery concludes with capsule summaries, leading to application questions, used to take stock and to consider the action implications of any change in understanding (e.g., 'What do you think you might change in our clinical relationships?'; 'What is the worst possible scenario, and what could you do about it?'). Prasko et al. (2020) helpfully provide copious verbatim examples of guided discovery, including an illustration of how it can strengthen ethical reflection.

Questioning and challenging need to be balanced with support, so that it is properly understood as something of an academic exercise, personally 'stretching' and stimulating (Kemer, 2020), but not overly challenging or personally threatening. An example is development of cultural competence, which should be given active attention in supervision, including the supervisory relationship. According to Barnett and Molzon (2014, p. 1056), 'Thoughtful supervisors will ... push supervisees to consider and address how these factors may be affecting the supervisees' in their clinical work ... It is essential that cultural competence (really, diversity competence) ... is integrated ... into all aspects of clinical supervision'. Discussion alone is usually insufficient for behaviour change (Bearman et al., 2017), but it represents an important and frequently used component within a blended approach to developing competence, one that combines various experiential methods such as modelling, role-play, and feedback (Bailin et al., 2018).

- **Be a role model**: Discussion and other verbal techniques should be supplemented by behavioural demonstrations by the leader, showing what competent professional practice looks like (or through presenting relevant video material). Demonstrating how to be an ethical supervisor involves active modelling of how to manage boundaries, ensuring proper pacing and closure. Modelling of ethical conduct should also be implicit, based on the supervisor's general manner, or explicit through specific ethical skill-development work. Demonstrating should remove any possible confusion about how to behave ethically, enabling the supervisee to imitate the general manner or specific skills of the supervisor correctly. This also boosts confidence and helps socialise the supervisee into the moral ways of the profession and the workplace. In an analogue study of therapy supervision (Bearman et al., 2017), role-play resulted in significant increases in therapist competence when provided for a significant portion of supervision sessions (39%).

  An example of the value of modelling is related to malpractice, where certain behaviours appear to be particularly significant. According to Knapp et al. (2013), primary care physicians who have fewer malpractice claims and disciplinary incidents used more orienting statements (explaining the procedures to their patients) and more facilitating statements (statements that encourage patients to express their opinions or concerns). From the patients' perspective, their claims were partly triggered by feeling that their physician had devalued their opinions, failed to understand their point of view, or had tried to withhold information. Supervision is an opportunity to demonstrate more appropriate communication skills, which may also improve adherence within both supervision and treatment.

- **Educate and train:** Education is a technique that develops capability: the capacity for critical thinking and intellectual problem-solving, when faced with novel situations (Fraser & Greenhalgh, 2001). This is another verbal technique, including discussion (see previous paragraphs), teaching, and reading about ethics, but epitomised by research activity (e.g., designing an action research study to solve a problem). With growing capability, the supervisee develops a deeper understanding, which may help them to improve their insight (e.g., how guidelines apply), as well as their logical reasoning and willingness to explore issues in a balanced but critical fashion (e.g., seeking evidence).

Teaching involves providing information about theories, facts and figures, ideas, and methods, in a didactic fashion (e.g., traditional 'academic' or 'information transmission' teaching). However, education of this kind is unlikely to lead to a change in behaviour, a significant concern in dealing with unethical conduct. Falender (2020) notes that ethics teaching tends to focus on developing a rote knowledge of an ethics code, without encouraging practitioners to consider ethical dilemmas in context, and without the teacher demonstrating positive ethical conduct in a way that would enhance the transfer of this teaching to the workplace. Therefore, we need to supplement teaching with training.

By contrast, training that targets behavioural proficiency helps rectify inadequate or incompetent supervision, so that standards of performance can be achieved (Beidas & Kendall, 2010; Rakovshik & McManus, 2010). When providing training, supervisors engage supervisees in appropriate experiential activities, designed to encourage trial-and-error learning (e.g., simulations, behavioural rehearsal, and educational role play). Training is primarily a practical, problem-based, and experimental activity that promotes competence in supervisees through strengthening their skill repertoire (e.g., how to best manage relationship boundaries). Through its experiential emphasis, training complements verbal and visual methods, creating a rounded, balanced experience that is more likely to succeed (as reflected in the old saying: 'I hear and I forget; I see and I remember; I do and I understand').

For optimal effectiveness, training methods address the learning needs of the supervisee, related to their stage of development (e.g., novice or expert). Also, training activity should have agreed upon learning goals (objectives and outcomes), and the supervisor needs to be sensitive to the anxiety that is often encountered when conducting experiential learning activities, taking care to create a safe and facilitating environment. Supervisees need to be encouraged to play an active role in their own learning; as in preparing carefully for training, raising questions for the leader, and anticipating problems in applying the training. An example related to ethical issues concerns the sexual exploitation of patients. Knapp et al. (2013) suggest that this risk can be reduced by rigorously maintaining boundaries, by seeking social support (e.g., the advice of a peer), and through training that develops professional skills in addressing the effective management of such strong feelings. The next chapter considers training in depth.

- **Observe:** The best way to ensure clinical oversight and the objective monitoring of ethical conduct is to observe representative samples of clinical work. This helps to ensure patient protection, and fulfills an ethical duty in supervision. Observation was employed in 79% of studies in a review of 52 successful manipulations of supervision (Milne et al., 2008; Milne & James, 2000), but it appears that the observation of clinical skills is 'rarely used' under routine clinical conditions (Dorsey et al., 2018, p. 1). Informative exceptions include systematic implementation efforts (e.g., including manualised supervisor training), such as IAPT programme in England (Improving Access to Psychological Therapies: Clark, 2018), and the multi-systemic approach to troubled families in the USA

(Schoenwald et al., 2009). In a third example, Dorsey et al. (2018) used observation in a public mental health service in the USA (Trauma-focused CBT: Cognitive Behavioural Therapy) to objectively describe workplace-based clinical supervision (involving 18 supervisors and 61 clinicians). They noted the potential of supervision to foster evidence-based practice, but added that observation of supervisees by their supervisors was infrequent (as were two other related 'gold-standard' techniques: the observation-based supervision methods of behavioural rehearsal in supervision, and supervisor modelling).

Comparisons between the use of observation versus relying on the supervisees' reports have indicated that there is greater agreement on the severity of clinical problems when observation occurred, together with other benefits (Galanter et al., 2014). From their review of the literature, this included positive changes in both patient care and education, increased hospital discharges, decreases in medical errors, and stronger compliance with care management protocols. These authors concluded that the absence of observation 'handicapped' the supervisors' evaluations of patients, advocating 'direct supervision' (where the supervising physician is physically present with the supervisee and patient). Galanter et al. (2014) also recognised that this observation required more time, but believed that the benefits made this worthwhile (potential gains in educational outcomes, patient safety, and patient satisfaction).

As this example indicates, observation can be live (e.g., co-working), or can occur through video/audio recordings (or other 'permanent products', such as clinical letters/reports). Observing should complement self-report and other sources of information, providing a relatively objective and richly detailed insight into the supervisees' work. This nourishes and stimulates supervision, representing a valuable resource for learning and feedback. Observation can also help to review strengths and weaknesses, improving the prioritisation of the supervision agenda, and enabling self-evaluation. This is a vital skill and can be especially informative for the supervisor. For example, self-evaluations can indicate self-serving or negative biases that are obstacles to learning (e.g., 'I was thinking that the patient was angry, so I tried to change the topic, as I am not good at handling emotions'). There is reason to expect that novices will have a bias to overestimate their competence, while experts will tend to underestimate their competence, consistent with the 'unskilled and unaware of it' bias (Kruger & Dunning, 1999). Such a review process could lead into an educational role-play, where the supervisor can again observe how the supervisee copes, with opportunities to demonstrate some ways to handle emotions, concluding with additional rehearsal and refinement of these coping skills.

An example of using observation was provided by Barnett and Molzon (2014), who suggested a gradual approach, starting with the supervisee observing the supervisor. This can proceed to joint working, then to live supervision (including feedback in real time). Recordings may be used next, with supervisees taking the lead in reflecting on self-selected recorded material in non-threatening ways. This can progress to more challenging work incidents or topics, and the review process can also become more thorough. Technological advances can boost these valuable opportunities for learning (e.g., online observation and feedback in real time: the 'bug-in-the-eye' approach: Weck et al., 2015), as can the review of clinical outcome monitoring data in supervision (e.g., Grossl et al., 2014).

A major example of the wide-scale implementation of observing can be found within the IAPT programme (Clark, 2018). IAPT training is part of a systematic process of post-qualification continuing professional development (CPD), and includes a five-day workshop in supervision, and the subsequent regular supervision and monitoring of therapist competence in relation to protocol-driven interventions recommended within a national competency framework (Roth & Pilling, 2008). This monitoring includes the review of a minimum number of clinical recordings by a supervisor, with the aim of maintaining competence, ensuring treatment fidelity, and contributing to clinicians' continued professional accreditation (Kellett et al., 2020).

Observing is also a critical aspect of clinical oversight, a term used in medicine to describe patient care activities performed by supervisors to ensure quality of care including patient safety, especially where the supervisee (trainee) sees patients in the presence of their supervisor. Kennedy et al. (2007) distinguished between several types of oversight that they observed, based on extensive interviews and observational fieldwork (e.g., 88 physicians were observed during their clinical activities for a total of 216 hours), conducted in Emergency Department and General Internal Medicine in-patient teaching wards in Canada. 'Routine oversight' referred to the planned monitoring of trainees' clinical work; 'responsive oversight' was a double-check or elaboration of trainees' clinical work when there are concerns; 'backstage oversight' was undertaken without the trainees' awareness, and 'direct patient care' referred to when the supervisors took over.

- **Provide feedback**: It is a truism that there is no learning without feedback, but it is also the case that not all feedback facilitates learning. The best feedback provides precise information on any gaps between the objectives of supervision and the supervisee's performance, rather than covering peripheral issues (e.g., the supervisee's personal style). Good feedback is also supportive, constructive, linked to a demonstration of the desired behaviour, and timely (the sooner the better, usually). According to Haarman (2013), the lack of timely feedback is often the most common basis for complaints about supervision. He recommends ongoing feedback related to any evaluation process (see following text), to minimise misunderstandings, and to maximise the time available for making improvements. Typically, effective feedback provides a concise and clear summary of the important information, helping the follower gain insight and develop competence, as well as validating and consolidating any good practice. Improvements in the relevant competencies should form a definite part of supervision, ideally based in part on the supervisee's understanding and self-monitoring. This includes role-plays or other experiential simulations, which enable feedback to be immediate, refined, and precise. Agreed objectives would ensue naturally, and the supervisor should consolidate this by demonstrating the competencies to the required standard, so providing a role model. Feedback may be verbal or written, and may also include a general summary of the positives and negatives in the supervisee's performance (e.g., using praise). The bottom line is that feedback addresses the supervisee's professional practice, as indicated at least partly through observation, and seeks to ensure patient safety. Feedback was the most frequently used method (employed in 81% of studies) in a review of 52 successful manipulations of supervision (Milne et al., 2008; Milne & James, 2000). In these studies, feedback included praise and constructive criticism. In an analogue study of therapy supervision (Bearman et al., 2017), corrective feedback for 75% of the sampled session time was the most frequent method used and resulted in significant increases in therapist competence.

It is also important to seek feedback on the leadership provided. This can be awkward and unnatural at first, but makes educational, professional, and ethical sense. The quality of the feedback can be boosted by asking the follower about helpful events (e.g., how a problem was resolved; what was useful clinically). Some workplaces routinely use standard feedback forms to help the process. The leader should encourage honesty and candour (e.g., prompting the follower for 'three positives and a negative', and by responding professionally to feedback).

An example where feedback can be vital is when supervision is of poor quality and hence unethical and potentially harmful. Ellis et al. (2014, p. 7) defined harmful supervision as 'the supervisor's actions or inactions resulting in psychological, emotional, or physical harm to the supervisee'. These authors distinguished harmful from inadequate supervision, pointing out that inadequate supervision may not be harmful, but that it is of such poor quality as to create risks. This was because inadequate supervision may fail to meet legal and ethical standards (e.g., supervisor incompetence, disinterest, or unavailability). Other characteristics of inadequate supervision were a failure to provide accurate and timely feedback to supervisees regarding competencies; and disrespecting or disregarding supervisee input.

- **Facilitate reflection**: Effective leaders encourage thoughtful deliberation on ethically relevant issues and past actions (especially including boundary issues and managing multiple relationships). The function of reflection is to draw on the supervisee's personal understanding of relevant ethical experiences, to make sense of their perceptions and experiences and to learn to construct ethically informed decision-making.

    An example comes from 'disciplinary' or 'mandated' supervision, which is supervision required by a professional registration or licensing board, intended for professionals who are judged to have violated ethical or practice standards or relevant laws (Thomas, 2014). This type of supervision seeks to correct the supervisee's misunderstandings and skill deficiencies and may include guided reflection on the personal and professional factors behind ethical errors. Reflection may also extend to the actual or potential consequences of their ethical violations on patients, and others. Reflecting in such ways can help supervisee's gain insight into their own behaviour, helping them to better recognise risk factors. A heightened awareness of the kinds of events, circumstances, and subjective experiences (e.g., strong emotions) that flag the presence of risk can improve objectivity and enable improved ethical conduct.
- **Problem-solve**: Leaders facilitate ethical problem-solving work by jointly defining ethical issues, and by undertaking task analysis. This includes 'positive' ethics (i.e., strengthening skills in the absence of an incident), and 'routine' ethics (i.e., making ethical topics a regular part of supervision, for instance, by discussing recent issues mentioned in the media). A negative stressor worthy of problem-solving is workload management, since work overload is such a common concern among clinicians. This can

include a review of the options, and the joint generation of possible options (e.g., more efficient ways of working). Problem-solving work should continue with an evaluation of these options, leading to an action plan. Some actions may benefit from some behavioural rehearsal (e.g., a role-play to practise a challenging skill).

An example of a topic requiring problem-solving work is dual relationships. We have already noted some suggestions earlier in this chapter (e.g., jointly considering the consequences). According to Knapp et al. (2013), it is also wise to document all multiple relationships that might be contraindicated or exploitative. This record should note the facts or circumstances, and the reasons for the selected option (e.g., unavoidable multiple relationships). Particularly in a high-risk situation, it is helpful to seek consultation to evaluate a proposed boundary crossing with a senior colleague. This analysis of the problem may well clarify the best option or will at least represent the ethical management of the situation.

- **Encourage self-care:** Managing our health is an ethical obligation, given that illness or distress may compromise our clinical performance or judgement, putting others at risk (Health and Care Professions Council (HCPC), 2016). This includes managing our ability to behave ethically (Barnett & Molzon, 2014). Conversely, actively practicing self-care can foster our physical and mental well-being, encouraging us to achieve our potential and strengthening our capacity to support colleagues. Such virtuous behaviour includes striking a balance between our professional and our private lives. While at work, it means coping with the pressures to remain resilient and committed, rather than slipping towards disengagement and burnout. Similarly, ethical supervision will model and address issues of self-care, to help encourage followers to proactively address any well-being issues, and to socialise them into a culture of self-care (Bernard & Goodyear, 2014). Good supervision contributes to well-being, leading to a virtuous cycle of increasing work engagement and improved outcomes for healthcare organisations (Boorman, 2009). As we noted in our prior book (Milne & Reiser, 2020), supervision can play its role by providing social support (especially emotional support), increasing feelings of choice and control, enhancing communication, and by aiding workload management. In that book we also summarised the affirmative evidence for several self-care techniques.

An example of self-care is cultivating your social support system. This starts with the support you get from a leader, and depends primarily on the quality of the emotional support element. Other valuable aspects of support are the provision of information (e.g., advice), practical help (e.g., co-working), and companionship support (e.g., being made to feel that you belong). Rather than passively expecting these types of support, we can actively facilitate them by firstly ensuring that we reciprocate the support that we do receive. Regulating any negative reactions or emotions also helps, as does enough openness to discussing our feelings about the work (including our relationships). Shared activities (at work and socially), including helping to reduce the stressors faced by colleagues, also tend to boost social support (Lakey & Orehek, 2011). These authors concluded from their review of the literature that such support can improve well-being, especially when support is flexible enough to include different sources and methods, and when it includes ordinary conversations that help individuals regulate their emotions (e.g., seeking support or comforting from someone who shares your approach to coping).

- **Mentor:** This aspect of supervision involves taking a personal interest in the supervisees' overall professional growth, welfare, and development, helping to shepherd them through difficult transitions. It may involve modelling, guidance, teaching, and general support, enabling them to become full members of a profession (Johnson, 2007). The mentoring role is similar to that of a consultant, though the mentor in many professions is only slightly more experienced than the mentee, and mentoring may also be obligatory. For example, pre-registered student nurses have mentors whose role is to facilitate learning, offer role modelling, and to provide support and encouragement (e.g., The Mentors Behaviour Scale in Nursing: Chen et al., 2018). Mentoring has also been established as a peer support strategy within physiotherapy (Thomson et al., 2016), and peer mentoring has been used successfully with medical students, with self-report data indicating that it led to enhanced competence in conducting physical exams and interacting with patients (Choudhury et al., 2014), and in decision-making and other clinical skills (Eisen et al., 2014).

  In a study with psychology trainees acquiring skills in psychological assessment, mentees reported that having a peer mentor helped their assessment training, especially in the development of technical skills such as scoring and report writing (89% of the participating mentees rated that having a peer mentor was *somewhat* or *very* helpful: Danzi et al., 2020).

  However, some skills reportedly benefitted little through mentoring, such as the development of multicultural competency, possibly because the mentors gave such topics little attention. Within supervision, other examples include discussions on career planning, advice on work-life balancing, getting involved in the profession, and becoming engaged in scholarship (e.g., working jointly on a research or writing project; serving together on a professional committee (Barnett & Molzon, 2014)).

- **Evaluate and provide gatekeeping:** Feedback is a kind of evaluation, but with a formative function (i.e., to foster competence development). By contrast, evaluation is summative, usually entailing a quantitative rating of competence using a standard form (e.g., a checklist), linked to a qualitative judgement about overall progress (e.g., a pass or fail decision on a placement/programme, a 'gatekeeping' function). Supervisors are ethically bound to provide professional evaluations on their supervisees, while supervisees are legally entitled to receive such evaluations. Evaluations should be as accurate, fair, and objective as possible (Haarman, 2013), based on formally monitoring the supervisee's competence, drawing on explicit public criteria applied to representative work samples (e.g., direct observation; a summary of the results of patient satisfaction measures; clinical outcome monitoring). In order to ensure clinical oversight, the supervisor should directly observe work performance, through audio/video-recordings (see 'observing'). Standard evaluation forms and criteria should be applied to such data, and the supervisee should know in advance about these evaluation procedures. The supervisor should routinely present and explain their evaluations, encouraging clarifications, action-planning (especially how to improve evaluations), and fostering a sense that this was a fair and just appraisal experience (i.e., that 'due process' was followed, a core aspect of procedural justice and ethical supervision).

When it comes to 'gatekeeping', ultimately the supervisor has a duty to ensure that those who are not suited to their profession are excluded (Bernard & Goodyear, 2014). Barnett and Molzon (2014) note that gatekeeping is inherently difficult, making it tempting to adopt a monitoring approach where possible. They noted how supervisees who have created concern can be passed on to the next supervisor like a 'hot potato', but stress that supervisors must take their obligations more seriously, addressing any difficulties for the sake of future patients. A survey of nearly 1500 placements by Gonsalvez et al. (2021) indicated that 17 were failed (1.2%), a figure that reduced as trainees progressed through their programmes. Yepes-Rios et al. (2016) agreed that there was a 'failure to fail', and conducted a literature review to define the barriers and boosters to gatekeeping, finding many issues that were common to various disciplines. Gatekeeping may include more comfortable options, such as remedial arrangements (e.g., repeating a placement with a different supervisor), or a leave of absence, when personal impairment compromises competence. In noting such options, Haarman (2013) adds that any such plan should be recorded and signed by all parties, and that all other aspects of due process are followed scrupulously. He points out that gatekeeping is especially tricky ethically and legally, and advocates consulting with appropriate authorities, to avoid liability or blame. We might add that it may also be tricky interpersonally, for the very reasons that a negative evaluation is being considered (e.g., because a supervisee has poor impulse or anger control). Also, a counterattack can be expected from most supervisees, given what is at stake. Indeed, both peers and supervisors may join in criticising or even ostracising the evaluator, often pursuing aversive forms of due process. Some further helpful suggestions on gatekeeping can be found in Homrich and Henderson (2018).

How can we minimise such disquiet? In our experience from within an initial professional training programme, we found it helpful to share the gatekeeping responsibility. Instead of requiring the supervisor alone to make the difficult decision, we altered the procedure so that the supervisors involved only made a recommendation, and in turn that was considered by more than one other person, ultimately including an external examiner and exam board. In one instance, an external examiner was able to study a recording and made their own independent evaluation. We also consulted with the university's experts, to ensure that our procedure was appropriate to the context. This procedure was included in the supervisees' handbooks, and they also had related teaching that encouraged them to familiarise themselves with their role in making this procedure work fairly (e.g., careful documentation and evidence gathering). In one sad instance, resulting in excluding a supervisee from the training programme, this procedure was judged robust by the university and withstood a legal challenge by the supervisee, although it was nonetheless very difficult for all those involved. Unfortunately, evaluation done properly will occasionally identify incompetence, unethical conduct, or other reasons for ending a supervisee's career. But only by behaving ethically as evaluators will supervisors and other leaders protect patients and their own profession. Supervisors can also be helped to do what is right through relevant training, peer and institutional support, and by identifying alternative career options for failing supervisees (Yepes-Rios et al., 2016).

However, behaving ethically over evaluations can be complex and quite challenging. Echoing our emphasis on peer consultation, Haarman (2013) advocates seeking supervision-of-supervision, when contemplating such negative gatekeeping decisions. This can help to ensure that any judgements are carefully reasoned and are not affected by strong feelings on gatekeeping or the supervisee. Key points again reflect due process: whether multiple methods of evaluation were used, related to previously established criteria; whether ongoing feedback was provided; and whether appropriate efforts were made to remedy any deficiencies. Haarman (2013) also suggests running an imaginary test of the proposed evaluation: how would the evaluation sound to a court, or to a professional registration (certification) board?

The unpleasant emotions associated with gatekeeping have also been noted across disciplines. In physiotherapy, Sellberg et al. (2020) created a focus group of 12 clinical supervisors, and a content analysis of their views indicated the value of support within their social network. They described how difficult feedback situations undermined their self-confidence as supervisors, but how talking to a colleague represented great support, provided new insights, and created a feeling of participation in a community of supervisors (including a teaching team). Dory et al. (2020) addressed the same kind of problem by adopting a 'nudges' approach to form-filling in medicine. Nudge theory proposes that small, straightforward environmental prompts can help to shape desirable behaviours, such as the supervisors' accurate completion of evaluation forms, so reducing the traditional emphasis on pressuring supervisors. Dory et al. (2020) found that nudges such as improvements to the layout of the evaluation form led to significantly higher quality, more detailed, balanced and actionable feedback, and better information for decision-makers. These examples underline the importance of ensuring that supervisors receive support and guidance when making difficult evaluations.

Illustration: Who Is Ultimately Responsible for Gatekeeping?

This vignette involves the supervision of doctoral students who completed a second-year practicum (placement) in a university clinical psychology training clinic. It is the same clinic as described in Chapter 3. As noted there, supervisors were a combination of university faculty and part-time independent contractors, hired solely to provide supervision in the clinic. Supervisors were responsible for evaluating their students on a quarterly basis, with a summative evaluation after 9 months. The university had developed a standardised evaluation form to record the supervisor's ratings, reflecting the major competencies of clinical psychology practice, based on Fouad et al. (2009). Procedures for dealing with problem students were detailed in two documents: the clinic procedure manual (the clinic policy on supervision), and the supervision agreement (the contract between supervisor and supervisee). According to the clinic manual, when problems with individual students arose, the clinic director was to be notified and then participated in the development of a performance improvement plan with the supervisor. The supervision agreement specified procedures for handling problems with a student's performance, including a series of steps to be taken, starting with an informal oral discussion with the supervisee, a follow-on written documented discussion with the supervisee specifically identifying the performance problems, and, finally, a comprehensive performance improvement plan with a specific time frame for remediating problems. In this final stage of remediation, if the problem had not been resolved a referral was made to the clinic director for remedial supervision. If necessary, students could also be referred for review by the university's student disciplinary committee.

However, in practice supervisors rarely referred students to the clinic director until extremely late in the disciplinary process, where a pervasive pattern of problematic behaviour had already occurred. For example, despite the availability of a monthly meeting designed to assist supervisors in managing problem students, supervisors very rarely addressed individual performance problems, often focusing on more general questions about clinic policy. Also, despite clear guidance on the need for procedural documentation in the supervision agreement, when students were referred to the director, there was typically no written documentation or evidence of a clear plan for remediation on the part of the supervisor, even when significant problems had occurred. This was true even in some cases where the student was in danger of failing their practicum experience. As a result, there was often a hurried, last-minute effort by the supervisor to document past problems with the student from memory, incorporating them into the formal performance improvement plan. This plan would then be discussed directly with the student, including specific expectations for improvement and a time frame, usually resulting in an additional term of required supervision with the clinic director, so that the supervisee could demonstrate that the problem had been resolved. The great disadvantage to this process was that often students were unaware of impending disciplinary actions against them, by which time it was too late to informally remediate the problem. They had not received sufficiently clear and specific feedback from their supervisor to really have a fighting chance to address the problem early on. This often seemed to occur through a process of wishful thinking ('things will get better') and procrastination. In a worst-case scenario, the problem student would simply get 'passed' and transferred to the next supervisor. In one unfortunate instance, this resulted in a student who repeatedly demonstrated minimal competence and performance problems only being referred for remediation towards the end of their practicum.

In a second case, a student was referred to the clinic director extremely late in the disciplinary process, based on a critical event where the student had not obeyed a specific request by the supervisor that he immediately follow up and consult on a possible report to child protection authorities. Despite the supervisor's very direct order that he do so, the student then also failed to show up for a specially scheduled ad-hoc supervision session. When he eventually did attend for his regular supervision, the student then argued with the supervisor as to the appropriateness of filing a report (the student argued that a report did not jibe with his beliefs about what constituted 'common sense'). Although not obeying the request and not attending timely supervision (child abuse neglect reports have a mandated 24-hour notification period in the US) constituted significantly more egregious conduct, this problematic behavior had actually been preceded by periodic problems with unprofessional conduct in the clinic, in terms of the student's attire and manner. The student seemed unaware of the need to differentiate between a professional therapist role and the casual demeanour typical of his personal style. This problematic behaviour had been formally documented by the clinic staff, but this history of marginally inappropriate behaviour raised the question as to whether this student had really been sufficiently closely monitored before a critical event had occurred. Ultimately, the student was formally reprimanded and given a performance improvement plan. This required that he receive an additional period of ongoing probationary supervision by the clinic director. In addition, the plan included the suspension of any new cases, several reflection assignments (entailing review of appropriate laws, regulations, and policies), and finally, a referral to the student ethics committee for further action.

Reflections

While the final outcome of this particular case was positive, in that after three months of remedial supervision, the student was able to reflect appropriately on his problematic behaviour and recognised that he had been overconfident and had misconstrued his role as a student in training, the vignette reflects considerable confusion and boundary issues as to the role of supervisors as gatekeepers. While clinic disciplinary procedures were clearly spelled out in a clinic procedure manual, and within the supervision agreement, some supervisors were reluctant to assume an authoritative position vis a vis problematic conduct, with the consequence that they avoided confronting the issues in a timely and direct fashion. Gatekeeping is an inherently uncomfortable aspect of supervision and also highlights a dialectical tension between the supervision alliance and the need for summative evaluation. Many supervisors in the clinic enjoyed a relaxed and rather collegial relationship with their students, and so clinic discipline was often perceived as 'split off', as something to be tended to by clinic managers and the clinic director. This can contribute to an avoidant style of coping when supervisors have to confront problematic behaviour, and result in remedial actions being postponed in the hope that things will improve ('kicking the can down the road'). Therefore, in this instance the 'avoidant' supervisor was actually conforming to an informal convention within the supervisor's group.

Among other things, this illustration shows how having disciplinary procedures that are clearly outlined may nonetheless be undermined by peer pressure and other interpersonal factors. This includes avoidant supervisor behaviours, the minimal training provided in supervision, and the limited oversight of supervisors. This situation could have been significantly ameliorated if supervisors had followed the guidance from the clinic's feedback, evaluation and gatekeeping-related guidelines, including providing timely, clear, and documented feedback. In this and other ways, this illustration reflects much of the discussion of gatekeeping presented earlier in the chapter. Specifically, Barnett and Molzon (2014) noted how gatekeeping is inherently difficult, making it tempting to adopt a monitoring approach where possible. In that discussion we mentioned how the organisational system should support and guide leaders, such as the clinic director. Unfortunately, in this illustration supervision leadership was potentially compromised by lack of institutional support processes and the gap between necessary oversight and actual 'conditions on the ground'. As we will explain in Chapter 10 (the workplace context), directors should share responsibility as a part of a management team, or other suitable arrangement (e.g., consultancy, peer support group). Addressing trainee performance problems through appropriate gatekeeping needs to be managed systemically.

Conclusions and Action Implications

The previous chapter offered a classification and formulation of unethical conduct, which represents a large proportion of the critical issues that occur in supervision. The present chapter offered extensive guidelines on resolving such issues, in terms of 12 evidence-based techniques that can be used to promote ethical clinical practice. These 12 intervention techniques have been presented separately for clarity, but in reality supervision will blend several of them together for optimal effect. An illustration is the detect-articulate-respond approach (DAR: Dunn et al., 2017) for addressing value conflicts in supervision. We describe this approach in Chapter 6. This chapter and the preceding one address the first two kinds of negative critical issues outlined in Chapter 1, issues that we suggest are due to 'faulty design' (flawed planning and unprofessional conduct). In the next chapter we move on to the third critical issue, 'faulty training'.

As with other guidelines, we add the disclaimer that these guidelines require professional judgement for their proper application, such as factoring in individual differences, culture, and local conditions. Those who apply these guidelines should be fully qualified, and must take full responsibility for judging the suitability of these techniques in relation to their particular situation, including any appropriate adjustments, taking into account their own profession's guidance, and other relevant considerations (e.g., the guidance of their managers, leaders, and employers).

We conclude that ethical issues can and should be addressed routinely, as a 'standing item' on supervision agendas. Against a backdrop where ethical issues are rarely mentioned (Novoa-Gomez et al., 2019), we should strive to normalise ethical discussion, and work to develop virtuous clinicians. Supervision is an excellent way to pursue these objectives. The 12 techniques outlined in this chapter can be used to promote ethical clinical practice in relation to the routine consideration of ethics, and can guide corrective interventions in the case of problems. Although research is scarce, we believe that these techniques have a robust foundation in expert consensus, relevant theory, and through extrapolation. However, systematic organisational support for complex ethical issues like gatekeeping is required to guide and support supervisors in being virtuous. We address organisational support in Chapter 10.

Action Implications

The main implications for supervisors or other leaders are the importance of familiarity with the above techniques and the development of competence in using them to promote ethical practice. Leaders might also consider undertaking suitable evaluations, and collaborating with researchers in other forms of action research. Training programmes might consider drawing on these guidelines on ethical conduct to boost their curriculum in this neglected sphere of professional practice. There are also pointers for supervisees, and for other stakeholders (e.g., service managers; meta-supervisors), which we hope will stimulate a constructive review of their arrangements. It is important that healthcare leaders play their part in ensuring that the system supports and guides supervisors, especially in trying to resolve tricky ethical matters.

References

Bailin, A., Bearman, S. K., & Sal, R. (2018). Clinical supervision of mental health professionals serving youth: Format and micro-skills. *Administration and Policy in Mental Health and Mental Health Services Research*,*45*(5), 800–812. https://doi.org/10.1007/s10488-018-0865-y

Barnett, J.E., & Molzon, C. H. (2014). Clinical supervision of psychotherapy: Essential ethics issues for supervisors and supervisees. *Journal of Clinical Psychology, 70*(11), 1051–1061. https://doi.org/10.1002/jclp.22126

Bearman, S.K., Schneiderman, R. L., & Zoloth, E. (2017). Building an evidence base for effective supervision practices: An analogue experiment of supervision to increase EBT fidelity. *Administration and Policy in Mental Health and Mental Health Services Research, 44*(2), 293–307. https://doi.org/10.1007/s10488-016-0723-8

Beidas, R.S., & Kendall, P. C. (2010). Training therapists in evidence-based practice: A critical review of studies from a systems-contextual perspective. *Clinical Psychology: Science & Practice, 17*, 1–30. https://doi.org/10.1111/j.1468-2850.2009.01187.x.

Bernard, J.M., & Goodyear, R. K. (2014). *Fundamentals of clinical supervision*. Pearson.

Boorman, S. (2009). *The final report of the independent NHS health and well-being review*. Department of Health.

Gabalda, I.C., Stiles, W. B., & Pérez Ruiz, S. (2016). Therapist activities preceding setbacks in the assimilation process. *Psychotherapy Research, 26*(6), 653–664. https://doi.org/10.1080/10503307.2015.1104422

Chen, Y., Watson, R., & Hilton, A. (2018). The structure of mentors' behaviour in clinical nursing education: Confirmatory factor analysis. *Nurse Education Today, 68*, 192–197. https://doi.org/10.1016/j.nedt.2018.06.018

Choudhury, N., Khanwalkar, A., Kraninger, J., Vohra, A., Jones, K., & Reddy, S. (2014). Peer mentorship in student-run free clinics: The impact on preclinical education. *Family Medicine, 46*(3), 204–208.

Clark, D.M. (2018). Realising the mass public benefit of evidence-based psychological therapies: The IAPT programme. *Annual Review of Clinical Psychology, 14*, 159–183. https://doi.org/10.1146/annurev-clinpsy-050817-084833

Danzi, B. A., Tawfik, S. H., Mora Ringle, V. A., & Saez-Flores, E. (2020). Enhancing profession-wide competencies in supervision and assessment: An evaluation of a peer mentorship approach. *Training and Education in Professional Psychology, 14*(3), 176. http://dx.doi.org/10.1037/tep0000256

Dorsey, S., Kerns, S. E. U., Lucid, L., Pullmann, M. D., Harrison, J. P., Berliner, L., Thompson, K., & Deblinger, E. (2018). Objective coding of content and techniques in workplace-based supervision of an EBT in public mental health. *Implementation Science, 13*(19), 1–12. https://doi.org/10.1186/s13012-017-0708-3

Dory, V., Cummings, B. A., Mondou, M., & Young, M. (2020). Nudging clinical supervisors to provide better in-training assessment reports. *Perspectives on Medical Education, 9*(1), 66–70. http://dx.doi.org/10.1007/s40037-019-00554-3

Dunn, R., Callahan, J. L., Farnsworth, J. K., & Watkins, C. E. (2017). A proposed framework for addressing supervisee-supervisor value conflict. *The Clinical Supervisor, 36*(2), 203–222. https://doi.org/10.1080/07325223.2016.1246395

Eisen, S., Sukhani, S., Brightwell, A., Stoneham, S., & Long, A. (2014). Peer mentoring: Evaluation of a novel programme in paediatrics. *Archives of Disease in Childhood, 99*(2), 142–146. http://dx.doi.org/10.1136/archdischild-2013-304277

Ellis, M.V., Berger, L., Hanus, A. E., Ayala, E. E., Swords, B. A., & Siembor, M. (2014). Inadequate and harmful clinical supervision: Testing a revised framework and assessing occurrence. *The Counseling Psychologist, 42*(2), 434–472. https://doi.org/10.1177/0011000013508656

Falender, C. (2020). Ethics of clinical supervision: An international lens. *Psychology in Russia: State of the Art, 13*(1), 43–54. https://doi.org/10.11621/pir.2020.0104

Fouad, N. A., Grus, C. L., Hatcher, R. L., Kaslow, N. J., Hutchings, P. S., Madson, M. B., Collins, F. L., Jr., & Crossman, R. E. (2009). Competency benchmarks: A model for understanding and measuring competence in professional psychology across training levels. *Training and Education in Professional Psychology, 3*(4 Suppl), S5–S26. https://doi.org/10.1037/a0015832

Fraser, S.W., & Greenhalgh, T. (2001). Complexity science: Coping with complexity: Educating for capability. *British Medical Journal, 323*(7316), 799–803. https://doi.org/10.1136/bmj.323.7316.799

Gailey, J.A., & Lee, M. T. (2005). An integrated model of attribution of responsibility for wrongdoing in organizations. *Social Psychology Quarterly, 68*(4), 338–358.

Galanter, C.A., Nikolov, R., Green, N., Naidoo, S., Myers, M. F., & Merlino, J. P. (2014). Direct supervision in outpatient psychiatric graduate medical education. *Academic Psychiatry*. https://doi.org/10.1007/s40596-014-0247-z

Gonsalvez, C., Terry, J., Deane, F., Nasstasia, Y., Knight, R., & Hoong Gooi, C. (2021). End-of-placement failure rates among clinical psychology trainees : Exceptional training and outstanding trainees or poor gate-keeping? *Clinical Psychologist, 25*(3), 294–305. https://doi.org/10.1080/13284207.2021.1927692

Greenberg, L. S., & Malcolm, W. (2002). Resolving unfinished business: Relating process to outcome. *Journal of Consulting and Clinical Psychology, 70*(2), 406–416. https://doi.org/10.1037/0022-006X.70.2.406

Grossl, A.B., Reese, R. J., Norsworthy, L. A., & Hopkins, N. B. (2014). Client feedback data in supervision: Effects on supervision and outcome. *Training and Education in Professional Psychology, 8*(3), 182. https://doi.org/10.1037/tep0000025

Haarman, G.B. (2013). *Clinical supervision: Legal, ethical and risk management issues*. Foundations: Education & Consultation.

Health and Care Professions Council (HCPC). (2016). *The Standards of Conduct, Performance, and Ethics*. The Health and Care Professions Council.

Homrich, A.M., & Henderson, K. L. (2018). *Gatekeeping in the Mental Health Professions*. American Counselling Association.

Johnson, W.B. (2007). Transformational supervision: When supervisors mentor. *Professional Psychology: Research and Practice, 38*(3), 259–267. https://doi.org/10.1037/0735-7028.38.3.259

Kadushin, A., & Harkness, D. (2002). *Supervision in Social Work* (4th ed.). Columbia University Press.

Kellett, S., Wakefield, S., Simmonds-Buckley, M., & Delgadillo, J. (2020). The costs and benefits of practice-based evidence: Correcting some misunderstandings about the 10-year meta-analysis of IAPT studies. *British Journal of Clinical Psychology, 60*(1), 42–47. Retrieved on September 2 from https://bpspsychub.onlinelibrary.wiley.com/doi/abs/10.1111/bjc.12268 https://doi.org/10.1111/bjc.12268

Kemer, G. (2020). A comparison of beginning and expert supervisors' supervision cognitions. *Counselor Education & Supervision, 59*(1), 74–92. https://doi.org/10.1002/ceas.12167

Kennedy, T.J.T., Lingard, L., Baker, G. R., Kitchen, L., and Regehr, G. (2007). Clinical oversight: Conceptualizing the relationship between supervision and safety. *Journal of General Internal Medicine, 22*(8), 1080–1085. https://doi.org/10.1007/s11606-007-0179-3

Knapp, S., Younggren, J. N., VandeCreek, L., Harris, E., & Martin, J. N. (2013). *Assessing and managing risk in psychological practice* (2nd ed.). American Psychological Association.

Kolb, D.A. (1984). *Experiential Learning: Experience as the Source of Learning and Development* (2nd ed.). Prentice-Hall.

Kruger, J., and Dunning, D. (1999). Unskilled and unaware of it: How difficulties in recognising one's own incompetence lead to inflated self-assessments. *Journal of Personality and Social Psychology, 77*(6), 1121–1134. https://doi.org/10.1037/0022-3514.77.6.1121

Lakey, B., and Orehek, E. (2011). Relational regulation theory: A new approach to explain the link between perceived social support and mental health. *Psychological Review, 118*(3), 482–495. https://doi.org/10.1037/a0023477

Milne, D., & James, I. (2000). A systematic review of effective cognitive-behavioural supervision. *British Journal of Clinical Psychology, 39*(2), 111–127. https://doi.org/10.1348/014466500163149

Milne, D., & Reiser, R. P. (2020). *Supportive clinical supervision: From burnout to well-being, through restorative leadership*. Pavilion.

Milne, D.L., Aylott, H., Fitzpatrick, H., & Ellis, M. V. (2008). How does clinical supervision work? Using a best evidence synthesis approach to construct a basic model of supervision. *The Clinical Supervisor, 27*(2), 170–190. https://doi.org/10.1080/07325220802487915

Milne, D.L., and Reiser, R. (2014). SAGE: A scale for measuring competence in CBT supervision. In C. E. Watkins & D. L. Milne (Eds.), *The Wiley international handbook of clinical supervision* (pp. 402–415). Wiley-Blackwell.

Milne, D.L., & Reiser, R. P. (2017). *A Manual for Evidence-based CBT Supervision*. Wiley-Blackwell.

Newman, C.F., & Kaplan, D. A. (2016). *Supervision Essentials for Cognitive-Behavioural Therapy*. American Psychological Society.

Novoa-Gómez, M., Córdoba-Salgado, O., Rojas, N., Sosa, L., Cifuentes, D., & Robayo, S. (2019). A descriptive analysis of the interactions during clinical supervision. *Frontiers in Psychology, 10*, 669. https://doi.org/10.3389/fpsyg.2019.00669

Prasko, J., Krone, I., Burkauskas, J., Ociskova, M., Vanek, J., Abeltina, M., Dicevicius, D., Juskiene, A., Slepecky, M., & Bagdonaviciene, L. (2020). Guided discovery in cognitive behavioural supervision. *Activitas Nervosa Superior Rediviva, 62*(1), 17–28.

Rakovshik, S.G., & McManus, F. (2010). Establishing evidence-based training in CBT: A review of current empirical findings and theoretical guidance. *Clinical Psychology Review, 30*(5), 496–516. https://doi.org/10.1016/j.cpr.2010.03.004

Reiser, R.P., Cliffe, T., & Milne, D. L. (2018). An improved competence rating scale for CBT supervision: Short-SAGE. *The Cognitive Behaviour Therapist, 11*, Article e7. https://doi.org/10.1017/S1754470X18000065

Roth, A.D., & Pilling, S. (2008). Using an evidence-based methodology to identify the competences required to deliver effective cognitive and behavioural therapy for depression and anxiety disorders. *Behavioural and Cognitive Psychotherapy, 36*(2), 129–147. https://doi.org/10.1017/S1352465808004141

Safran, J.D., Muran, C. J., Stevens, C., & Rothman, M. (2007). A relational approach to supervision: Addressing ruptures in the alliance. In C. A. Falender & E. P. Shafranske (Eds.), *Casebook for clinical supervision: A competency-based approach* (pp. 137–157). American Psychological Association.

Schoenwald, S.K., Sheidow, A. J., & Chapman, J. E. (2009). Clinical supervision in treatment transport: Effects on adherence and outcomes. *Journal of Consulting and Clinical Psychology, 77*(3), 410–421. https://doi.org/10.1037/a0013788

Sellberg, M., Skavberg Roaldsen, K., Nygren-Bonnier, M., & Halvarsson, A. (2020). Clinical supervisors' experience of giving feedback to students during clinical integrated learning. *Physiotherapy Theory and Practice*, *38*(1), 122–131. https://10.1080/09593985.2020.1737996

Stiles, W.B., Elliott, R., Llewelyn, S., Firth-Cozens, J., Margison, F. R., Shapiro, D. A., & Hardy, G. (1990). Assimilation of problematic experiences by clients in psychotherapy. *Psychotherapy*, *27*(3), 411–420. https://doi.org/10.1037/0033-3204.27.3.411

Thomas, J.T. (2014). Disciplinary supervision following ethics complaints: Goals, tasks, and ethical dimensions. *Journal of Clinical Supervision: In Session*, *70*(11), 1–11. https://doi.org/10.1002/jclp.22131

Thomson, K., Nguyen, M., & Leithhead, I. (2016). Peer mentoring for clinical educators: A case study in physiotherapy. *Focus on Health Professional Education*, *17*(3), 30–44. https://doi.org/10.11157/fohpe.v17i3.175

Watkins, C.E., & Milne, D. L. (Eds.). (2014). *The Wiley International Handbook of Clinical Supervision*. Wiley.

Weck, F., Jakob, M., Neng, J. M. B., Höfling, V., Grikscheit, F., & Bohus, M. (2015). The effects of bug-in-the-eye supervision on therapeutic alliance and therapist competence in cognitive-behavioural therapy: A randomized controlled trial. *Clinical Psychology and Psychotherapy*, *23*(5), 1–11. https://doi.org/10.1002/cpp.1968

Yepes-Rios, M., Dudek, N., Duboyce, R., Curtis, J., Allard, R. J., & Varpio, L. (2016). The failure to fail underperforming trainees in health professions education: A BEME systematic review: BEME Guide No. 42. *Medical Teacher*, *38*(11), 1092–1099. https://doi.org/10.1080/0142159X.2016.1215414

6

Resolving Critical Issues in Training for Supervision

Introduction

Historically, supervision was a neglected duty that came automatically with seniority, but without training. Instead of training, supervisors based their practice on the way that they were themselves supervised (Lee et al., 2019), utilising incidental learning ('experience') and relevant clinical skills in order to provide a framework for supervision. This kind of 'reflexive' strategy is insufficient for competent supervision (Milne, 2008), partly because supervision 'is a distinct professional competency that requires formal education and training' (American Psychological Association: APA, 2015, p. 35). Without training, supervision is impaired (e.g., Schriger et al., 2020), ineffective (Bailin et al., 2018), and possibly harmful (Ellis et al., 2014).

Latterly, supervision training has become more common, but it remains problematic: 'Supervisors typically receive little or no formal training for their supervision role …' (Lee et al., 2019, p. 2). This is a widespread concern, both internationally (Watkins & Wang, 2014) and across the healthcare professions (e.g., in Occupational Therapy: Gaitskell & Morley, 2008; Tsutsumi, 2011). For example, in medicine, Bogie et al. (2017, p. 430) stated that: '… most medical educators receive little to no formal training in teaching before assuming the role of supervisor/teacher'. In summary, 'there is collective amazement, angst, and alarm about the neglect of supervisor training' (Gonsalvez & Milne, 2010, p. 234). The situation may be better within some professions (e.g., psychology and social work), but survey figures still indicate that at best only about two-thirds of the supervisors in these groups have received any training whatsoever, and that far fewer supervisees have been fully trained to provide competent supervision (Gonsalvez & Milne, 2010). As Watkins (1997) pointed out, given the importance of supervision, 'Something does not compute…' (p. 604).

In the present era of evidence-based practice, this lack of training is unacceptable as well as illogical, failing to support and guide supervisors, and failing to ensure safe and effective clinical practice, among other concerns (Milne & Reiser, 2020). Our stance is consistent with perspectives on training in general, namely that it plays a necessary role in developing competence among healthcare staff (e.g., Beidas & Kendall, 2010); and is also consistent with healthcare policy (e.g., Ockenden, 2022). We know too that training is necessary from

Resolving Critical Issues in Clinical Supervision: A Practical, Evidence-based Approach, First Edition.
Derek L. Milne and Robert P. Reiser.
© 2023 John Wiley & Sons Ltd. Published 2023 by John Wiley & Sons Ltd.

our own in-depth supervision studies, as we have repeatedly found that even highly experienced supervisors have a surprising lack of competence prior to training (e.g., Milne & James, 2002; Milne et al., 2013). Seemingly without exception, our findings have been corroborated by observational and survey-based studies, indicating that, without training, supervision tends to be excessively didactic and hence largely ineffective (e.g., Accurso et al., 2011; Bailin et al., 2018; Dorsey et al., 2017; Schriger et al., 2020). We regard the failure to ensure that supervisors are properly trained as the greatest critical issue threatening clinical supervision.

Even when training is provided, there may continue to be critical issues, such as unsatisfactory training. For example, a survey of 110 supervisors and supervisor trainers indicated that satisfaction with their training was modest, with only 66% reporting that they were 'Satisfied' or 'Very Satisfied' (Reiser & Milne, 2016). Such problems are due in part to the scarcity of research on the variables influencing the effectiveness of supervision training (Gosselin et al., 2015; Rees et al., 2020). For instance, how much training is 'enough', and how can we ensure that training resources are adequate and properly utilised? Should supervisees receive training alongside their supervisors? Without an empirical evidence-base, how can we answer such questions and provide successful training? A weak underpinning evidence-base contributes to poorly designed training, which is expensive, wasteful, and ultimately uneconomical and unsuccessful. Poorly informed training may even be harmful, as indicated by the history of training in critical incident debriefing. This became a required intervention in many US police departments, intended to reduce the likelihood of post-traumatic stress disorder. However, a review indicated that it was not only ineffective, but might actually cause harm by unnecessarily targeting those who would naturally recover from traumatic experiences (NICE, 2018).

Chapter Plan

How can we cope with a weak evidence base in the research literature, and make supervision training 'compute'? Our answer incorporates a selective review of the best-available research, supplemented by relevant theory and expert consensus statements (e.g., Pilling & Roth, 2014). For instance, our theoretical understanding is guided by popular thinking on experiential learning (Kolb, 1984), and also by the less well-known 'fidelity framework', including ways in which training can go wrong (added). These conceptions alert us to what matters in training, including the threats and opportunities. We also draw on neighboring research literatures, especially in the fields of staff training (e.g., Goldstein & Ford, 2002) and expertise development (Rousmaniere et al., 2014).

But in particular we are influenced by the most directly relevant research on supervisor training (Milne & Reiser, in press; Milne et al., 2011), alongside other reviews of similar research (e.g., Bluestone et al., 2013; Watkins & Wang, 2014). This is how we define evidence within our 'evidence-based clinical supervision' approach (EBCS: Milne & Reiser, 2017).

In terms of this chapter's content, we start by defining, describing, and formulating five ways in which training may fail to compute. We then focus on two of them (inadequate and misguided training), addressing the remaining three in Chapter 10 (i.e., absent, insufficient, and unsupported training), as we deem these latter issues best addressed within the organisational context.

Definition, Description, and Formulation of the Main Critical Issues

We have previously defined supervisor training as 'A systematic approach using evidence-based instructional methods (e.g., feedback, role-play, modeling, and teaching) in order to develop the participating mental health professionals' supervision competences to the required standard, including knowledge, skills, and attitudes.' Traditionally, supervisor training is conducted in brief educational workshops. According to Falender (2018), training is 'typically 1- or 2-day sessions ...' (p. 4) (e.g., 1-day workshop by Gillieat et al., 2014). Optimal training entails longer workshops, such as the 5–7 days within the Improving Access to Psychological Therapies programme (IAPT, e.g., Newman-Taylor et al., 2012). Workshops should be supplemented by periodic consultation and supervision-of-supervision (or equivalent support and guidance), alongside specialty workshop training or other appropriate methods designed to increase expertise over time (Milne & Reiser, 2017). We should add that supervisees also require training, as do other participants, such as consultants, and even trainers themselves. We note that different healthcare professions or organisations use different terminology, such as 'faculty development' (Bearman et al., 2018), though the assumptions and objectives are the same (i.e., that training is necessary for competence, requiring an integrated system of continuing education/continuing professional development arrangements: CE/CPD). Various terms are also used to refer to those receiving these various forms of training, such as 'participant', 'learner', 'faculty', and 'trainee', as well as 'supervisor' and 'supervisee'. In turn, those leading training may be referred to as 'trainers', educators', or 'workshop leaders/facilitators' We will use these terms interchangeably, and assume one trainer, except where a specific emphasis is required. Also, we will refer mostly to 'supervision training', so as to include both supervisors and supervisees, since we believe that both groups require training in supervision if we are to make it optimally effective.

These different training arrangements help to address the changing educational needs that accompany the development of supervisory expertise. Development is an adaptive process based on optimal individual improvements in supervision competencies and capabilities, facilitated through trainer-led experiences, within a collaborative relationship where trainees contribute to the learning experience (e.g., by drawing on their expertise as learners: Bransford & Schwartz, 2009). Improvements gradually lead towards supervisory expertise, provided that the training provides the conditions for deliberate practice, including extensive practise (DP: Tracey et al., 2014). This includes training, in terms of 'coaching', which plays a central role in providing trainees with support and guidance (e.g., structuring learning opportunities, goal-setting, monitoring, providing feedback, and motivating (Ericsson, 2009)). In essence, DP assumes that 'it takes expertise to make expertise' (Bransford & Schwartz, 2009). By expertise, we refer in particular to supervisors' optimal combination of cognitive competencies and capabilities (e.g., decision-making and problem-solving skills); to behavioral proficiency (e.g., conducting training methods correctly and with skill); and to sophisticated professional attitudes (e.g., cultural competence). To be perceived as expertise, these defining features also need to be effective and to demonstrate excellence (Milne & Reiser, 2017). We next apply these concepts.

Description and Formulation of Five Common Critical Issues

We next sketch out and suggest ways to make sense of five broad examples of critical issues in supervision training, starting with the most common critical issue: no training at all.

No Training

Training may be absent when supervision itself is absent, because supervisors avoid training opportunities, or because organisations fail to arrange or discourage supervision training (perhaps as leaders or policies prioritise alternative staff development arrangements, such as coaching or peer supervision; see Chapter 10). Similarly, professional bodies, clinical managers, peers, and others may devalue training. For example, Buus et al. (2016) cited the instance where nursing staff were only offered supervision at weekends (i.e., in their own free time). Their analysis included administrative databases (e.g., training attendance information) and self-report data, recorded over a three-month period. This indicated that 47% of 171 survey respondents did not participate in their supervision, reporting in interviews that this was due to excessive stress at work, a lack of encouragement (from peers or managers), and because of negative perceptions of supervision (e.g., it is ineffective). If supervision is poorly implemented or absent, then the training of supervisors is also likely to be absent.

Individual factors may combine with organisational factors to explain the absence of training, and Buus et al. (2016) cited the example of nurses experiencing group supervision as anxiety-provoking. Another factor can be traced to the inherent tensions that a normative approach creates for professionals in general, especially in professions with strongly egalitarian or democratic values, such as social work (Kadushin & Harkness, 2002). From such perspectives, the very idea of being trained may seem inappropriate or even offensive to some staff. Such feelings and perspectives can lead to avoidance behaviours and irrational thinking processes, such as supervisors absenting themselves from training because they genuinely believe that they do not need it. For instance, Kruger and Dunning (1999) provided this classic empirical analysis of positive (self-serving) bias, 'We argue that when people are incompetent in the strategies they adopt to achieve success and satisfaction, they suffer a dual burden: Not only do they reach erroneous conclusions and make unfortunate choices, but their incompetence robs them of the ability to realize it' (p. 1121). That is, they are unskilled, but unaware of it, carrying huge consequences. To illustrate, in one study (Gillieat et al., 2014), 71% of participating supervisors self-rated their pre-training competence as either 'good' or 'very good'. However, after a mere one-day introductory workshop 83% reported improved competence, suggesting that the workshop had led to heightened awareness and a more realistic self-evaluation. Therefore, even a brief workshop can carry benefits, which can be adequately evaluated through simple instruments, and help to lay a foundation for future learning. For instance, this self-serving bias may lead those lacking awareness or skill to dismiss as irrelevant or inaccurate the kind of feedback that might heighten self-awareness and prompt skill acquisition. In addition, individuals with this self-serving positive bias have also been found to be far less motivated to learn and develop skills than their more competent peers (Sheldon et al., 2014).

Insufficient Training

More commonly, training may be arranged by managers and attended by staff, but prove too brief to develop the requisite competence. This is due to the dominance of brief 'one-off' workshops (Falender, 2018), in that they are not followed by continuing education/continuing professional development (CE/CPD: career-long development of supervisors). To illustrate, in a review related to medical faculty development, Steinert et al. (2016) critiqued the reliance on workshops and seminars: 'The current literature demonstrates a continuing overreliance on formal, structured approaches such as workshops, short courses and seminars' and noted the lack of 'other methods that take advantage of experiential learning in the workplace, which include guided reflection, peer coaching and mentorship ... educational projects; intentional community building; longitudinal program design; and institutional support' (p. 781). To these we would add career-long consultancy, coaching, and supervision-of-supervision, which have proven vital in ensuring the successful transfer of training (Milne & Reiser, 2017).

Inadequate Training

A further problem is that training may be poorly organised. A thorough professional approach to training follows the steps in the 'training cycle', or a similar systematic approach (Goldstein & Ford, 2002). These steps start with an institutional commitment, then a clarification of the training goals (initially through educational and organisational needs assessments for training). For example, in a large survey of clinical supervisors in the medical profession, clinical supervisors indicated that: 'The top three areas for improvement ... included: giving feedback, promoting reflection and insight, and developing a range of teaching strategies'" (Bearman et al., 2017, p. 36).

The training cycle also requires proper preparation of educational resources (e.g., guidelines and video-demonstrations), effective leadership, blended didactic and experiential training methods (including corrective feedback), and evaluation. Similarly, the review by Steinert et al. (2016) summarised the most effective methods of training as evidence-informed educational design (e.g., adherence to the principles of teaching and learning, and the use of multiple instructional methods); relevant content; experiential learning, providing opportunities for practise and application; and opportunities for feedback and reflection. Similar recommendations can be found across healthcare professions, and also within the science of learning, related to vocational training in general (e.g., Tonhäuser & Büker, 2016). Poor organisation of training appears to be a significant problem across a wide range of medical, nursing, counseling, and clinical psychology specialties (e.g., Hutman et al., 2021; Weallans et al., 2022), frequently failing to provide opportunities for experiential learning because it is overly didactic (Bluestone et al., 2013). We detail these steps in the training cycle below, treating it as the best way to resolve issues with inadequate training.

Misguided Training

Training is rarely empirically or theoretically grounded (Lee et al., 2019), more commonly being designed by a trainer on the basis of their experience, and then unfolding in unpredictable and unsatisfactory ways as a result of group pressures (e.g., colluding to avoid the stress of educational role-plays: Milne et al., 2009). Like 'inadequate' training, it is pseudo-training, carrying the promise of learning, but not developing competence. This is also partly due to the paucity of helpful or rigorous research on supervisor training (Gosselin et al., 2015; Rees et al., 2020), including limited or absent local evaluations of supervision training, and few demonstration or action-research (cf., Lynch & Happel, 2008). Trainers may also lack the necessary competence to lead certain learning experiences, suffer from personal impairments that undermine competence, and consequently avoid experiential work (e.g., offering corrective feedback because it is interpersonally challenging (Milne, 2020). The problems associated with feedback are partly explained by the scarcity of direct observation (and other experiential methods), which might be due to differing values or practices. For example, in a survey of 791 psychotherapy trainees in Germany, Weck et al. (2017) reported that 46% of their supervisors never used audio or video recordings in supervision, preferring case discussion and information exchange. By contrast, in a survey of CBT supervisors in the UK, Reiser and Milne (2017) found that nearly 99% reported using direct observation 'sometimes' or 'frequently', and were far more likely to employ other experiential methods in supervision. There are other good reasons for avoiding observation. In their review, Fromme et al. (2009) noted that 'Residents and students report rarely being observed during their educational process, even though they value the experience. Reasons for this include a lack of faculty time, a lack of faculty skills, a potential stressful effect on the learner, and a perceived lack of validation of the assessment.' (p. 365).

Unsupported Training

Even the best training and CPD requires a supportive environment (see Chapter 10). This starts with a workplace in which clinical managers base training commissions on an assessment of the organisational need for staff training, motivate staff to participate, ensure that it is evaluated, and monitor the outcomes so that improvements can be made (e.g., including training on dealing with any barriers to the transfer of training). Unfortunately, such supportive environments seem to be the exception within healthcare, which can have disastrous consequences (e.g., Ockenden, 2022), and more commonly managers and clinicians prefer inappropriate alternatives to authentic clinical supervision, such as peer group supervision (Martin et al., 2018). Nonetheless, peer supervision is widely used by organisations and in private practice (Borders, 2012), perhaps as it saves managers and clinicians from engaging in the more challenging and expensive option of authentic clinical supervision. Perversely, professional and government bodies generally also contribute to these critical issues by endorsing peer group supervision as an acceptable alternative to authentic clinical supervision (e.g., The British Association for Behavioural and Cognitive Psychotherapy). All of these factors undermine support for supervisor training.

Conclusions on Faulty Training

As this description indicates, there are in theory at least five ways in which supervision training may fail. All five pose significant problems, as they hamper support and guidance to supervisors (Milne & Reiser, 2020) and undermine the quality of supervision. This increases the risk of incompetent or unethical clinical practices by supervisees, practices which can harm patients (Panagioti et al., 2018) and result in expensive litigation (Naczenski et al., 2017). Thankfully, we believe that there is now sufficient evidence to guide supervisor and supervisee training in a more positive direction, towards a variety of developmentally appropriate and effective CPD methods, leading to the acquisition of supervisory expertise and enhanced clinical outcomes. Because we believe that absent, insufficient, and unsupported supervision training are best understood and resolved within the organisational context, we will address them in Chapter 10. In this chapter, we want to next concentrate on the critical issues of inadequate and misguided training. But first the illustration that follows highlights some true examples of these issues, after which we will suggest ways to resolve these two issues by adopting the systematic 'ADDIE' approach to effective training.

Illustration

A state-wide agency in the USA contracted with a large training organisation to provide training on the evidence-based treatment of post-traumatic stress disorder (PTSD) to counsellors working with first responders (i.e., service staff first on the scene of emergencies and disasters, such as firefighters or police officers). Most of the counsellors targeted for the training already provided some form of counselling for first responders, but had extremely limited expertise in either structured trauma-informed cognitive behavioral treatments, or in related evidence-based treatments (e.g., prolonged exposure; Cognitive Processing Therapy). Hence, a great majority of the counselling was likely to be a supportive and rather generic form of 'talking therapy', one that did not utilise the evidence-based exposure treatment methods. Therefore, it was probable that many first responders were not receiving effective treatments, at a time when demand for treatment during the COVID-19 pandemic was increasing, especially for treatment of trauma and PTSD related to the pandemic.

In this context, an organisation negotiated a contract for training, but limited funds budgeted for this training only allowed for a maximum of three days (18 hours) of workshop-based training for large groups, with only partial support for small group follow-up consulting. The workshops were provided through a video-based platform that provided an interactive experiential format, including multiple video demonstrations of prolonged exposure (the selected, evidence-based treatment), and repeated opportunities for small group practice, together with encouragement to reflect on the required key competencies. However, follow-up consulting was limited to five one-hour long sessions, in small groups (six participants, or less). Consultation utilised a case presentation format, but there was no requirement that participants provided audio or video recordings of their counselling sessions for review or rating (e.g., using a competence evaluation instrument, such as the Cognitive Therapy Rating Scale). This is a standard requirement for achieving competency in cognitive therapy training. Also, both the workshops and the follow-up consultation groups were completely voluntary, and there was no requirement for ongoing attendance. As a result, while the initial workshop was well attended, follow-up consultation groups were unevenly attended, with several participants cancelling their agreed-upon case presentations and not attending. The outcome was that about 75% of attendees actually completed the full course of training, including the five follow-up consultation groups.

Reflections

Although an experienced trainer delivered this training program, he was fully aware that the training was insufficient, and inadequately implemented. He was faced with a dilemma. On the one hand, introducing counsellors to evidence-based treatment for PTSD offers the possibility of improving outcomes for clients. It was also possible that some counsellors would undertake more formal training in evidence-based treatments for PTSD, further improving their treatment outcomes. On the other hand, many counselors would probably not opt for further training, and, since there was no formal evaluation of their newly trained skills, the counsellors may have assumed incorrectly that they were now competent to provide the new prolonged exposure treatment. This could harm their clients, or at least increase client dropout, early termination, or abandonment of therapy, limiting the likelihood of successful outcomes. The trainer was especially concerned about these possibilities, since exposure-based treatments require considerable expertise (e.g., to motivate clients to confront directly their anxiety-provoking thoughts and feelings, also preparing them for the temporary worsening of their symptoms).

On the positive side, the trainer was encouraged by the highly interactive and experiential nature of the workshop, including multiple demonstrations of the competent use of prolonged exposure, and opportunities for small group practice, which conformed to a well-established training model with a strong empirical basis. However, a further concern was that this method was undermined by the brevity of this training, meaning that it was unlikely to be effective in helping counsellors achieve basic competence. This reflection process highlighted the associated ethical concerns for the trainer: was it ethical for him to provide training within this brief and superficial format? Was there a significant possibility of harm to the counsellors' clients? In retrospect, he would have been further reassured by a more formal workshop disclaimer: 'You should not consider this brief workshop and consultation a substitute for more intensive professional training, to the standard required to demonstrate competence. And always bear in mind that you should make your own professional judgement about your use of treatments, preferably following discussion with your supervisor'.

Resolving Critical Issues within Supervisor Training

To try and resolve the critical issues of inadequate and misguided training, as exemplified in the previous illustration, we next suggest how supervisor training can be properly organised and evidence-based. Systematically organised training typically follows an instructional design cycle of activities designed to maximise training effectiveness (Aguinis & Kraiger, 2009; Goldstein & Ford, 2002; Steinert et al., 2016). There are various approaches, but they all describe the process of designing, developing, and delivering instructional activities to foster learning among trainees. A popular example is the ADDIE approach, so long-established that its origins are unclear (Molenda, 2003). It is not a formal model of training, more of a practical approach that embraces many better-researched elements, such as training delivery (Bell et al., 2017). ADDIE represents a 'training cycle' (Goldstein & Ford, 2002), and stands for Analyze, Design, Develop, Implement, and Evaluate. Evidence in support of this cycle comes from a review by Steinert et al. (2016), from recommendations within the science of learning related to vocational training (e.g., Tonhäuser & Büker, 2016), and also this training cycle matches the 'cycle of excellence' within the expertise literature (Rousmaniere et al., 2017), though with an emphasis on the trainer as well as the learner (Milne & Reiser, 2017). A detailed illustration of the training cycle in action can be found in the blueprint for the workshop-based training of novice supervisors (Milne & Reiser, 2020), using the kinds of slideshows, video clips, guidelines, and other supporting materials provided within our supervision manual (Milne & Reiser, 2017). Evidence to guide the activities within the training cycle, as described below, will also be drawn from the most directly relevant research studies (e.g., Schriger et al., 2020), together with reviews of such research on supervision training (e.g., American Psychological Association, 2015; Birden et al., 2013; Lee et al., 2019; Milne & Reiser, in press). This evidence-base consistently indicates that effective supervisor training includes developmentally appropriate training objectives, learning resources that help to facilitate relevant experiential learning (especially recordings that demonstrate specific competencies), a judicious blend of targeted training methods (didactic and experiential techniques, applied responsively and collaboratively), opportunities for behavioral rehearsal, feedback to trainees, and an evaluation of training that highlights whether the objectives have been achieved, contributing to future effectiveness. We next draw on this evidence-base to suggest how we might best tackle each ADDIE step, adding more specifically relevant evidence where appropriate.

Analyze: Clarify the Goals of Training

This initial step develops a problem specification, based on a 'training needs analysis'. This analysis should help to define gaps between baseline knowledge, skills, and attitudes and the intended learning outcomes (ILO's), such as the competencies to be demonstrated, taking account of the organisational context and the trainees' characteristics. Establishing the baseline competencies also provides a comparison point for individual feedback and for the overall evaluation of training.

Establishing clear and moderately challenging training objectives leads to improved task performance (e.g., Hattie & Timperley, 2007), part of the 'deliberate practice' approach (DP: Ericsson, 2009). An illustrative list of supervisor training objectives was compiled by Milne (2016), drawn from published training manuals and supervision guidelines (e.g., 'Address relevant professional guidelines and supervision standards'). These should create the conditions for the learners to achieve their ILO's. An example from the Roth and Pilling (2008) supervision competence framework is 'Ability to use a range of methods to give accurate and constructive feedback'. The trainer's objectives and the learners' outcomes should be tied to what the employing organisation needs, based on first clarifying what the clinical service requires in order to provide evidence-based care (e.g., the competencies of greatest relevance to patients' needs). Competencies derived from expert consensus statements should also inform this needs assessment process (e.g., Roth & Pilling, 2008), as should professional bodies' standards. Of course, training goals should also encompass the training methods, an evaluation of outcomes, and so forth. We tackle these below.

A strategic issue in the analysis of training concerns the involvement of supervisees, historically excluded from supervisor training, and in our experience typically given little practical training for their role within supervision. But there are good reasons to include supervisees, and for starting while they are undertaking their initial professional training ('graduate school' in the USA), while they are actively receiving supervision (Bearman et al., 2019). There is empirical support for this kind of shared learning approach (e.g., Bell et al., 2017).

Suggestions for Resolving Critical Issues Concerning Training Goals

- Use the training cycle to guide the overall training process, to ensure that training is properly organised. Start with an educational needs assessment, based on the host organisation's clinical needs. This should profile the current and intended competencies of the trainees, thereby defining the training task.
- Summarise the training objectives and ILO's within a training programme, so that everyone understands the goals. Refer to them repeatedly during training (e.g., to justify activities or to motivate).
- Start training events by clarifying participants' expectations and strengths/weaknesses, related explicitly to the programme. Use a variety of assessment techniques to gather this information (e.g., quizzes; reactions to a video demonstration), then refine/confirm the ILO's, encouraging the trainees' involvement in ensuring that they are appropriate and moderately challenging. This illustrates a collaborative process that remains crucial throughout the training cycle.
- Involve supervisees (and any other key participants) in shared learning about supervision (i.e., alongside their supervisors).
- Example study: specifying competencies as objectives, and as workshop evaluation criteria: Newman-Taylor et al. (2012).

Designing Training

Next, trainers should develop a plan to address these needs, including deciding on the nature of training, and how it will be evaluated. They should also take account of national standards, professional guidelines, and other helpful recommendations on training and quality control (e.g., accreditation criteria). The training needs assessment that underpins the initial step of problem analysis contributes directly to the design of training, so that appropriate methods are planned, and make the objectives achievable. As far as the trainee is concerned, the welcome tangible result of such planning is a workshop programme, being a detailed specification of training (i.e., clarifying the date, venue, and schedule; the aim or purpose of training, plus intended learning outcomes; the content to be covered; the contributors/trainers; the intended methods; and how the training will be evaluated. Linked standards or CPD credits may also be noted). Such a programme will help to highlight the required training materials (e.g., video presented demonstrations of competent supervision), and associated learning resources (e.g., supervision guidelines), the next steps in the training cycle. Relevant theory (e.g., Kolb, 1984), personal preferences, and prior participant feedback can also guide planning, indicating how best to lead the training.

As far as the trainer is concerned, planning will ideally result in a training manual, being 'a written statement designed to inform and facilitate the trainers' capacity to lead experiential workshops. For instance, a manual may suggest programmes of activity (e.g., learning objectives; links to competence frameworks), may suggest learning exercises, or may link to training resources (e.g., slide shows, video material, supervision guidelines). The goal is implementation fidelity: the consistent repetition of a particular approach to training' (Milne, 2016, p. 2).

To illustrate planning, consider how national standards can help shape high-quality training. Standards can be defined as generally accepted quality criteria, being highly specific and uniform benchmarks, generally accepted requirements, rules, or codes of practice concerning how training should be conducted and what it should achieve. In healthcare, standards are commonly established through authoritative statements (e.g., what is expected by professional bodies), or through expert consensus statements, or comparative data. Standards are quantifiable where possible, and also clarify what can be expected from training (e.g., 'Following training, supervisors will be able to provide competent feedback to their supervisees'). By indicating the most essential features, they can additionally help to streamline the design and delivery of training, and can generally increase the consistency or uniformity of training, such that it conforms to what is expected across trainers, timing, or location. These features can help increase participant confidence in training as a uniform and predictable educational intervention, including reliable learning processes that achieve well-established and widely accepted outcomes (e.g., external professional validation of training programmes). They can also help to drive up training quality, for example, by guiding trainers as to the most appropriate educational methods.

The term 'guideline' is closely related in meaning, which we define as a written workshop handout, offering general suggestions or broad recommendations for achieving a standard. Guidelines are voluntary (standards are mandatory), and guidelines also differ in offering background information (e.g., explaining or justifying a standard). But standards and guidelines share an emphasis on quality-control and quality-enhancement, so both should play a significant role in designing training. Together they can clarify what constitutes competent supervisory practice, and what kind of training is required. As an example of best practices and relatively high training standards for clinical psychology supervisors in Australia, the following requirements are noted: passing a knowledge-based assessment (including seven hours of self-study, reading, and reflection); 12 hours of face-to-face workshop training, emphasising the integration of knowledge and practical skills; and a competence evaluation, based on the submission of a recording of a supervision session, plus a written reflection, incorporating a self-evaluation. This is followed by a requirement for refresher training of at least six hours' duration every five years (Australian Board of Psychology, 2018). Similarly high standards are also evident in UK medicine, where the clinical ('educational') supervisor ('trainer') must furnish evidence concerning their compliance with standards in seven domains, one being 'Continuing professional development as an educator'. Courses must fully prepare the supervisors for supervision, and are provided by higher education institutions, externally accredited, and approved by the Director of Medical Education. Refresher training is also required. The initial training is typically a brief module delivered through a blend of self-paced on-line learning, and four half-day sessions of face-to-face training. Other domains require evidence of effective supervision practice (e.g., 'Supporting and monitoring educational progress'). The six supervisor CPD standards include: 'Takes action to improve own practice on the basis of feedback received (e.g., appraisal, informal feedback)', and a distinction is made between 'effective' and 'excellent' CPD. An example of the latter is: 'Actively seeks the views of colleagues through e.g., 360 degree appraisal, peer observation'. The evidence selected by supervisors is independently appraised on an annual basis (Health Education England, 2020). Such standards provide useful guidance when designing training.

Suggestions for Resolving Critical Issues in Designing Supervisor Training

Time invested in planning will probably be rewarded, as it will contribute enormously to the training process and communicate to participants that the training is an important and highly professional activity. The trainer is also likely to be more relaxed and effective, knowing that everything is organised.

- The design of supervisor training should be based on the educational/organisational needs assessments, supplemented by relevant standards and guidelines, so that appropriate methods are planned and the training objectives are achievable.
- A suitable standard is that initial training should be at least five full days (30 hours) in duration, consisting of didactic and experiential learning methods (e.g., discussions and demonstrations). Large and small group activities should be included, addressing relevant competencies, standards, and other core content. Blended learning opportunities should also be planned, combining traditional workshops with modern systems of technology-assisted learning (Rousmaniere, 2014).
- Evidence of sound planning includes a workshop programme, listing evidence-based content (e.g., theories and research; roles and responsibilities; ethical and legal aspects; supervision methods; evaluation: Watkins & Wang, 2014).
- Plans should include the trainer's leadership style, especially skills in managing the learning environment, monitoring progress towards training goals, motivating trainees, and thinking how the training environment will be structured and supportive.
- Example study: analyzing the trainer's leadership: Culloty et al. (2010).

Developing Training Resources

The next step for trainers is to prepare or locate educational resources to support instruction (e.g., slideshows, video demonstrations, and written guidelines), materials designed to ensure the active engagement of the participants (e.g., learning exercises or assignments), and evaluation instruments.

Such resources were judged inadequate in a survey of 110 CBT supervisors and supervisor trainers in the UK: only 36% of these respondents reported that they were 'satisfied' or 'very satisfied' with the available training resources (Reiser & Milne, 2016). But the situation appears much better within the IAPT programme in England (Richards, 2014), as supervisor training included demonstration video-tapes, supervision checklists, students' and supervisors' guides, written support materials (e.g., supervision record sheets) and a reference list. These should contribute directly to the training objectives, forming an integral and stimulating part of the workshop. Learning exercises represent a bridge between the various training methods, creating essential opportunities for trainees to engage in the experiential learning cycle (i.e., enabling their involvement in conceptualising, planning, experimenting, experiencing, and reflecting (Kolb, 2014)). Other forms of advanced training, such as individual coaching and supervision-of-supervision, are more reliant on instruction, teaching, demonstration, and detailed feedback on supervision (Milne & Reiser, in press).

Unfortunately, we fear that much training is pseudo-training, as it does not actually involve taking participants around the experiential learning cycle, and so is probably more accurately described as 'teaching' or 'lecturing' (i.e., information transmission). Of course, there is a necessary place for information transmission within workshops, to increase declarative knowledge and capability, but it should be a minor element that sets the scene for experiential learning (Beidas & Kendall, 2010; Watkins & Wang, 2014). In our experience, pseudo training is a common phenomenon, as even established trainers from prestigious universities have required training as trainers, having initially been observed to rely heavily on lecturing (e.g., Milne, et al., 2000).

Sadly, publicly available and professional quality resources to support genuine supervision training are scarce (e.g., video demonstrations: Milne, 2016a). Guidelines on supervision are another essential resource, to be provided to delegates as handouts. Formal guidelines are systematically developed recommendations, founded on research evidence, as moderated by expert consensus (NICE, 2012). They should capture the essence of the available knowledge in a highly readable format, highlighting key variables in a practical context, while acknowledging the quality of the available research evidence. These recommendations are designed to improve communication, clarify standards, enable training, and enhance decision-making (Milne, 2016a). Learning exercises are also rarely published (i.e., problem-based learning assignments, undertaken by trainees during training), meaning that trainers usually have to develop their own. However, our training 'blueprint' for restorative supervision (Milne & Reiser, 2020) details several learning exercises, illustrating how they combine with other training resources.

Suggestions for Resolving Critical Issues in Developing Training Resources

- Prepare or locate educational resources to support training (e.g., slideshows, video demonstrations, and guidelines), being materials designed to ensure the active engagement of the participants (e.g., learning exercises or assignments). Develop a training programme that uses these resources imaginatively, facilitating experiential learning. Study successful examples (e.g., Richards, 2014).
- Learning exercises and problem-based learning tasks should make extensive use of training resources, creating essential opportunities for trainees to engage in the experiential learning cycle (i.e., enabling their involvement in conceptualising, planning, experimenting, experiencing, and reflecting (Kolb, 2014)). Ensure sufficient resources to make experiential learning the dominant part of training.
- Guidelines and other written resources (e.g., record/observation sheets; questionnaires) should consolidate learning, which can be maintained through a well-prepared reading list and access to ongoing support and training. To aid training transfer, workshops should include an action-planning episode. This can be organised as a learning exercise where small groups of participants identify their perceived barriers and boosters to transfer, together with their preferred coping strategies. Large group discussion can

extend and refine this action planning effort, leading to individual transfer objectives. Ideally, progress is assessed and supported at a later date (e.g., through consultancy or a follow-up workshop).
- Full participation in training is essential as participants contribute through their knowledge of the workplace and learning expertise. But often staff are prevented from participating in training, as there are too many other pressing demands and simply 'not enough time in the day'. Sometimes staff cope by attending training in their own (off duty) time, but this is unreasonable and inadequate (see the first illustration in Chapter 10). Recent healthcare disasters have emphasised the need for protected training time, to include human factors training (e.g., Ockenden, 2022, p. 168). A specific example of the human factors approach cited in this report is for managers to ensure that all staff have training time allocated in their job plans, which managers should then monitor. Time also needs to be protected within supervision, or we risk rendering it superficial and ineffective (Pullman et al., 2018). We return to the vital role of managers in Chapter 10.

Implement Training

Traditionally, training commences with face-to-face educational interactions within workshops. Latterly, these have been supplemented by (or blended with) virtual learning methods (e.g., O'Neill et al., 2020). Subsequent career-long training (CPD/CE) continues with training based primarily on consultancy, individual coaching, and supervision-of-supervision, increasingly emphasising trainee participation and co-construction. From a manager's normative perspective, training implementation is the delivery of the instructional programme so that the participants learn their roles, develop the necessary competence, and are motivated to engage in supervision as a means to improve organisational efficiency (Kadushin & Harkness, 2002).

It is now possible to define 'gold-standard' supervisor training, through a combination of the findings from supervisor training research and by extrapolation to the most relevant approaches to training in neighbouring literatures. We have cited supervision research examples throughout this chapter, while the general guidance on training staff was sourced from neighbouring literatures, including 'Behavioural skills training' (Sarokoff & Sturmey, 2004), 'Deliberate practice' (Ericsson, 2009), Educational psychology (Hattie & Timperley, 2007), Evaluation in Medicine and health-care (Rossi et al., 2003), 'Instructional design' (van Merrienboer & Boot, 2009), 'Learner expertise' (Bransford & Schwartz, 2009), 'Problem-based training' and related approaches, and the system-contextual perspective (Beidas & Kendall, 2010). These gold standards underpin our suggested resolutions for critical issues in implementing supervisor training.

Suggestions for Resolving Critical Issues Concerning Training Implementation
- Use didactic instruction appropriately, to teach essential concepts and core material (e.g., developmental models and methods), building on existing knowledge (conveying facts and declarative information, such as guidelines). Use a stimulating variety of didactic methods, especially teaching (lecturing), large group discussions, Socratic questioning, and other forms of intellectual challenge. Diagnose thinking errors and

provide explicit advice. Encourage critical thinking, activating the participants' conceptualisation and planning processes, and ultimately developing their problem-solving capability (Fraser & Greenhalgh, 2001). Create a foundation for experiential learning.
- Emphasise experiential learning methods, to allow declarative knowledge to be applied and transformed into procedural knowledge (behavioural proficiency), in an experimental/exploratory way (e.g., methods of behavioural rehearsal, such as educational role-play). Provide modelling/demonstrations of competent practice, combined with corrective feedback; throughout supervisors' careers, aim for gradual automation, based on refinements and the elimination of errors.
- Engage supervisees' learning expertise, to accelerate learning and to address relevant critical issues. Normalise and reframe setbacks, such as 'freezing' or 'deskilling' episodes.
- Exemplar study: successful experiential learning and training: Milne et al. (2013).

Evaluate Training

Evaluation entails making judgements about the degree to which training objectives and ILO's are achieved by the end of training. A major critical issue concerns measurement: what is the most appropriate focus for evaluation? Unresolved debate has continued for years over the suitability of patient benefit as the 'acid test' of supervision (Ellis et al., 1996), but this is disputed by many scholars and researchers, including ourselves, who prioritise the supervisees' learning, and patient safety (Reiser & Milne, 2014). To consider patient benefit as a training outcome measure seems even more contentious, on logical and scientific grounds, given the difficulty of establishing valid causal inferences when there are three successive complex interventions (i.e., training, supervision, and clinical work). Further critical issues are the outcome criteria and type of measurement. The most popular outcome is some form of trainee reaction, such as 'satisfaction' with the training processes and outcomes, usually assessed through self-report on an ad hoc questionnaire (O'Donovan & Kavanagh, 2014). Not only is there good reason to believe that favourable trainee reactions are inversely related to their learning outcomes (e.g., that challenging and even 'disagreeable' leaders actually do best at developing competence: Rieck et al., 2015); there is also reason to be suspicious of self-report data (e.g., on account of the typical absence of any psychometric instrument development, and the significant biases present). Nonetheless, simple ratings can be useful: in one instance, a one-day introductory workshop for 90 members of 12 different health professions in Australia relied exclusively on simple self-ratings of the workshops content (especially the Proctor model) and outcomes, but this evaluation was sufficient to address participants' willingness to provide supervision, a pressing local concern (Gillieat et al., 2014). Additionally, we believe that the current convention among supervision trainers is that reactions are a necessary part of training evaluation.

However, if we want to know if training succeeded in developing competence, then outcomes should also be evaluated objectively, supplementing trainees' reactions with more objective measures. An illustration is SAGE (Supervision: Adherence and Guidance Evaluation: Milne & Reiser, 2014). The 23 SAGE items are rated on a seven-point competence scale, ranging from 0 (not yet competent) to 6 (expert). These items fully address the Roth and Pilling (2008) competence framework. More recent progress heralds some promising competence evaluation instruments (e.g., Hamilton et al., 2021; Swank et al., 2021). Focussing on competence has a clear educational value (due to the specificity, in relation to current and desired proficiency), aiding improvement efforts, and raising the objectivity of assessments. A self-rating example using the Roth and Pilling (2008) competence framework was provided by Newman-Taylor et al. (2012). Some reviews have indicated that the most frequently used instruments within supervision research have used similar competence measures to assess learning outcomes, plus the transfer of learning to the workplace (e.g., Milne, 2018; Wheeler & Richards, 2007). These reviews also indicated the popularity of complementary qualitative instruments, and of employing multiple measures. But other reviews have indicated a much wider range of topics and tools, sadly lacking 'a clear, coherent, collective and cumulative research agenda' (Wheeler & Barkham, 2014, p. 380), leading them to recommend a 'core battery'.

The evaluation of training in general enjoys greater coherence, with a popular approach being the evaluation of training in terms of successive outcomes: trainee reactions, learning, transfer to routine work, and clinical outcomes (Kirkpatrick, 1967). This approach remains popular, supplemented by a growing emphasis on trainee characteristics and workplace environments (e.g., team dynamics: Bell et al., 2017). There have been some similar approaches within supervision training, such as Culloty et al. (2010), who operationalised the 'fidelity framework' by measuring the impact of supervision training in terms of the workshop's design, the training delivery (the trainer's adherence to the training manual), the delivery of the workshop (the trainer's competence), the learning of the participants, and the clinical outcomes. An illustration of the participants' learning is the Feedback Quality Instrument, derived from collaborative research involving physiotherapists, nurses, and physicians (FQI: Johnson et al. (2021)). We believe that the FQI could also be useful within training (e.g., based on the trainers' rating of supervisors' feedback), or as a follow-up evaluation tool, to assess the maintenance of any training effects.

Suggestions for Resolving Critical Issues Concerning Feedback and Evaluation

- Seek ongoing feedback: invite trainees' reactions and self-evaluations, and observe evidence from training (e.g., learning exercises, questions/comments), to gain a better perspective on progress and the influential factors (e.g., which training methods are most helpful); use such information to pinpoint the gaps between the actual/observed performance and the intended competence or standard.
- Evaluate whether training achieved its objectives: To guide reflection on the training, conduct a participative evaluation using multiple measures, ideally including process evaluations (Watkins & Milne, 2014) and more objective instruments; interpret the findings with other stakeholders, to best draw out the lessons. Providing training is a complex skill, so assume that it can always improve. Review regularly, including consultancy and peer review; attend workshops with admired leaders, and study guidance documents.
- Take the long view: workshops should start a multi-phase, career-long training strategy, including in-depth coaching, and ongoing feedback (Falender, 2018). Keep in mind

organisational, cultural, and other factors that might affect participants' motivation and ability to transfer training, addressing barriers collaboratively (e.g., Buus et al., 2016).
- Exemplar studies: outline of a typical but minimal training evaluation approach: Tebes et al. (2011); summary of a thorough system of supervisor training and evaluation, to foster quality control (Schoenwald, 2016).

Conclusions

We set out to explain how supervisor training could be made to compute, since 'competence in clinical supervision does not fall from the sky' (Watkins & Wang, 2014, p. 178). There are now uplifting signs that training in supervision is belatedly becoming more common (Watkins & Wang, 2014), and also is an accepted part of workforce development (e.g., Health Education England, 2020). For instance, Ten Cate and Billet (2014) summarised the changing zeitgeist within medicine: 'Many medical schools now offer or even require teachers to take training in teaching skills' (p. 1). Although supervision training may thankfully be more common, there remain many critical issues that require resolution for training to succeed. Based on the normative or managerial perspective taken throughout this book, success in training helps healthcare organisations to be efficient in achieving their clinical goals, in essence by enabling staff to do their jobs cooperatively and properly (especially with respect to risk management and ethical practice). Efficiency should be supported by related mechanisms, such as quality control and staff management (e.g., monitoring supervisors' competence; evaluating supervisees' clinical outcomes: Kadushin & Harkness, 2002).

But unlike other chapters, in the present one we have struggled to locate detailed evidence of the critical issues that impair training and organisational effectiveness. Therefore, in suggesting the resolution of critical issues, we adopted the strategy of assuming that they generally arise when the gold-standards for training are not achieved (e.g., when the goals are absent, or the instructional methods are inappropriate). For example, Steinert et al. (2016) noted the following key features of effective supervisor training programmes in medicine: the use of evidence-informed educational design; experiential learning and opportunities for practice; feedback and reflection. Based on such advice, and because we lacked reliable details of the full range of issues, we assumed that some critical issues included the opposite features (e.g., poor design and overly didactic instruction). This was consistent with the few studies that directly identified training issues (e.g., Culloty et al., 2010; Milne & Reiser, in press) and with reviews of the most relevant studies (e.g., Lee et al., 2019), but research on supervision training is scarce and generally methodologically compromised (e.g., weak measurement: Wheeler & Barkham, 2014).

Based on our evidence-based strategy, we defined, described and formulated five ways in which supervision training could fail, due to critical issues. In this present chapter we addressed two of them, inadequate and misguided training, as exemplified in our illustration (the remaining three issues are addressed in Chapter 10, being best construed as organisational issues). We then used the ADDIE training cycle to detail how exactly training could be inadequate and misguided, leading to our evidence-based suggestions on resolving the critical issues. As a result, we believe that we have described how supervision training can be made to 'compute', but there are some remaining issues that we should note.

Limitations of Our Approach

In identifying the critical issues in training supervisors for this chapter we relied heavily on relevant theory, extrapolation to neighbouring literatures, and expert consensus. This was adequate in some respects, such as clearly supporting the use of a blend of didactic and experiential training methods (e.g., Roth & Pilling, 2007; Rousmaniere et al., 2017). However, to date research on supervisor training has been narrowly focused on participant reactions and learning outcomes, meaning that we actually know very little about what actually happens during training to produce such outcomes. Specifically, there are very few process evaluation studies of the actual delivery of supervisor training (i.e., manipulation checks), studies which measure which training methods are used, how competently they are conducted, or other questions concerning training fidelity. Rare exceptions are the exploratory observational study by Culloty et al. (2010), which explicitly adopts the fidelity perspective, and the studies by Henggeler et al. (2009). Therefore, one weakness of this chapter is that we have not been able to define the selected critical issues empirically, meaning that we may have ignored some critical issues that are actually common, but not yet identified.

A related limitation has been the scarcity of methodologically sound research on supervision training, which, within the mental health field, may number only 21 studies (Milne & Reiser, in press). Although a systematic review by Gosselin et al. (2015) identified 52 supervisor training papers, these authors only deemed 12 of these as interpretable research. And though these 12 studies reported positive impacts of training, in turn only five of these studies directly measured learning. Although these small samples include some controlled evaluations indicating that supervisor training can be effective (e.g., Milne et al., 2011), there clearly remain many possibilities for advancing supervisor training, such as the science-informed implementation of instructional methods. According to Dorsey et al. (2013), 'there is little empirical guidance around which strategies are most critical, which combinations are most effective, and how these elements can be implemented effectively and efficiently' (p. 2).

In this context, we must acknowledge that our awareness of the extant, multi-disciplinary research literature has been limited by the fact that we are both clinical psychologists, working within the mental health field. These biases will no doubt have blinded us to a greater fund of empirical evidence.

Action Implications

Researchers are not alone in having work to do, in order to make training compute. Trainers can consider drawing on the science of learning in designing their training (Borders, 2019), and in delivering evidence-based training (e.g., The Yale programme on supervision: Hoge et al., 2014). These guides to training encourage the use of highly interactive and experiential techniques, revolving around problem-based learning, in which participants identify their current supervisory problems, then collaborate as a group to generate resolutions.

Supervisors and supervisees can play a vital role in helping to design such training, and hopefully this will include ways of reducing their experiential avoidance (e.g., Ellis et al., 2015; Milne et al., 2009). According to Hoge et al. (2014), clinical managers (or quality improvement directors, etc.) can contribute by developing supervision implementation plans, including the establishment and leadership of peer learning communities to support supervisors. This support arrangement follows a common training, in order to help supervisors' transfer, maintain, and develop their supervisory skills. In Chapter 10 we resume our discussion of collaborative and systemic resolutions to the issues undermining supervision training.

In conclusion, as far as training itself is concerned, we know that training is necessary for the development of supervisory expertise, and without it supervision is superficial, impaired, and possibly harmful (Ellis et al., 2014). But training is itself a complex intervention and requires its own expertise. Thankfully, there is a strong consensus that training can succeed if it is done right. This means that a skilled leader with supervision expertise ensures that career-long training is developmentally appropriate, of adequate duration, meets the learners' needs, is collaborative, and responsively blends multiple evidence-based didactic and experiential methods (especially teaching, modelling, behavioral rehearsal, and feedback (Ericsson, 2009; Milne & Reiser, in press; Rees et al., 2020; Tracey et al., 2014)). Feedback and evaluation should guide improvements, benchmarked against a suitable range of process and outcome criteria. Given the weak evidence-base for supervision training, trainers should also study the best-available evidence as it emerges, seeking expert training and guidance, since 'it takes expertise to make expertise' (Bransford & Schwartz, 2009). The other necessary condition is that training and supervision are consistently enabled and supported within the workplace (Beidas & Kendall, 2010; Buus et al., 2016: see Chapter 10).

References

Accurso, E. C., Taylor, R. M., & Garland, A. F. (2011). Evidence-based practices addressed in community-based children's mental health clinical supervision. *Training and Education in Professional Psychology*, 5(2), 88–96. https://doi.org/10.1037/a0023537

Aguinis, H., & Kraiger, K. (2009). Benefits of training and development for individuals and teams, organizations, and society. *Annual Review of Psychology*, 60, 451–474. https://doi.org/10.1146/annurev.psych.60.110707.163505

American Psychological Association. (2015). Guidelines for clinical supervision in health service psychology. *The American Psychologist*, 70(1), 33–46. https://doi.org/10.1037/a0038112

Australian Board of Psychology. (2018). Guidelines for supervisors.

Bailin, A., Bearman, S. K., & Sal, R. (2018). Clinical supervision of mental health professionals serving youth: Format and micro-skills. *Administration and Policy in Mental Health and Mental Health Services Research*, 45(5), 800–812. https://doi.org/10.1007/s10488-018-0865-y

Bearman, S. K., Bailin, A., & Sale, R. (2019). Graduate school training in CBT supervision to develop knowledge and competencies. *The Clinical Supervisor*, 39(1), 66–84. https://doi.org/10.1080/07325223.2019.1663459

Bearman, M., Tai, J., Kent, F. et al. (2018). What should we teach the teachers? Identifying the learning priorities of clinical supervisors. *Advances in Health Science Education*, 23, 29–41. https://doi.org/10.1007/s10459-017-9772-3

Bearman, S. K., Schneiderman, R. L., & Zoloth, E. (2017). Building an evidence base for effective supervision practices: An analogue experiment of supervision to increase EBT fidelity. *Administration and Policy in Mental Health*, 44(2), 293–307. https://doi.org/10.1007/s10488-016-0723-8

Beidas, R. S., & Kendall, P. C. (2010). Training therapists in evidence-based practice: A critical review of studies from a systems-contextual perspective. *Clinical Psychology: Science & Practice*, 17(1), 1–30. https://doi.org/10.1111/j.1468-2850.2009.01187.x

Bell, B. S., Tannenbaum, S. I., Ford, J. K., Noe, R. A., & Kraiger, K. (2017). 100 years of training and development research: What we know and where we should go. *Journal of Applied Psychology*, 102(3), 305–323. https://doi.org/10.1037/apl0000142

Birden, H., Glass, N., Wilson, I., Harrison, M., Usherwood, T., & Nass, D. (2013). Teaching professionalism in medical education: a Best Evidence Medical Education (BEME) systematic review. BEME Guide No. 25. *Medical Teacher*, 35(7), e1252–e1266. https://doi.org/10.3109/0142159X.2013.789132

Bluestone, J., Johnson, P., Judith Fullerton, J., Carr, C., Alderman, J., & BonTempo, J. (2013). Effective in-service training design and delivery: Evidence from an integrative literature review. *Human Resources for Health*, 11(51), 1–26. https://doi.org/10.1186/1478-4491-11-51

Bogie, B. J. M., Harms, S., Saperson, K., & McConnell, M. M. (2017). Learning the tricks of the trade: The need for specialty-specific supervisor training programmes in competency-based medical education. *Academic Psychiatry*, 41(3), 430–433. https://doi.org/10.1007/s40596-016-0598-8.

Borders, D.-A. (2019). Science of learning: Evidence-based teaching in the clinical supervision classroom. *Counselor Education & Supervision*, 58(1), 64–79. https://doi.org/10.1002/ceas.12124

Borders, L. D. (2012). Dyadic, triadic, and group models of peer supervision/ consultation: What are their components, and is there evidence of their effectiveness? *Clinical Psychologist*, 16(2), 59–71. https://doi.org/10.1111/j.1742-9552.2012.00046.x

Bransford, J. D., & Schwartz, D. L. (2009). It takes expertise to make expertise: Some thoughts about why and how and reflections on the themes in chapters 15–18. In K. A. Ericsson (Ed.), *Development of professional expertise* (pp. 432–448). Cambridge University Press.

Buus, N., Lisa Lynch, L., & Gonge, H. (2016). Developing and implementing 'meta-supervision' for mental health nursing staff supervisees: Opportunities and challenges. *The Cognitive Behaviour Therapist*, 9, e22. https://doi.org/10.1017/S1754470X15000434

Culloty, T., Milne, D. L., & Sheikh, A. I. (2010). Evaluating the training of clinical supervisors: A pilot study using the fidelity framework. *The Cognitive Behaviour Therapist*, 3(4), 132–144. https://doi.org/10.1017/S1754470X10000139

Dorsey, S., Pullmann, M. D., Deblinger, E., Berliner, L., Kerns, S. E., Thompson, K., ... & Garland, A. F. (2013). Improving practice in community-based settings: a randomized trial of supervision–study protocol. *Implementation Science*, 8(1), 1–11. https://doi.org/10.1186/1748-5908-8-89

Dorsey, S., Pullmann, M. D., Kerns, S. U., Jungbluth, N., Meza, R., Thompson, K., & Berliner, L. (2017). The juggling act of supervision in community mental health: Implications for supporting evidence-based treatment. *Administration and Policy in Mental Health and Mental Health Services Research*, *44*(6), 838–852. https://doi.org/10.1007/s10488-017-0796-z

Ellis, M. V., Berger, L., Hanus, A. E., Ayala, E. E., Swords, B. A., & Siembor, M. (2014). Inadequate and harmful clinical supervision: Testing a revised framework and assessing occurrence. *The Counseling Psychologist*, *42*(4), 434–472. https://doi.org/10.1177/0011000013508656

Ellis, M. V., Hutman, H., & Chapin, J. (2015). Reducing supervisee anxiety: Effects of a role induction intervention for clinical supervision. *Journal of Counseling Psychology*, *62*(4), 608. https://psycnet.apa.org/doi/10.1037/cou0000099

Ellis, M. V., Ladany, N., Krengel, M., & Schult, D. (1996). Clinical supervision research from 1981 to 1993: A methodological critique. *Journal of Counseling Psychology*, *43*(1), 35–50. https://doi.org/10.1037/0022-0167.43.1.35

Ericsson, K. A. (2009). *Development of professional expertise*. Cambridge University Press.

Falender, C. A. (2018). Clinical supervision—the missing ingredient. *American Psychologist*, *73*(9), 1240–1250. https://doi.org/10.1037/amp0000385

Fraser, S. W., & Greenhalgh, T. (2001). Complexity science: Coping with complexity: Educating for capability. *British Medical Journal*, *323*(7316), 799–803. https://doi.org/10.1136/bmj.323.7316.799

Fromme, H. B., Karani, R., & Downing, S. M. (2009). Direct observation in medical education: a review of the literature and evidence for validity. *Mount Sinai Journal of Medicine: A Journal of Translational and Personalized Medicine*, *76*(4), 365–371. https://doi.org/10.1002/msj.20123

Gaitskell S, & Morley M. (2008). Supervision in Occupational Therapy: How are We Doing? *British Journal of Occupational Therapy*, *71*(3), 119–121. https://doi.org/10.1177/030802260807100310

Gillieatt S, Martin R, Trudi Marchant T, Angela Fielding A, & Kate Duncanson K. (2014). Evaluation of an inter-professional training program for student clinical supervision in Australia. *Human Resources for Health*, *12*, 60. https://human-resources-health.biomedcentral.com/articles/10.1186/1478-4491-12-60

Goldstein, I. L., & Ford, J. K. (2002). *Training in organizations: Needs assessment, development, and evaluation* (4th ed.). Brooks/Cole.

Gonsalvez, C. J., & Milne, D. L. (2010). Clinical supervisor training in Australia: A review of current problems and possible solutions. *Australian Psychologist*, *45*(4), 233–242. https://doi.org/10.1080/00050067.2010.512612

Gosselin, J., Barker, K. K., Kogan, C. S., Myriam Pomerleau, M., & Pitre d'Ioro, M.-P. (2015). Setting the stage for an evidence-based model of psychotherapy supervisor development in clinical psychology. *Canadian Psychology*, *56*(4), 379–393).

Hamilton, S. J., Briggs, L., Peterson, E., Slattery, M., & O'Donovan, A. (2021). Supporting conscious competency: Validation of the Generic Supervision Assessment Tool (GSAT). *Psychology and Psychotherapy: Theory, Research and Practice*, *95*(1), 113–136. https://doi.org/10.1111/papt.12369

Hattie, J., & Timperley, H. (2007). The power of feedback. *Review of Educational Research*, *77*(1), 81–112. https://doi.org/10.3102/003465430298

Health Education England. (2020). *Recognition of trainers: Standards & guidance*. HEE.

Henggeler, S. W., Schoenwald, S. K., Borduin, C. M., Rowland, M. D., Cunningham, P. B. (2009). *Multisystemic Therapy for Antisocial Behavior in Children and Adolescents* (2nd ed.). New York: Guilford Press.

Hoge, M. A., Migdole, S., Cannata, E., & Powell, D. J. (2014). Strengthening supervision in systems of care: Exemplary practices in empirically supported treatments. *Clinical Social Work Journal*, 42(2), 171–181. https://doi.org/10.1007/s10615-013-0466-x

Hutman, H., Enyedy, K., Ellis, M., Goodyear, R., Falender, C., Campos, A., ... & Zetzer, H. (2021). Training public sector clinicians in competency-based clinical supervision: Methods, curriculum, and lessons learned. *Journal of Contemporary Psychotherapy*, 51(3), 227–237. https://doi.org/10.1007/s10879-021-09499-3

Johnson, C. E., Keating, J. L., Leech, M., Congdon, P., Kent, F., Farlie, M. K., & Molloy, E. K. (2021). Development of the Feedback Quality Instrument: a guide for health professional educators in fostering learner-centred discussions. *BMC Medical Education*, 21(1), 1–17. https://doi.org/10.1186/s12909-021-02722-8

Kadushin, A., & Harkness, D. (2002). *Supervision in social work* (4th ed.). Columbia University Press.

Kirkpatrick, L. D. (1967) Evaluation of training. In: R.L. Craig & L.R. Bettel (Eds.), *Training and development handbook* (pp. 87–112). NY: McGraw-Hill

Kolb, D. A. (1984). *Experiential learning: Experience as the source of learning and development.* Englewood Cliffs, NJ: Prentice-Hall

Kolb, D. A. (2014). *Experiential learning: Experience as the source of learning and development* (2nd ed.). Prentice-Hall.

Kruger, J., & Dunning, D. (1999). Unskilled and unaware of it: How difficulties in recognising one's own incompetence lead to inflated self-assessments. *Journal of Personality and Social Psychology*, 77(6), 1121–1134. https://doi.org/10.1037/0022-3514.77.6.1121

Lee, M. C. C., Idris, M. A., & Tuckey, M. (2019). Supervisory coaching and performance feedback as mediators of the relationships between leadership styles, work engagement, and turnover intention. *Human Resource Development International*, 22(3), 257–282. https://psycnet.apa.org/doi/10.1080/13678868.2018.1530170

Lynch, L., & Happel, B. (2008). Implementation of clinical supervision in action: Part 2: Implementation and beyond. *International Journal of Mental Health Nursing*, 17(1), 65–72. https://doi.org/10.1111/j.1447-0349.2007.00512.x

Martin, P., Milne, D. L., & Reiser, R. P. (2018). Peer supervision: International problems and prospects. *Wiley Online Library*. https://doi.org/10.1111/jan.13413

Milne, D. L. (2008). CBT supervision: from reflexivity to specialization. *Behavioural and Cognitive Psychotherapy*, 36(6), 779–786. http://dx.doi.org/10.1017/S1352465808004773

Milne, D. L. (2016). Guiding CBT supervision: how well do manuals and guidelines fulfil their promise? *The Cognitive Behaviour Therapist*, 9 (Article), e1. https://doi.org/10.1017/S1754470X15000720

Milne, D. L. (2016a). How can video recordings best contribute to clinical supervisor training? *The Cognitive Behaviour Therapist*, 9, https://doi.org/10.1017/S1754470X15000562

Milne, D. L., (2018) *Evidence-based CBT Supervision.* Chichester: Wiley-Blackwell.

Milne, D. L. (2020). Preventing harm related to CBT supervision: A theoretical review and preliminary framework. *The Cognitive Behaviour Therapist*, *13*, E54. https://doi.org/10.1017/S1754470X20000550.

Milne, D. L. & James, I. A. (2002). The observed impact of training on competence in clinical supervision. *British Journal of Clinical Psychology*, *41*(1), 55–72. https://doi.org/10.1348/014466502163796

Milne, D. L., Keegan, D., Westerman, C., & Dudley, M. (2000). Systematic process and outcome evaluation of staff training in psychosocial interventions for severe mental illness. *Journal of Behaviour Therapy and Experimental Psychiatry*, *31*(2), 87–101. https://doi.org/10.1016/S0005-7916(00)00013-6

Milne, D. L., Leck, C., & Choudhri, N. Z. (2009). Collusion in clinical supervision: Literature review and case study in self-reflection. *The Cognitive Behaviour Therapist*, *2*, 106–114. https://psycnet.apa.org/doi/10.1017/S1754470X0900018X

Milne, D. L., & Reiser, R. (2014). SAGE: a scale for measuring competence in CBT supervision. In C. E. Watkins & D. L. Milne (Eds.). *The Wiley International Handbook of Clinical Supervision*. Chichester: Wiley-Blackwell (pp.402–415).

Milne, D. L., & Reiser, R. P. (2017). *A manual for evidence-based CBT Supervision*. Chichester:Wiley-Blackwell.

Milne, D. L., & Reiser, R. P. (2020). *Supportive Clinical Supervision: From burnout to well-being, through restorative leadership*. Pavilion.

Milne, D. L., & Reiser, R. P. (in press). Evidence-based methods for training CBT supervisors: Recommendations for career-long development. In T. Del Vecchio & M. Terjesen (Eds.) *Handbook of training and supervision in cognitive-behavioral therapy*. Springer.

Milne, D. L., Leck, C., & Choudhri, N. Z. (2009). Collusion in clinical supervision: literature review and case study in self-reflection. *The Cognitive Behaviour Therapist*, *2*(2), 106–114. https://psycnet.apa.org/doi/10.1017/S1754470X0900018X

Milne, D. L., & Reiser, R. P. (2017). *A manual for evidence-based CBT supervision*. Wiley-Blackwell.

Milne, D. L., Reiser, R. P., & Cliffe, T. (2013). An n=1 evaluation of enhanced CBT supervision. *Behavioural & Cognitive Psychotherapy*, *41*(2), 210–220. https://psycnet.apa.org/doi/10.1017/S1352465812000434

Milne, D. L., Reiser, R. P., Cliffe, T., & Raine, R. (2011). SAGE: Preliminary evaluation of an instrument for observing CBT supervision. *The Cognitive Behaviour Therapist*, *4*(4), 123–138. https://psycnet.apa.org/doi/10.1017/S1754470X11000079

Molenda, M. (2003). In search of the elusive ADDIE model. *Performance improvement*, *42*(5), 34–37. https://doi.org/10.1002/pfi.4930420508

Naczenski, L. M., de Vries, J. D., Madelon, L. M., & Kompier, M. A. (2017). Systematic review of the association between physical activity and burnout. *Journal of Occupational Health*, *59*, 477–494. https://doi.org/10.1539/joh.17-0050-RA

National Institute for Health and Care Excellence. (2012). The guidelines manual. *NICE Guidline*.

National Institute for Health and Care Excellence. (2018). Post-traumatic Stress Disorder. *NICE Guideline*.

Newman-Taylor, K., Gordon, K., Grist, S., & Olding, C. (2012). Developing supervisory competence: Preliminary data on the impact of CBT supervision training. *The Cognitive Behaviour Therapist*. https://doi.org/10.1017/S1754470X13000056

O'Donovan, A., & Kavanagh, D. J. (2014). Measuring competence in supervisees and supervisors: Satisfaction and related reactions to supervision. In C. E. Watkins & D. L. Milne (Eds.), *Wiley international handbook of clinical supervision* (pp. 458–467). Wiley.

O'Neill, N., Albiston, M., Ferguson, S., & Nicklas, L. (2020). Improving CBT supervision. Four years of implementing NES specialist supervision training for CBT in Scotland. *The Cognitive Behaviour Therapist, 13*. https://doi.org/10.1017/S1754470X20000136

Ockenden, D. (2022). Findings, conclusions and essential actions from the independent review of maternity services at The Shrewsbury and Telford Hospital NHS Trust. London: Crown publications.

Panagioti, M., Geraghty, K., Johnson, J., Zhou, A., Panagopoulou, E., Chew-Graham, C., ... Esmail, A. (2018). Association between physician burnout and patient safety, professionalism, and patient satisfaction: A systematic review and meta-analysis. *Journal of the American Medical Association, Internal Medicine, 178*(10), 1317–1330. https://doi.org10.1001/jamainternmed.2018.3713

Pilling, S., & Roth, A. D. (2014). The competent clinical supervisor. In C. E. Watkins & D. L. Milne (Eds.), *The Wiley International Handbook of Clinical Supervision* (pp. 20–37).

Pullman, M. D. Lucid, L. Harrison, J.P. Martin, P. Deblinger, E. Benjamin, K.S. & Dorsey, S. (2018). Implementation climate and time predict intensity of supervision content related to evidence-based treatment. *Frontiers in Public Health, 6*(280). https://doi.org.frontiersin.org/articles/10.3389/fpubh.2018.00280

Rees, C. E., Huang, E., Denniston, C., Edouard, V., Pope, K., Sutton, K., Palermo, C., Waller, S., & Ward, B. (2020). Supervision training in healthcare: A realist synthesis. *Advances in Health Sciences Education, 25*(3), 523–561. https://doi.org/10.1007/s10459-019-09937-x

Reiser, R. P., & Milne, D. L. (2014). A systematic review and reformulation of outcome evaluation in clinical supervision: Applying the fidelity framework. *Training & Education in Professional Psychology, 8*(3), 149–157. https://doi.org/10.1037/tep0000031

Reiser, R. P., & Milne, D. L. (2017). A CBT formulation of supervisees' narratives about unethical and harmful supervision. *The Clinical Supervisor, 36*(1), 102–115. https://psycnet.apa.org/doi/10.1080/07325223.2017.1295895

Reiser, R. P., & Milne, D. L. (2016). A survey of CBT supervision in the UK: methods, satisfaction and training, as viewed by a selected sample of CBT supervision leaders. *The Cognitive Behaviour Therapist, 9*(e20), 1–14. https://doi.org/10.1017/S1754470X15000689

Richards, D. A. (2014). Clinical case management supervision: Using clinical outcome monitoring and therapy progress feedback to drive supervision. In C. E. Watkins & D. L. Milne (Eds.), *Wiley international handbook of clinical supervision* (pp. 518–529). Wiley.

Rieck, T., Callahan, J. L., & Watkins, C. E. (2015). Clinical supervision: An exploration of possible mechanisms of action. *Training and Education in Professional Psychology, 9*(2), 187–194. https://psycnet.apa.org/doi/10.1037/tep0000080

Rossi, P.H., Freeman, H.E. & Lipsey, M.W. (2003). *Evaluation: A systematic approach* (7th ed.). Thousand Oaks, CA: Sage.

Roth, A. D., & Pilling, S. (2007). *A competence framework for the supervision of psychological therapies*. University College London. The full set of competences referred to in this document are available for downloading from the CORE website: www.ucl.ac.uk/CORE

Roth, A. D., & Pilling, S. (2008). Using an evidence-based methodology to identify the competences required to deliver effective cognitive and behavioural therapy for depression and anxiety disorders. *Behavioural and Cognitive Psychotherapy*, *36*(2), 129–147. https://doi.org/10.1017/S1352465808004141

Rousmaniere, T. (2014). Using technology to enhance clinical supervision and training. In C. E. Watkins & D. L. Milne (Eds.), *The Wiley International Handbook of Clinical Supervision* (pp. 204–237).

Rousmaniere, T., Goodyear, R. K., Miller, S. D., & Wampold, B. E. (2017). *The Cycle of Excellence: Using deliberate practice to improve supervision and training*. Wiley-Blackwell.

Rousmaniere, T. G., Swift, J. K., Babins-Wagner, R., Whipple, J. L., & Berzins, S. (2014). Supervisor variance in psychotherapy outcome in routine practic. *Psychotherapy Research*, *26*, 196–205. https://doi.org/10.1080/10503307.2014.963730

Sarokoff, R. I., & Sturmey, P. (2004). The effects of behavioural skills training on staff implementation of discrete-trial teaching. *Journal of Applied Behavior Analysis*, *37*(4), 535–538. https://doi.org/10.1901/jaba.2004.37-535

Schoenwald, S. K. (2016). Clinical supervision in a quality assurance/quality improvement system: Multisystemic therapy® as an example. *The Cognitive Behaviour Therapist*, *9*, e21. https://doi.org/10.1017/S1754470X15000604

Schriger, S. H., Becker-Haimes, E. M., Skriner, L., & Beidas, R. S. (2020). Clinical supervision in community mental health: Characterizing supervision as usual and exploring predictors of supervision content and process. *Community Mental Health Journal*. https://doi.org/10.1007/s10597-020-00681-w

Sheldon, O. J., Dunning, D., & Ames, D. R. (2014). Emotionally unskilled, unaware, and uninterested in learning more: Reactions to feedback about deficits in emotional intelligence. *Journal of Applied Psychology*, *99*, 125–137. https://doi.org/10.1037/a0034138

Steinert, Y., Mann, K., Anderson, B., Barnett, B. M., Centeno, A., Naismith, L., … Dolmans, D. (2016). A systematic review of faculty development initiatives designed to enhance teaching effectiveness: A 10-year update: BEME Guide No. 40. *Medical Teacher*, *38*, 769–786. https://doi.org/10.1080/0142159X.2016.1181851

Swank, J. M., Liu, R., Neuer Colburn, A. A., & Williams, K. M. (2021). Development and Initial Validation of the Supervision Competencies Scale (SCS). *International Journal for the Advancement of Counselling*, *43*(2), 195–206. https://doi.org/10.1007/s10447-021-09427-z

Tebes, J. K., Matlin, S. L., Migdole, S. J., Farkas, M. S., Money, R. W., Shulman, L., & Hoge, M. A. (2011). Providing competency training to clinical supervisors through an interactional supervision approach. *Research on Social Work Practice*, *21*(2), 190–199. https://doi.org/10.1177/1049731510385827

Ten Cate, O., & Billett, S. (2014). Competency-based medical education: origins, perspectives and potentialities. *Medical Education*, *48*(3), 325–332. https://doi.org/10.1111/medu.12355

Tonhäuser, C., & Büker, L. (2016). Determinants of transfer of training: A comprehensive literature review. *International Journal for Research in Vocational Education and Training*, *3*(2), 127–165. https://doi.org/10.13152/IJRVET.3.2.4

Tracey, T. J. G., Wampold, B. E., Lichtenberg, J. W., & Goodyear, R. K. (2014). Expertise in psychotherapy: An elusive goal? *American Psychologist*, *69*(3), 218–229. https://psycnet.apa.org/doi/10.1037/a0035099

Tsutsumi, T. (2011). Development of an evidence-based guideline for supervisor training in promoting mental health: literature review. *Journal of Occupational Health*, *53*(1), 1–9. https://onlinelibrary.wiley.com/doi/abs/10.1539/joh.R10002

Van-Merrienboer, J.J.G. & Boot, E.W. (2009). Research on past and current training in professional domains: The emerging need for a paradigm shift. In K.A. Ericsson (Eds.), *Development of Professional Expertise*. Cambridge University Press (pp. 157–179).

Watkins, C. E. (Ed.). (1997). *Handbook of psychotherapy supervision*. Wiley.

Watkins, C. E., & Milne, D. L. (Eds.). (2014). *The Wiley International Handbook of Clinical Supervision*. Wiley-Blackwell.

Watkins, C. E., & Wang, C. D. C. (2014). On the education of clinical supervisors. In C. E. Watkins & D. L. Milne (Eds.), *The Wiley International Handbook of Clinical Supervision* (pp. 177–203). Wiley-Blackwell.

Weck, F., Kaufmann, Y. M., & Witthoft, M. (2017). Topics and techniques in clinical supervision in psychotherapy training. *The Cognitive Behaviour Therapist*, *10*(Article), e3. https://doi.org/10.1017/S1754470X17000046

Weallans, J., Roberts, C., Hamilton, S., & Parker, S. (2022). Guidance for providing effective feedback in clinical supervision in postgraduate medical education: a systematic review. *Postgraduate Medical Journal*, *98*(1156), 138–149. https://doi.org/10.1136/postgradmedj-2020-139566

Wheeler, S., & Barkham, M. (2014). A core evaluation battery for supervision. In C. E. Watkins & D. L. Milne (Eds.), *Wiley International Handbook of Clinical Supervision* (pp. 367–385). Wiley.

Wheeler, S., & Richards, K. (2007). The impact of clinical supervision on counsellors and therapists, their practice and their clients. A systematic review of the literature. *Counselling and Psychotherapy Research*, *7*(1), 54–65. https://doi.org/10.1080/14733140601185274

7

Skills in Dealing with Incompetent Supervisors

Introduction

We started this book by setting out 10 critical issues in supervision and have now reached issue number four: the faulty delivery of supervision (see Table 1.2, Chapter 1). Unlike Chapters 4 and 5 which revolved around character weaknesses, this chapter considers faulty delivery in terms of supervisory incompetence. Incompetence was also an aspect of Chapter 4, but there we focussed on unethical aspects of incompetence (such as irresponsibility and neglect). Chapter 6 addressed supervisor training, the obvious way to tackle incompetence, but as we noted there, not all supervisors receive training, and those that do usually only receive a brief training with no follow-up. This makes it likely that many supervisors require additional support and guidance. This chapter sets out the evidence-based options for resolving such issues.

The definition we use for supervisory incompetence is the opposite of competence: *Incompetent supervision is the inability to perform relevant techniques or competencies proficiently, appropriately, or effectively within the practice and professional context, falling below the standard that is expected in employment. The incompetent supervisor may also be unqualified, lack basic understanding, and behave inappropriately (i.e., inconsistent with relevant standards, guidelines, professional values, and ethical practice). Consequently, incompetent supervisors are likely to harm supervisees and patients.* This definition is based on the integration of US and UK definitions of competence in clinical psychology (e.g., Watkins & Milne, 2014, pp. 8–9); on the medical education literature (as reviewed by ten Cate et al., 2010); and is also consistent with the fidelity framework underpinning this book (see Chapter 1, Table 1.2). As noted in these sources, there are many different competence terms, concepts, and approaches, but no question about the positive influence that competence frameworks in general have had on supervision internationally (Pilling & Roth, 2014). Based on expert consensus, such frameworks have replaced the traditionally vague and idiosyncratic statements about supervision with detailed blueprints, providing unprecedented consistency, specificity, and transparency.

Based on this overview, incompetence creates these critical issues:

- **Supervisor lacks proficiency**: Issues include unskilled and generally low fidelity supervision (i.e., 'doing it wrong'). This presents as a behavioural skill deficit, featuring

Resolving Critical Issues in Clinical Supervision: A Practical, Evidence-based Approach, First Edition.
Derek L. Milne and Robert P. Reiser.
© 2023 John Wiley & Sons Ltd. Published 2023 by John Wiley & Sons Ltd.

errors, inconsistency, clumsiness, slowness, a rigid and inflexible style, or a lack of self-management. It manifests itself in multiple areas, such as inadequate goal-setting (e.g., failing to agree a supervision contract), and bad planning (e.g., poorly structured sessions, with no effective agenda). A promising way to resolve a lack of proficiency is through training (see Chapter 6), ideally in the form of supervision coaching.
- **Supervisor fails to adhere to the correct procedure**: Issues include methods that do not represent the intended or proper technique, perhaps due to a 'drift' away from competence following training (i.e., 'not doing the right thing'). The correct techniques may also be avoided, especially experiential learning methods that create anxiety (e.g., not demonstrating a technique to a supervisee). In this sense, we will address non-adherence as a problem of experiential avoidance, which functions to avoid anxiety. Skills for resolving a lack of adherence due to avoidance are primarily ones that resolve these aversive underlying feelings (e.g., fearing that one is an imposter). These include dealing with such feelings through self-care and social support arrangements (e.g., peer groups or proctoring).
- **Supervision is ineffective**: The issue is that supervision may be skilfully provided and adherent, yet prove ineffective (i.e., 'not getting the right result'). We will treat this as due to a failure to relate effectively, perhaps due to interpersonal conflicts or collusion. It may include avoiding challenges or overlooking complications (e.g., ignoring a supervisee's non-compliance), with the result that supervision fails to influence the supervisee as intended. This may result in harm to patients. Skills in resolving ineffective supervision include the guidance methods used by consultants (e.g., cognitive restructuring), and systems for providing corrective feedback (e.g., clinical outcome monitoring).
- **Supervisor adopts an inappropriate approach**: The issue includes a reluctance to accept the role of supervisor (e.g., professional identity conflicts), or other primarily cognitive difficulties (miscommunication; misunderstandings). These may be linked to behavioural difficulties, including a failure to use suitable techniques ('doing the wrong thing'). Promising options include participation in peer groups or mentoring, drawing on didactic information (e.g., guidelines, video demonstrations). As this aspect of incompetence has already been addressed in Chapter 5, here we will only discuss peer groups and mentoring.

Following the structure in earlier chapters, we will next expand on the first of these three types of incompetence, consider how it can best be formulated, list some guidelines on the skills for dealing with incompetence, before drawing our main conclusions. Reflecting Chapter 1, these different kinds of incompetence indicate that the critical issues primarily concern the supervisor, rather than the supervisee. Therefore, we will now view the supervisor as the follower, the person with incompetence issues that are in need of resolution. It follows that the leader here will be someone like a consultant who supports and guides the supervisor towards expertise, or other similar leader (e.g., supervision coach, peer support group). Our illustration below presents a supervisor who lacks competence in some supervision skills, but who is receiving supervision coaching. However, we recognise that the supervisor should also play their part in developing competence (e.g., by self-monitoring). And similarly, the supervisee and other colleagues can play their important roles.

Supervisor Lacks Proficiency

A lack of proficiency is usually defined as a lack of skill or talent, a behavioural deficit. It is the inability to perform supervision techniques smoothly and without error. Proficiency may also be regarded as approximating to 'expertise'. The Dreyfus model of skill acquisition clarifies their relationship, ranging through five skill levels: novice, advanced beginner, competent, proficient, and expert (Dreyfus, 2004). As illustrated in medical education (Humphrey et al., 2013), the Dreyfus model captures how learners attain skills with practice, becoming competent and able to progress through their careers. Becoming a supervisor is part of this developmental process, and the same competence issues apply to this phase of professional growth. The Dreyfus model indicates the characteristic features of each of these five levels of expertise, which are set out fully in the next chapter. For example, a novice characteristically makes multiple errors in a faltering, rigid style, whereas the expert performs techniques quickly, smoothly, and accurately (Ericsson, 2009). The Dreyfus scale is a starting point in assessing competence, but measurement instruments can add much more useful information, helping us to guide efforts to resolve critical issues in supervision.

Proficiency ratings using the Dreyfus scale are usually linked to competence statements. For example, Orakzai et al. (2020) surveyed 37 clinical supervisors and 135 of their medical trainees in Pakistan, in order to assess the supervisors' ability. A modified version of the Maastricht Clinical Teaching Questionnaire was used, consisting of 24 items that were rated on a 5-point Likert scale (1 = fully disagree, through to 5 = fully agree). Items included 'I consistently demonstrate how to perform clinical tasks' and 'I observe students multiple times during patient encounters'. There was little agreement between supervisors and supervisees on the ability demonstrated by supervisors on these items, with supervisors rating their competence significantly more highly than the supervisees. The authors concluded that these survey data highlighted several issues with supervision, particularly insufficient observation of trainee-patient encounters, and limited demonstration of clinical tasks. Similar disappointment with supervision was also reported in a UK survey of 871 medical students (e.g., little consultant feedback on supervisees' clinical performance: Tasker et al., 2014).

Roth and Pilling (2007) have developed a competency framework for supervisors, based on an expert consensus statement on what constitutes competent supervision in relation to therapy. Newman-Taylor et al. (2013) conducted an evaluation of a 5-day supervisor training workshop based on this framework. Competence examples included 'Demonstrates ability to give accurate and constructive feedback'. Participants rated themselves on 18 of these competencies, using a simple 'traffic light' competence rating scale, ranging from 'not/barely achieved' (red), through 'partially achieved' (amber), to 'well/fully achieved' (green). This approach provides a simple and user-friendly evaluation of supervision skills. These kinds of instruments can help to define and quantify incompetence, which benchmarks the problem and provides the basis for formulating any difficulties.

Formulation

According to the expertise approach (Ericsson, 2009), there are five main reasons for incompetence:

a) **Challenging tasks are avoided**, goals are too easily achievable, or are already within an individual's current competence. This is especially true following the completion of initial post-licensure professional training, and is exacerbated because clinicians and supervisors form positively biased judgements about their competence (Tracey et al., 2014);
b) **feedback is absent or inaccurate**, failing to correctly define gaps between the performance of a skill and a standard or goal, such as a competence statement (when what is required is systematic, ongoing, formal feedback, from empirical outcome measures and experts);
c) **training opportunities are rare**, typically during the post-licensure period, and feedback is ignored (there is no attempt to learn from errors made);
d) **competence development efforts are superficial** when there needs to be repeated, intensive practise of what we do least well, until eventually the competence has become automatic; and
e) **there is little or no help from experts** to address these and other reasons for incompetence and to enable the necessary expertise to be developed (e.g., cognitive errors in understanding competence development; biases in interpreting feedback).

By contrast, when these five elements are tackled properly, training constitutes 'deliberate practice', the favoured method for developing competence within the expertise literature (Ericsson, 2009; Rousmaniere et al., 2017). From its roots in behavioural psychology, deliberate practice integrates well-established methods for developing competence, such as Vygotsky's (1978) Zone of Proximal Development, criterion-referenced instruction (Mager, 1997), performance-related feedback (Locke & Latham, 2006), and mastery learning (McGaghie et al., 2014). By definition, deliberate practice creates the necessary learning experiences to benefit from one's practice (Tracey et al., 2014). Because this deliberate practice formulation of incompetence is so relevant to this chapter, and broad enough to encompass the different types of incompetence that we discuss, we will treat this as our 'core' formulation. This means that we will simply note which of these five conditions for competence are most relevant to the sections that follow on non-adherence and ineffectiveness, rather than introducing additional formulations. We say more about deliberate practice in the next chapter since it also illuminates supervisee incompetence (see Table 8.2).

We should also acknowledge that proficiency problems arise in a social and organisational context, so may also be due to factors such as a lack of social support, or to an unsupportive supervision setting (ten Cate et al., 2010). The social aspect was illustrated in a study by McCutcheon and Duchemin (2021), who surveyed 223 supervisors working in an American medical centre to assess their experiences of using feedback. Of these respondents, 37% reported fearing damaging their rapport with colleagues, 25% reported resistance to feedback from supervisees, over 20% of them lacked confidence in providing feedback, and 16% even feared retaliation from these colleagues (or from training programme directors). Only 12% of this sample experienced no such barriers to providing feedback. Buus et al. (2016) have described some of the significant organisational barriers to supervision, including low prioritisation by managers and peers, leading to nearly half of the 171 staff in their sample not receiving any supervision over the three-month study period.

In summary, competence should be understood in context. We now turn to supervision-of-supervision, a method for developing supervisory competence that comes closest to embodying deliberate practice.

Guidelines for Supervisor Coaching (Supervision-of-supervision)

Supervision-of-supervision involves a senior supervisor or subject expert providing training and support to one or more supervisors. This is usually an individualised and intensive approach, and may not always be voluntary (e.g., in the case of remedial or disciplinary involvement), but also occurs in small groups. It is intended to tackle a lack of proficiency, or to promote expertise. Unlike consultancy (also known as 'metasupervision': Newman, 2013), as we define it, supervision-of-supervision is based on an accountability relationship. This means that the supervisor-of-the-supervisor has the authority to instruct the supervisor, and similarly may also play a gatekeeping role (e.g., recommending promotion or a pay rise). But unlike supervision, the supervisor-of-the-supervisor only shoulders responsibility for the supervisor's supervision, not for the supervisee's clinical work (which remains the supervisor's responsibility: see Chapter 2). Assuming that this proper authority is in place, supervision-of-supervision comes closest to the practice of 'coaching the coaches'. In this relationship, the supervising coach provides technical assistance to coaches through demonstrating how to perform coaching skills, and by organising practise opportunities with feedback, to improve the coaching process (Joyce & Showers, 2002).

We now present more detailed guidelines on supervision-of-supervision, drawing on the steps in the 'doctor coach' approach, as used to help educational leaders in medicine to use deliberate practice (Gifford & Fall, 2014):

- **Introduce core concepts:** define the role as an expert supervisor, placing it in the organisational context (e.g., part of a quality control system). The methods to be used include a collaborative working alliance; managing the learning environment (including the 'scaffolding' of training); and using deliberate practice in a structured and supportive environment.
- **Clarify the goals:** use measurement instruments and self-assessments to define the supervisor's current competencies; jointly identify development goals that address the learning needs (e.g., select those competence statements from supervision frameworks that represent suitable goals for the supervisor); agree any other intended learning outcomes and training objectives (e.g., to train the supervisor to think like an expert).
- **Facilitate experiential learning**: use a blend of instructional methods (symbolic, iconic, and enactive) to teach essential concepts, and to develop supervision competencies (e.g., use case-studies and realistic/representative vignettes to build on existing knowledge). Use didactic instruction to convey facts and procedural information (e.g., guidelines); for skill-development, use techniques such as behavioural rehearsal, simulations, educational role-plays, demonstrations, and feedback. Monitor the learning process and motivate the supervisor (e.g., encourage repetition and corrections, reinforcing the supervisor when competence is demonstrated). Encourage over-learning (practising a skill beyond the point of achieving competence), and weave in evidence

(i.e., refer to research findings). Coaching in this way provides a clear model of best practice for the supervisor. Draw attention to the parallels between supervision-of-supervision and supervision.
- **Evaluate progress**: determine training effectiveness using multiple instruments to evaluate multiple outcomes and perspectives. For example, measure the resources used, in terms of the time and money required ('structure' data); measure the supervisor's experience of receiving training ('process' data, such as reactions or satisfaction with training); and measure whether the goals were achieved ('outcome' data, such as an evaluation of the targeted competencies following training).
- **Plan the transfer of training**: identify the boosters and barriers to maintaining supervisory competence, making a plan to harness these factors through supervisor self-regulation (e.g., by reviewing critical supervision issues with a peer); follow-up on progress, and provide booster sessions.

Conclusions

It appears that the methods used within initial pre-licensure clinical training normally address these five necessary elements of deliberate practise, and so successfully develop proficiency (e.g., Hill et al., 2015; Mason et al., 2016). This is a reassuring conclusion, as it indicates that post-licensure experience should also continue to develop expertise, if it conforms to deliberate practice. Unfortunately, it rarely does so, which is why we emphasise the value of career-long clinical supervision, which usually addresses these necessary conditions for deliberate practice (McMahan, 2014).

Supervisor Fails to Adhere to the Correct Procedure

Supervisors may be proficient but incompetent, due to their non-adherence to the appropriate supervision competencies or standards after they have been demonstrated (i.e., post-proficiency departure from the correct contents, processes, procedures, or outcomes of supervision). This includes failing to ensure the right amount of these factors (the wrong 'dose'), or a 'drift' away from performing tasks in a timely, responsive fashion, despite adequate training and resources (e.g., Schriger et al., 2020; Waller & Turner, 2016). Non-adherence also implies that patients will probably receive ineffective or inappropriate treatment, and as a result may be harmed or at least may fail to obtain the expected benefits of a treatment (Waller & Turner, 2016). An example of non-adherence is an observation-based case study in CBT supervision-of-supervision, which identified a drift into a collusive relationship between the supervisor and the supervisee (the supervisor allowed the supervisee to provide extensive and unnecessary details of his self-selected casework, thus avoiding exposure to the experiential supervisory methods that should have been used). In this example, the supervisor agreed that this collusion served as a 'safety behaviour', which was corrected through training (Milne et al., 2009).

This kind of avoidance may be common. Schriger et al. (2020) measured how often supervisors adhered to evidence-based methods, finding that their sample of 32 supervisors in Philadelphia rarely used key experiential methods such as observing, role-playing, and modelling. Of the 18 supervisory techniques rated, observing (i.e., review of audio or video tapes) was the least utilised, as supervisors instead prioritised administrative tasks. In addition, Schriger et al. (2020) found a negative correlation between how long supervisors had worked in their organisations and their use of experiential methods, consistent with a drift to non-adherence over time. This study was based on a self-report version of the instrument SAGE (Milne et al., 2011). As SAGE was originally designed as an observational tool, it can provide a more objective behavioural breakdown of adherence. In one of our own studies, based on the intensive analysis of one experienced supervisor, we found that he did not adhere to the majority of the 18 SAGE items during the baseline period (Milne et al., 2013). As detailed in the illustration, prior to receiving training the supervisor was not using several supervision techniques competently (e.g., demonstrations and educational role plays). Another instrument for rating adherence is the Supervisor Adherence Measure (SAM; Schoenwald, 2016). This is a 36-item instrument that (like SAGE) was designed to measure supervisors' adherence to a supervision manual (e.g., 'following the recommended structure and process of supervision'). It is completed by the supervisees at two-month intervals, taking about 10 minutes to complete their rating of the group supervision that they received (e.g., using a standardised scale ranging from 1 = *not at all*; to 5 = *very much*).

Competence frameworks and performance standards are complementary ways of judging adherence. For instance, the generic Roth and Pilling supervision framework includes the competence: 'Ability to use direct observation and contingent feedback to enhance learning in supervision'. Such frameworks provide a valuable point of reference, helping to pinpoint possible non-adherence to what the GMC (General Medical Council (GMC), 2013, p. 14) refer to rather vaguely as 'appropriate supervision'. More helpfully, Falender et al. (2004) developed a formal consensus among supervision experts. Their competencies framework included 'relationship skills – ability to build supervisory alliance', and they also considered that supervisor training should include experiential methods (e.g., 'observation of supervision, with critical feedback'). This degree of specificity helps supervisors to judge their adherence to best practices.

Formulation

The initial core formulation discussed earlier suggests that non-adherence to supervision methods is most likely when feedback is absent or inaccurate; training opportunities are rare; feedback is ignored (e.g., McLoughlin et al., 2021); and competence development efforts are superficial.

Guidelines on Improving Supervisory Adherence

- **Join a peer group:** If we formulate non-adherence as a safety behaviour, driven by relief from anxiety (like the example of collusion), then our intervention should aim to reduce the anxiety. Peer support groups are a popular and promising option, taking many forms (e.g., Balint and Resilience groups; see, Taylor et al., 2018). Although there is enthusiastic support for peer groups and high user satisfaction, few of these groups have been evaluated (Borders, 2012). Perhaps the most evidence-based option is the Schwartz Centre Rounds, which in one review were found to be associated with significant improvements in staff well-being, including increased empathy for colleagues and positive changes in practice (Maben et al., 2018). Schwartz Centre Rounds are regular meetings that are open to all healthcare staff, designed to encourage compassionate patient care, enabling reflection on emotional and other challenging healthcare experiences in a safe and supportive group environment, with the aim of promoting insight, peer support at work, and staff well-being (Taylor et al., 2018). However, the method would also suit a peer supervision support group, and indeed peer support is part of the purpose of Rounds. Whatever the type of group, it is vital that a peer support group creates the right conditions. The key mechanisms appear to be that there is effective leadership, to ensure that there is a supportive, safe and trusting group environment (social support, emotional containment); that members can say what they want to get out of the discussion (e.g., seeking information on how peers have managed their anxiety successfully); that group members share a critical issue or stressful experience (disclosure); and that processing of issues is encouraged (reflection, insight). Although the research evidence is not yet strong, in theory these mechanisms are likely to help reduce anxiety and thereby limit supervisory drift.

- **Find a mentor or proctor:** Peer support groups may help practitioners to ventilate their uncomfortable feelings, and to better understand their anxiety (or safety behaviours), so creating the conditions for improved adherence. Some form of more direct advice may then bring about adherence, such as mentoring, a widely accepted practice in healthcare. For example, in the UK, The General Medical Council (General Medical Council (GMC), 2013) stated that physicians should be willing to participate in structured support opportunities such as mentoring, defined as 'a personal and reciprocal relationship in which a more experienced (person) acts as a guide, role model, teacher, and sponsor of a less experienced (person). A mentor provides the protégé with knowledge, advice, counsel, challenge and support in the protégé's pursuit of becoming a full member of a particular profession' (Johnson, 2007, p. 20). In this sense, mentoring can be thought of as complementary to supervision. 'Mentoring for supervisors would include: a partnership stance with their mentors, so that the mentor could shepherd them safely through vulnerable transitions and other stressors; showing concern for the supervisor's welfare and development; and attempting to offer wisdom, empathy and compassion' (Milne, 2018, p. 232).

  While a mentor is usually a senior colleague, a proctor is more likely to be only a year or two senior to the mentee. For example, Keenan-Miller and Corbett (2015) described how clinical psychology trainees in their fourth or fifth year of training acted as proctors, providing supervision to less experienced trainees within the same programme. To ensure effectiveness, the proctors' supervision was in turn supervised, according to the meta-supervision approach described by Newman (2013). This form of consultancy included group meetings to discuss assigned reading and developing supervision skills through video-based review of participants' supervision. Based on the analysis of 11 years of archival clinical outcome data for 255 patients, Keenan-Miller and Corbett (2015) reported promising clinical results.

- **Monitor your adherence:** Even with individual guidance and support, adherence may remain low, so it is vital to add information that guides informed adjustments. This can be defined as a self-monitoring process, in which a supervisor works independently, directing their own professional development by assessing and improving key skills. An example that is consistent with deliberate practice is self-monitoring by means of standard assessments. As already noted, Schriger et al. (2020) used the SAGE self-rating instrument to monitor supervision competence, retaining the same seven-point rating scale and asking supervisors to rate the extent to which they used various supervisory techniques in a recent supervision session. This could also serve as a self-monitoring instrument for supervisors concerned about non-adherence to experiential techniques.
- **Seek feedback from your supervisee:** Self-monitoring could complement or be replaced by feedback from your supervisee. As noted earlier in defining the conditions for developing expertise, feedback needs to specify the distance between the current and the expected supervision behaviour, as in rating supervision relative to a competence or standard (e.g., 'Ability to use a range of methods to give accurate and constructive feedback': Pilling & Roth, 2014). To be effective, feedback also needs to indicate how any gap can be bridged (e.g., as stated in a guideline, demonstrated in a video, or via detailed suggestions from the supervisee). Feedback should be timely, factual, clear, and precise. It applies to competence and incompetence: feedback that something was done well is also valuable, if less common (Bagwandeen & Singaram, 2016). These authors surveyed medical consultants on their use of feedback, and some of the questionnaire items may be helpful to readers (e.g., 'Feedback is given about procedures and techniques performed correctly').

Of course, being relative novices and subject to biased responding (given the power differential and a pressure to offer a 'grateful testimonial'), supervisees may not be best-placed to comment on a supervisor's proficiency. But supervisees do have an invaluable perspective on how the supervision skills were experienced, and on their perceived value or effectiveness (e.g., what they learned from supervision; see Tasker et al., 2014). This could be especially valuable in relation to a supervisor's experiential avoidance, in that a supervisee could give detailed feedback on how the supervisor set-up an experiential technique, and could collaborate with the supervisor on refining such methods (e.g., by using an anxiety hierarchy). In any case, supervisees (and anyone else receiving feedback) need to be engaged in the process (Molloy et al., 2020).

Supervision Is Ineffective

Competent supervision is effective, at least in terms of influencing supervisees (e.g., fostering attitude change, knowledge gain, skill acquisition). Benefits for patients should follow, but at worst, harm should be minimised. Incompetent supervision may be skilful and adherent yet prove ineffective. Another way to define incompetence is to ask supervision experts or supervisees for their opinions. To illustrate, Ellis et al. (2014) developed an initial classification of supervisory incompetence through an expert consensus-building procedure. This process added a theoretical foundation, together with a testable definition of 'inadequate' supervision (i.e., sub-standard or ineffective supervision). Empirical support was obtained through experts' ratings of the inadequate supervisor behaviours. The result was a list of 16 inadequate supervision descriptors (e.g., 'Relationship is cold and distant'; 'Does not know what to do'). Survey data were based on 363 supervisees' self-reports, drawn from a sample of USA trainees in social work and various branches of applied psychology. These reports indicated that 93% of the survey participants were currently receiving inadequate supervision (i.e., they reported currently receiving at least one of these 16 descriptions of inadequate supervision). In particular, the supervisors were reported as failing to use a supervision consent form or contract (reported by 54% of survey participants); and were failing to observe or monitor supervisees' clinical work (reported by 40% of survey participants).

Ineffective supervision has also been studied through direct observation, using the SAGE instrument already mentioned (Milne et al., 2011). In addition to measuring the supervisor's adherence to 13 supervision competencies, the final five SAGE items assessed the initial signs of the supervisee's experiential learning, regarded as the initial 'mini-outcome' of supervision. This provided an empirical definition of competent supervision, in that facilitating experiential learning was taken to represent effective supervision (e.g., enabling the supervisee to reflect, plan, conceptualise, experiment, and experience). In our main study (Milne et al., 2013), a comparison between standard and enhanced (more experiential) supervision indicated statistically significant differences between the supervisee's learning, favouring the enhanced approach. This was associated with observer's ratings of improved engagement in experiential learning on four of these five experiential learning items, amounting to a mean improvement of 32%.

This small n = 1 study (Milne et al., 2013) included consultancy for the supervisor, a major option in addressing ineffective supervision, and one we will focus on in this section. We term this consultancy as there was only an advisory relationship (i.e., the supervisor could take or leave the advice). During the baseline period the supervisor's competencies that were rated by the observer as 'not yet competent' on several of the SAGE items (e.g., there were low ratings for the items 'agenda-setting' and 'demonstrating'). Not surprisingly, this was associated with ineffectiveness, in that the data on three of the supervisee items indicated no change (i.e., in the mini-competencies defined as 'experiencing', 'planning', and 'experimenting'), although the supervisor was effective at encouraging the supervisee to 'reflect' and 'conceptualise' (i.e., the supervisor was effective in terms of traditional, didactic supervision). Over the 11-month study period, consultancy helped the supervisor to become significantly more effective in facilitating all of these mini learning outcomes. Therefore, this demonstrated that post-licensure supervisor training could be successful, through reinstating the deliberate practice of supervision.

Consultancy can also draw on a range of additional techniques. These methods are primarily designed to enhance the supervisor's thinking skills, such as self-awareness or reflection (Kilburg & Diedrich, 2007). We have drawn on the extensive review by Kilburg and Diedrich (2007) to outline a number of the more relevant methods (see Table 7.1). For instance, self-awareness depends on the ability to self-monitor, part of fostering more effective supervision and understanding incompetence. This has been demonstrated within the literature on expertise, which indicates that novices are less accurate than experts at judging their own performance. Novices are 'unskilled and unaware of it', which

Table 7.1 Major methods of consultancy for supervisors, based on outcome monitoring and self-monitoring (based on objectives in Kilburg & Diedrich, 2007), with examples drawn from the chapter's detailed illustration.

Consultancy objectives and consultant activities

Consultancy objectives	Options/possible actions	Examples of consultant's relevant feedback and activities (see the chapter's detailed illustration)
Heightening self-awareness	Reflecting on pleasing moments from interactions with other supervisors (e.g., to become more alert to own efforts to seek approval). Completing and presenting the results of a self-report questionnaire, to discuss my role in ineffective supervision episodes. Requesting advice on implementing a self-monitoring system (e.g., based on the routine use of supervisee satisfaction data as feedback on supervision).	Commenting on the 'culture' of supervision: 'And there's no "disagreement/challenge", just lots of that Californian positivity.... Remember that the theory of experiential learning requires modest "destabilisation" to occur, if there's going to be any real learning.' Using a manualised checklist of desirable supervisor behaviours (SAGE). Providing feedback on specific supervisory competencies, with great detail and specificity indicating gaps between desired behaviours and current supervision practice.
Improving self-care	'Ventilation' – ensuring that there are opportunities to express negative feelings, to reduce tension. Seeking other types of social support (information, practical help, sense of collegiality). Reviewing and strengthening relevant personal coping strategies (e.g., reframing upsetting incidents).	Consultant, despite providing very direct feedback, also uses humour and cultural sensitivity to undercut any defensiveness, or hostile reactions.
Enhancing evidence-based practice	Discussing personally relevant research and development activities (e.g., audits). Considering local applications of action research (e.g., introducing routine clinical outcome monitoring; seeking guidance on designing and implementing this monitoring system).	Consultant discusses regular use of an instrument designed to evaluate supervision (SAGE), options of more formal training of clinic supervisors, making monthly administrative meetings more clinically focused on supporting supervisors, etc.
Encouraging educational development	Studying and discussing personally relevant issues arising from guidelines, competence frameworks, important studies/books, workshops, and similar educational material. Viewing video material that demonstrates competent supervision.	Making reference to underlying competency frameworks relevant to supervision goals, structure, and process; introducing an experiential learning model that encourages reflection, processing, and experimenting with new behaviours, being more consistent with competency frameworks (i.e., setting and managing a clear agenda in future supervision sessions).

(Continued)

Table 7.1 (Continued)

Consultancy objectives and consultant activities

Consultancy objectives	Options/possible actions	Examples of consultant's relevant feedback and activities (see the chapter's detailed illustration)
	Taking the opportunity to experiment and practice key competencies arising from video material in a safe, respectful, confidential consulting environment.	Consultant's qualitative feedback: 'Good to see a role-play' – consider developing the supervisee's skills in this (e.g., introduce difficulties/complications, rehearsing coping strategies; 'might work best if you first demonstrate how you'd deal with these')
Deepening understanding	Questioning assumptions about how supervisees develop competence. Reviewing critical issues in own supervision (including positive episodes, such as 'sudden gains' made by the supervisee). Formulating why we prefer to use particular supervision techniques (including making sense of the avoidance of other techniques).	See previous remarks' on the effects of two little challenge, too much agreement, a problematic culture of being overly nice in supervision; and, consultant's concluding summary: 'I suggest to you that supervisees need a tolerable, effective degree of challenging work to do in supervision.'
Problem-solving	Provide and jointly view a recording of my supervision, to enable consultant to help me to identify reasons why my supervision is generally ineffective with a particular supervisee. Aim to: clarify problems; generate and appraise options; draw out implications for my future practice.	Consultant assists in developing a follow-up plan based on the feedback and review of the session that helps the supervisor identify priorities for affecting behavioural change.
Supporting self-monitoring	Facilitating reflection on key events. Considering sources of information (e.g., use a relevant supervision questionnaire). Interpreting results and Qualitative Information.	Consultant provides practical and direct feedback embedded in a supportive and affirming context: 'I hope that the suggestions above clarify how that might be achieved, and wish to encourage you to broaden your repertoire from a lovely, supportive, and pragmatic approach, to that of a significant facilitator of the supervisee's development, a "trainer".'

Source: Milne, D.L. (2018). Reproduced with permission of Derek Milne.

leads them to do things like discount feedback (Kruger & Dunning, 1999). But smart organisational systems can overcome such idiosyncrasies. For example, a review by Macdonald and Mellor-Clark (2014) suggested that clinical outcome monitoring may be effective because it raises awareness and corrects biases in clinicians' assessment of their work, which can then be integrated with ongoing supervision. Consultants can contribute to this monitoring effort, by guiding the design of the system, and by discussing data (see Table 7.1 for more examples of consultancy involvement).

Formulation

The most relevant deliberate practice explanations for ineffectiveness are probably that feedback is absent or inaccurate, competence development efforts are superficial, and there is little or no help from experts.

Guidelines

We focus now on how consultants can help supervisors to become more effective, using the examples of clinical outcome monitoring, and self-monitoring, incorporating educational approaches.

Clinical outcome monitoring (OM) can be viewed as a feedback system for the supervisor, indicating whether their supervisee (the clinician) is being effective with patients. OM requires that patient outcomes are monitored routinely, using norm-referenced measures. This allows comparisons to be made with data from hundreds of other patients, allowing judgements about progress to be formed, and representing feedback to guide the supervisor and/or supervisee. This feedback may have implications for the effectiveness of supervision (e.g., highlighting the need to alter the implementation of a treatment). OM within supervision can dramatically improve effectiveness, simply by ensuring that all relevant patients are reviewed, especially the problematic cases that the supervisee might otherwise not readily present in supervision. OM has consistently resulted in significant improvements in therapy outcomes (Swift et al., 2015), and is integral to well-designed healthcare systems (e.g., IAPT: Lambert et al., 2018; Richards, 2014).

Self-monitoring is similar to OM, in treating feedback as the mechanism for improving supervisory effectiveness. But instead of clinical outcome information, the data in self-monitoring relate to the personal processes that are judged to contribute to outcomes (e.g., avoiding experiential learning methods due to anxiety). These are potentially wide-ranging, including thoughts, feelings or behaviours. This diversity is reflected in the terms used historically to define self-supervision (e.g., self-management, self-regulation, and self-monitoring). To illustrate, in psychiatry self-monitoring may involve taping clinical sessions; listening to entire tapes independently; making process notes (reflections on what the psychiatrist identified in the tape), and discussing the notes in supervision (Basa, 2018). Another example is to audit one's supervision, aided by using published instruments with normative data (as per OM). To illustrate, The Manchester Clinical Supervision Questionnaire (Winstanley & White, 2014) contains seven sub-scales (e.g., 'support/advice' and 'improving care/skills'), and there are data from large samples of supervisors, providing the basis for a comparative supervision profile. That is, a supervisor could ask their supervisee to complete The Manchester Clinical Supervision Questionnaire in relation to their supervision, before comparing the resultant profile with these norms. This could then be reviewed in consultancy, and any gaps addressed to improve effectiveness.

Below we summarise guidelines for maximising the value of consultancy, illustrated in relation to a supervisor's use of OM and self-monitoring, but widely applicable. These guidelines draw on our own experience, from other sources in this book, and from several additional empirical and theoretical sources (e.g., Davidson et al., 2017; Lucock et al., 2015; Milne & Reiser, 2017; Schoenwald, 2016; Tracey et al., 2014; Weck et al., 2016):

- **Start with explanations:** Explain who you are and how you prefer to work as a consultant. Offer reasons for what you propose to do together by explaining these approaches, how to use them, and why we are doing this at this stage. Aim to boost collaboration through joint goal-setting, and an interactive approach to feedback. Place things in context demonstrating how planned changes are part of a solution, benefitting the supervisor in their workplace. Develop systems, methods, and a culture that encourages supervisors to value feedback.
- **Invite questions and reactions:** Clarify the supervisor's developmental and professional needs. Consider important factors together, such as structure, time/resources/equipment considerations, process (e.g., nature of activity), and outcomes (e.g., supervisory effectiveness). Where possible, feedback should be tailored to meet these needs and contextual factors (e.g., how feedback can be enhanced with more valued data or made less intrusive). Recognise the practical and personal challenges, empathising with the associated difficulties (e.g., risking damaging the supervisory alliance). Aim to integrate the feedback system with routine practice, and with the required quality assurance systems within the host organisation.
- **Define gaps:** Develop a system for tracking the patients' response to treatment longitudinally, comparing the data against norms for treatment response. When there is a discrepancy between the results from the local provision of treatment and the outcomes achieved within the normative sample, then a system is in place to alert clinicians and their supervisors to this relatively poor progress. This includes providing clinicians with a problem-solving decision tree, together with recommendations for possible interventions to boost progress (algorithms or brief guidelines). The same logic applies to the supervisor, in that regular profiling of supervisory skills could help define gaps and help to define consultancy objectives (e.g., the Supervisor Adherence Measure: Schoenwald et al., 1998). These kinds of data should be discussed in consultancy, to ensure that the chosen system is used correctly.
- **Monitor progress:** Something like a supervision adherence measure may be excessively arduous to use routinely, so additional brief instruments may be advantageous (in terms of involving different stakeholders, and due to using multiple measures for better validity). According to the underlying theory, feedback will work best when it is utilised to provide information that suggests a specific actionable improvement to the treatment provided by the supervisee, which is duly processed in supervision (e.g., learning from errors made; developing and executing an improvement plan). Technical adjustments may ease accessing and using feedback (e.g., use preferred data display formats, such as user-friendly 'traffic light' approaches). Link improvement efforts to support materials and individuals (e.g., peer support groups). Use signposting or similar approach to provide perspective on progress (current stage of progress, related to the plan).

- **Use multiple methods:** Together, the consultant and supervisor should draw on the feedback to design a suitable supervision development plan, intended to strengthen the highlighted competencies. The consultant should use a blend of methods to support and guide the supervisor, as per supervision. This can include supervision guidelines, illustrative video material, illustrative vignettes, and experiential work (including educational role-plays and behavioural rehearsal). Acknowledge the challenges inherent in responding to feedback (personal and professional). In general, feedback should be based on observable behaviours, defined concretely, and including specific constructive suggestions, phrased in descriptive, non-technical and non-judgmental language, and provided in a timely way. Emphasise replacing deficits with positive alternatives (rather than criticising or trying to prevent the weak instances). Competent behaviours should also be reinforced. Naturally, corrective mutual feedback on these kinds of efforts should also be included.
- **Demonstrate effective methods:** Ensure that there is a good understanding of the underlying principles, and clarity about how to apply this understanding. Consultants should demonstrate how principles apply, and illustrate how to perform key supervision techniques, stressing how they might be applied with a supervisee, while noting their clinical value: Booster training sessions will boost confidence and help to reduce 'drift'.
- **Learn the lessons:** Implementing new feedback systems entails dealing with the barriers to innovation and grappling with a succession of practical setbacks. The healthcare context is complex, and simple solutions are rare. Resources may be insufficient, calling on resourcefulness and realistic goal-setting. For some feedback systems, there may be great value in undertaking some action research, to best formulate and tackle the barriers and boosters. The organisational context surrounding supervision needs to include effective leadership (e.g., managers who can secure the technical resources to build and maintain the feedback system), and foster an innovation culture (e.g., creative planning and addressing resistance collectively).

Detailed Illustration

The director of a training clinic, a senior psychologist who was responsible for supervising graduate students and the oversight of supervision throughout the clinic, had never actually received formal training as a supervisor: he had never been directly observed, nor provided with feedback. The clinic director engaged a consultant to further develop his supervision skills. The supervision coaching process involved direct observation of the clinic director and use of a structured instrument to evaluate supervisory behaviours, with follow-up sessions to provide specific detailed feedback. Key elements of the consultant's feedback are summarised in Table 7.1 (see column three 'Examples of consultant's relevant activities') alongside a list of standard consultancy objectives. Summarising this feedback, despite a number of strengths (notably the supervision alliance), this initial review of supervision determined that there were deficits in the director's approach, when related to the 'evidence-based' approach operationalised by SAGE, including insufficient structuring of the session, and overuse of case-focused discussion. This approach resulted in a very modest level of experiential learning, which the consultant (DM) summarised in a direct but humorous manner as follows:

'To continue my James Bond impression, I think that this supervisee would feedback, in confidence to me, that: "That'll do nicely: not shaken or stirred". In contrast, I suggest to you that supervisees need a tolerable, effective degree of challenging work to do in supervision. I hope that the suggestions here clarify how that might be achieved, and wish to encourage you to broaden your repertoire from a lovely, supportive and pragmatic approach, to that of a significant facilitator of the supervisee's development, a "trainer".'

Personal Reflections

As the director of the training clinic, you might well imagine that I (RR) experienced a range of emotions upon receiving this feedback: shock, a good dose of 'imposter syndrome', and an immediate sense of defensiveness (including not wanting to fully accept or process the feedback). As a practicing psychologist, I had been supervising in some capacity for over 20 years, and for the past 6 years had been a primary supervisor in an APA approved graduate training clinic. How could I possibly not be fully competent, just based upon my experience and background? Unfortunately, as was common during the period of my graduate training 30 years ago, there were no dedicated courses on supervision and no observation of my supervision at any point. I had simply been 'nominated' to be a supervisor at a certain point in my career, but I never received specific training. There was an assumption that if you were a competent psychologist eventually you would simply become a competent supervisor, through some kind of osmosis – a magical absorption of skills. I had certainly never gotten direct feedback on my supervision, except from my student evaluations which were generally quite positive, and with hindsight I can see that none of the necessary conditions for expertise were met.

This feedback, while delivered with some tactful humour and recognition of some of the cultural differences, was quite divergent from my own self-assessment of my supervision (further examples can be found within Table 7.1, column 3). A quite challenging discussion ensued, one that highlighted the difficulty senior practitioners may experience when receiving direct feedback (Milne & Reiser, 2017, includes a similar video vignette). After working together with the consultant on processing the unpleasant emotions resulting from the feedback, we worked collaboratively together to develop to a very specific and concrete action plan involving deliberate practice, with continuing feedback and support from the consultant. This process helped me rapidly evolve my supervision towards more competent practice, as documented in our N = 1 study of supervision in which we demonstrated training effects over six sessions on a standardised instrument designed to observe supervision (Milne et al., 2013). However, without this direct observation, feedback and deliberate practice, it's likely I would have continued on a similar trajectory possibly throughout my career. Studies of developing expertise (e.g., Ericsson, 2009) have similarly noted the possibility of a flattening out of practitioner skills over time, due to drift and an automatised, routinised approach.

To put this challenging experience in historical context, at the time that this happened supervision had not received the necessary professional and programmatic support to prosper as an independent competency. For instance, alongside the rarity of training opportunities, video-presented demonstrations and supervision guidelines were not yet available, and managers gave little emphasis to supervision. Although my self-initiated experience was uncomfortable, I take some credit for tackling and resolving this critical competence issue.

Conclusions and Action Implications

There are many intervention methods for resolving critical issues related to incompetent supervision. In this chapter we have highlighted: supervisor coaching (supervision-of-supervision), proctoring, guidelines, video demonstrations, peer groups, supervisee feedback, consultancy, self-monitoring, and clinical outcome-monitoring. We linked these methods to three different types of incompetence: a lack of proficiency, non-adherence, and ineffectiveness. Inappropriateness was noted as a fourth type of incompetence, having already been addressed in Chapter 5. Based on the expertise literature, we provided a core formulation of why a lack of proficiency, non-adherence, and ineffectiveness might arise. We also drew heavily on the signature method for developing expertise, deliberate practice. Guidelines for resolving these issues were provided.

Although this chapter has offered a wide-ranging review of the most promising, evidence-based skills for resolving critical issues related to supervisory incompetence, it is not exhaustive. Also, we should clearly acknowledge that we largely linked the different types of incompetence with the various methods for resolving them on the basis of convenience: the approach that we adopted at the start of this chapter neatly partitioned the reasons for incompetence, as well as the various skills and methods for dealing with supervisory incompetence. In reality, these reasons and interventions are much less neat and tidy, and have a much wider relevance. It follows that those helping supervisors to develop competence should use their professional judgement in seeking to understand the reasons for critical issues, and also in intervening to deal with them.

Another possible criticism of this chapter is the risk of reductionism when discussing competence, so we wish to emphasise that we share with others (e.g., ten Cate et al., 2010) the perspective that competence (and incompetence) is best understood as a characteristic of individuals in interaction with their context. In this sense, some workplaces help us to demonstrate competence, while others render us incompetent (e.g., as a result of inadequate equipment). Of course, individuals need to do their best to get the most out of their environment, which is why we lay such store in coping strategies, social support, and self-regulation. Ultimately, competence is the ability to get the job done, given the circumstances. Therefore, we devoted a section to effectiveness and its enhancement. In later chapters we will go on to balance this emphasis on individuals against the role that the workplace needs to play in supporting them (see Chapter 10). There is also the risk that we might reduce competence to a list of techniques, technical actions to be ticked off a long list. Just as workplaces entail complex interactions, so does supervision. We share with others (e.g., Parry et al., 2020) the view that competence in these essentially human interactions entails a truly impressive degree of responsivity: making ongoing judgements and adjustments that are guided by our understanding, and designed to make relationships work. This includes choosing to use different techniques in particular ways, and is another reason for stressing that readers must exercise their professional judgement in following our guidelines.

Another concern with this chapter is that supervision research remains at an exceptionally early stage in demonstrating the effectiveness of the various methods and techniques discussed. This has meant that we have had to place much of our confidence in the available evidence on relevant theory, expert advice, and extrapolation (e.g., from what works in supervision, to what should work in consultancy or coaching). A particular research weakness rests in the causal assumptions that are made: that roles are enacted properly, that techniques are used competently, and that the desired changes ensue. For instance, it is tempting to assume that studies that report manipulating clinical outcome monitoring ensured that supervisors were properly trained for their role in facilitating the supervisees' assimilation of this feedback, and that assimilation duly occurred, and it led to behaviour changes observable in subsequent treatment sessions. Unfortunately, such assumptions are frequently unsupported by close scrutiny of these steps: the independent variable often lacks fidelity within supervision (see Table 1.1 in Milne, 2018). To illustrate in relation to this chapter, in one study supervisors were trained to implement outcome monitoring, which was evaluated through observations of supervision and linked supervisee reports (Fullerton et al., 2018). The findings suggested that, although the supervisors became more confident, competent, and positive about outcome monitoring following training, in supervision they were inconsistent in discussing with clinicians how the monitoring system was administered. That is, monitoring the outcome monitoring intervention itself indicated low fidelity to the system, possibly explaining the poor outcomes. Sadly, this is a common finding related to outcome monitoring and supervision (e.g., Davidson et al., 2017; Reese et al., 2009). This is partly due to the challenge of ensuring high fidelity with complex interventions: even in exemplary clinical trials supervision is often reported inconsistently and superficially, although it appears to have played an essential role (Roth et al., 2010). If we are to demonstrate causal links, we need better specificity regarding such instances of effective supervision. There are promising signs that, when steps are taken to ensure high fidelity, at least some of the causal steps can be demonstrated reliably (e.g., improvements in clinician competence as a result of feedback (Weck et al., 2016)).

In conclusion, we are struck by the parallel between the nature of these challenges and the four main reasons for incompetence, as set out previously. That is, it seems like a promising action implication to apply deliberate practice to methods such as outcome monitoring within supervision. This might be expected to raise fidelity and help to resolve some of the critical issues. It has been said that only with evidence-based supervision can we expect evidence-based practice (Fullerton et al., 2018, p. 2). To this we add that only with evidence-based support for supervisors can we expect evidence-based supervision.

References

Bagwandeen, C. I., & Singaram, V. S. (2016). Feedback as a means to improve clinical competencies: Consultants' perceptions of the quality of feedback given to registrars. *African Journal of Health Professions Education*, 8(1), 113–116. https://doi.org/10.7196/AJHPE.2016.v8i1.758

Basa, V. (2018). 'Self-supervision' in the therapeutic profession. *European Journal of Counselling Theory, Research and Practice*, 2(6), 1–7. Retrieved from http://www.europeancounselling.eu/volumes/volume-2-2018/volume-2-article-6

Borders, L. D. (2012). Dyadic, triadic, and group models of peer supervision/consultation: What are their components, and is there evidence of their effectiveness? *Clinical Psychologist*, *16*(2), 59–71. https://doi.org/10.1111/j.1742-9552.2012.00046.x

Buus, N., Lisa Lynch, L., & Gonge, H. (2016). Developing and implementing 'meta-supervision' for mental health nursing staff supervisees: Opportunities and challenges. *The Cognitive Behaviour Therapist*, *9*, e22. https://doi.org/10.1017/S1754470X15000434

Davidson, K. M., Rankin, M. L., Begley, A., Lloyd, S., Barry, S. J. E., McSkimming, P., Bell, L., Allan, C., Osborne, M., Ralston G., Bienkowski, G., Mellor-Clark, J., & Walker, A. (2017). Assessing patient progress in psychological therapy through feedback in supervision: The MeMOS randomized controlled trial. *Behavioural and Cognitive Psychotherapy*, *2017*(45), 209–224. https://doi.org/10.1017/S1352465817000029

Dreyfus, S. E. (2004). The five-stage model of adult skill acquisition. *Bulletin of Science, Technology& Society*, *24*(3), 177–181. https://doi.org/10.1177/0270467604264992

Ellis, M. V., Berger, L., Hanus, A. E., Ayala, E. E., Swords, B. A., & Siembor, M. (2014). Inadequate and harmful clinical supervision: Testing a revised framework and assessing occurrence. *The Counseling Psychologist*, *42*(4), 434–472. https://doi.org/10.1177/0011000013508656

Ericsson, K. A. (2009). *Development of Professional Expertise*. Cambridge University Press.

Falender, C., Cornish, J. A. E., Goodyear, R., Hatcher, R., Kaslow, N. J., Leventhal, G., Shafranske, E., Sigmon, S. T., Stoltenberg, C., & Grus, C. (2004). Defining competencies in psychology supervision: A consensus statement. *Journal of Clinical Psychology*, *60*(7), 771–785. https://psycnet.apa.org/doi/10.1002/jclp.20013

Fullerton, M., Edbrooke-Childs, J., Law, D., Martin, K., Whelan, I., & Wolpert, M. (2018). Using patient-reported outcome measures to improve service effectiveness for supervisors: A mixed-methods evaluation of supervisors' attitudes and self-efficacy after training to use outcome measures in child mental health. *Child and Adolescent Mental Health*, *23*(1), 34–40. https://doi.org/10.1111/camh.12206

General Medical Council (GMC). (2013). *2012 Annual Statistics: Fitness to Practise*. http://www.gmc-uk.org/2012_Annual_Statistics.pdf_53844772.pdf

Gifford, K. A., & Fall, L. H. (2014). Doctor-coach: A deliberate practice approach to teaching & learning clinical skills. *Academic Medicine*, *89*(2), 272–276. https://doi.org/.10.1097/ACM.0000000000000097

Hill, C. E., Baumann, E., Shafran, N., Gupta, S., Morrison, A., Rojas, A. E. P., Spangler, P. T., Griffin, S., Pappa, L., & Gelso, C. J. (2015). Is training effective? A study of counselling psychology doctoral trainees in a psychodynamic/interpersonal training clinic. *Journal of Counseling Psychology*, *62*(2), 184–201. https://psycnet.apa.org/doi/10.1037/cou0000053

Humphrey, H. J., Marcangelo, M., Rodriguez, E. R., & Spitz, D. (2013). Assessing competencies during education in psychiatry. *International Review of Psychiatry*, *25*(3), 291–300. https://doi.org/10.3109/09540261.2013.799460

Johnson, W. B. (2007). Transformational supervision: When supervisors mentor. *Professional Psychology: Research and Practice*, *38*(3), 259–267. https://psycnet.apa.org/doi/10.1037/0735-7028.38.3.259

Joyce, B., & Showers, B. (2002). *Student achievement through staff development*. Association for Supervision and Curriculum Development.

Keenan-Miller, D., & Corbett, H. I. (2015). Metasupervision: Can students be safe and effective supervisors? *Training and Education in Professional Psychology*, *9*(4), 315–321. http://dx.doi.org/10.1037/tep0000090

Kilburg, R. R., & Diedrich, R. C. (2007). *The wisdom of coaching: Essential papers in consulting psychology for a world of change*. APA.

Kruger, J., & Dunning, D. (1999). Unskilled and unaware of it: How difficulties in recognising one's own incompetence lead to inflated self-assessments. *Journal of Personality and Social Psychology*, 77(6), 1121–1134. https://psycnet.apa.org/doi/10.1037/0022-3514.77.6.1121

Lambert, M. J., Whipple, J. L., & Kleinstäuber, M. (2018). Collecting and delivering progress feedback: A meta-analysis of routine outcome monitoring. *Psychotherapy*, 55(4), 520–537. https://doi.org/10.1037/pst0000167

Locke, E. A., & Latham, G. P. (2006). New directions in goal-setting theory. *Current Directions in Psychological Science*, 15(5), 265–268. https://psycnet.apa.org/doi/10.1111/j.1467-8721.2006.00449.x

Lucock, M., Halstead, J., Leach, C., Barkham, M., Tucker, S., Randal, C., Middleton, J., Khan, W., Catlow, H., Waters, E., & Saxon, D. (2015). A mixed-method investigation of patient monitoring and enhanced feedback in routine practice: Barriers and facilitators. *Psychotherapy Research*, 25(6), 633–646. https://doi.org/10.1080/10503307.2015.1051163

Maben, J., Taylor, C., Dawson, J., Learny, M., McCarthy, I., Reynolds, E., Ross, S., Shuldham, C., Bennett, L., & Foot, C. (2018). A realist informed mixed methods evaluation of Schwartz Center Rounds in England. *First BMJ Open*, 8. https://doi.org/10.1136/bmjopen-2018-024254.

Macdonald, J., & Mellor-Clark, J. (2014). Correcting psychotherapists' blindsidedness: Formal feedback as a means of overcoming the natural limitations of therapists. *Clinical Psychology & Psychotherapy*, 22(3), 249–257. https://doi.org/10.1002/cpp.1887

Mager, R. F. (1997). *Preparing instructional objectives: A critical tool in the development of effective instruction* (3rd ed.). Center for Effective Practice.

Mason, L., Grey, N., & Veale, D. (2016). My therapist is a student? The impact of therapist experience and client severity on cognitive behavioural therapy outcomes for people with anxiety disorders. *Behavioural & Cognitive Psychotherapy*, 44(2), 193–202. https://doi.org/10.1017/s1352465815000065

McCutcheon, S., & Duchemin, A.-M. (2021). Faculty self-evaluation of experiences with delivering feedback to trainees across academic ranks. *Medical Science Educator*, 31, 355–358. https://doi.org/10.1007/s40670-020-01196-5

McGaghie, W. C., Issenberg, S. B., Barsuk, J. H., & Wayne, D. B. (2014). A critical review of simulation-based mastery learning with translational outcomes. *Medical Education*, 48(4), 375–385. https://doi.org/10.1111/medu.12391

McLoughlin, C., Casey, S., Feeney, A., Weir, D., Abdalla, A. A., & Barrett, E. (2021). Burnout, work satisfaction, and well-being among non-consultant psychiatrists in Ireland. *Academic Psychiatry*. Advance online publication. https://doi.org/10.1007/s40596-020-01366-y

McMahan, E. H. (2014). Supervision, a non-elusive component of deliberate practice toward expertise. *American Psychologist*, 69(7), 712–713. https://psycnet.apa.org/doi/10.1037/a0037832

Milne, D. L. (2018). *Evidence-based CBT Supervision*. Wiley-Blackwell.

Milne, D. L., Leck, C., & Choudhri, N. Z. (2009). Collusion in clinical supervision: Literature review and case study in self-reflection. *The Cognitive Behaviour Therapist*, 2(2), 106–114. https://doi.org/10.1017/S1754470X0900018X

Milne, D. L., & Reiser, R. P. (2017). *A manual for evidence-based CBT Supervision*. Wiley-Blackwell.

Milne, D. L., Reiser, R. P., & Cliffe, T. (2013). An n=1 evaluation of enhanced CBT supervision. *Behavioural & Cognitive Psychotherapy, 41*(2), 210–220. https://psycnet.apa.org/doi/10.1017/S1352465812000434

Milne, D. L., Reiser, R. P., Cliffe, T., & Raine, R. (2011). SAGE: Preliminary evaluation of an instrument for observing CBT supervision. *The Cognitive Behaviour Therapist, 4*(4), 123–138. https://psycnet.apa.org/doi/10.1017/S1754470X11000079

Molloy, E., Ajjawi, R., Bearman, M., Noble, C., Rudland, J., & Ryan, A. (2020). Challenging feedback myths: Values, learner involvement and promoting effects beyond the immediate task. *Medical Education, 54*, 33–39. https://doi.org/10.1111/medu.13802.

Newman, C. F. (2013). Training cognitive behavioural therapy supervisors: Didactics, simulated practice, and "meta-supervision". *Journal of Cognitive Psychotherapy: An International Quarterly, 27*(1), 5–18. https://doi.org/10.1891/0889-8391.27.1.5 https://psycnet.apa.org/doi/10.1037/pro0000171

Newman-Taylor, K., Gordon, K., Grist, S., & Olding, C. (2013) Developing supervisory competence: Preliminary data on the impact of CBT supervision training. *The Cognitive Behaviour Therapist, 5*(4), 83–92. https://doi.org/10.1017/S1754470X13000056

Orakzai, G. S., Sethi, A., Victor, G., & Aamir, H. S. (2020). Clinical supervision: What do the supervisors and residents think? *The Professional Medical Journal, 27*(11), 2529–2536. https://doi.org/10.29309/TPMJ/2020.27.11.4543

Parry, G., Bennett, D., Roth, A. D., & Kellett, S. (2020). Developing a competence framework for cognitive analytic therapy. *Psychology and Psychotherapy: Theory, Research and Practice, 94*(1), 151–170. https://doi.org/10.1111/papt.12306

Pilling, S., & Roth, A. D. (2014). The competent clinical supervisor. In C. E. Watkins & D. L. Milne (Eds.), *The Wiley International Handbook of Clinical Supervision* (pp. 20–37).

Reese, R. J., Usher, E. L., Bowman, D. C., Norsworthy, L. A., Halstead, J. L., Rowlands, S. R., & Chisholm, R. R. (2009). Using client feedback in psychotherapy training: An analysis of its influence on supervision and counsellor self-efficacy. *Training and Education in Professional Psychology, 33*(3), 157–168. https://psycnet.apa.org/doi/10.1037/a0015673

Richards, D. A. (2014). Clinical case management supervision: Using clinical outcome monitoring and therapy progress feedback to drive supervision. In C. E. Watkins & D. L. Milne (Eds.), *Wiley International Handbook of Clinical Supervision* (pp. 518–529). Wiley.

Roth, A. D., & Pilling, S. (2007). *A competence framework for the supervision of psychological therapies*. University College London. The full set of competences referred to in this document are available for downloading from the CORE website: www.ucl.ac.uk/CORE

Roth, A. D., Pilling, S., & Turner, J. (2010). Therapist training and supervision in clinical trials: Implications for clinical practice. *Behavioural and Cognitive Psychotherapy, 38*(3), 291–302. https://doi.org/10.1017/s1352465810000068

Rousmaniere, T., Goodyear, R. K., Miller, S. D., & Wampold, B. E. (2017). *The cycle of excellence: Using deliberate practice to improve supervision and training*. Wiley-Blackwell.

Schoenwald, S. K. (2016). Clinical supervision in a quality assurance/quality improvement system: Multisystemic Therapy® as an Example. *The Cognitive Behaviour Therapist, 9*, e21. https://doi.org/10.1017/S1754470X15000604

Schoenwald, S. K., Henggeler, S. W., & Edwards, D. (1998). *MST Supervisor Adherence Measure*. MST Institute.

Schriger, S. H., Becker-Haimes, E. M., Skriner, L., & Beidas, R. S. (2020). Clinical supervision in community mental health: Characterizing supervision as usual and exploring predictors of supervision content and process. *Community Mental Health Journal*. Advance online publication.https://doi.org/10.1007/s10597-020-00681-w

Swift, J. K., Callahan, J. L., Rousmaniere, T. G., Whipple, J. L., Dexter, K., & Wrape, E. R. (2015). Using client outcome monitoring as a tool for supervision. *Psychotherapy, 52*(2), 180–184. https://doi.org/10.1037/a0037659

Tasker, F., Newbery, N., Burr, B., & Goddard, A. F. (2014). Survey of core medical trainees in the United Kingdom 2013 – Inconsistencies in training experience and competing with service demands. *Clinical Medicine, 14*(2), 149–156. https://doi.org/10.7861/clinmedicine.14-2-149

Taylor, C., Xyrichis, A., Leamy, M. C., Reynolds, E., & Maben, J. (2018). Can Schwartz Center Rounds support healthcare staff with emotional challenges at work, and how do they compare with other interventions aimed at providing similar support? A systematic review and scoping reviews. *BMJ Open, 8*, e024254. https://doi.org/10.1136/bmjopen-2018-024254.

ten Cate, O., Snell, L., & Carraccio, C. (2010). Medical competence: The interplay between individual ability and the health care environment. *Medical Teacher, 32*(8), 669–675. https://doi.org/10.3109/0142159X.2010.500897

Tracey, T. J. G., Wampold, B. E., Lichtenberg, J. W., & Goodyear, R. K. (2014). Expertise in psychotherapy: An elusive goal? *American Psychologist, 69*(3), 218–229. https://doi.org/10.1037/a0035099

Vygotsky, L. S. (1978). *Mind in society: The development of higher psychological processes*. Harvard University Press.

Waller, G., & Turner, H. (2016). Therapist drift redux: Why well-meaning clinicians fail to deliver evidence-based therapy, and how to get back on track. *Behaviour Research and Therapy, 77*, 129e137. http://dx.doi.org/10.1016/j.brat.2015.12.005

Watkins, C. E., & Milne, D. L. (Eds.). (2014). *The Wiley International Handbook of Clinical Supervision*. Wiley-Blackwell.

Weck, F., Kaufmann, Y. M., & Höfling, V. (2016). Competence feedback improves CBT competence in trainee therapists: A randomized controlled pilot study. *Psychotherapy Research, 27*(4), 501–509. https://doi.org/10.1080/10503307.2015.1132857

Winstanley, J., & White, E. (2014). The Manchester Clinical Supervision Scale: MCSS-26. In C. E. Watkins & D. L. Milne (Eds.), *The Wiley International Handbook of Clinical Supervision* (pp. 386–401). Chichester.

8

Skills in Dealing with Challenging Supervisees

Introduction

Supervisees should be viewed as essential and valued partners in the pursuit of effective supervision: 'the optimal relationship between ... supervisor and supervisee is one in which both parties necessarily depend on the others' contribution, and benefit from the process' (Milne & Reiser, 2017, p. 44). This implies a major role for supervisees in making supervision a success. As Falender and Shafranske (2012) have expressed it, 'supervision is dynamically co-constructed, and effective supervision is the responsibility of both the supervisor and the supervisee' (p. 209). They provided a dozen examples of how supervisees could play their part, including self-care (e.g., enhancing their resilience), aspiring to ethical practice and personal effectiveness (e.g., managing stressors), using instruments to self-define their competence levels (to clarify their own learning needs), and improving their thinking (e.g., clarifying their own assumptions about patients). These contributions are consistent with expert consensus statements (American Psychological Association, 2015; Roth & Pilling, 2007). For instance, the Roth and Pilling (2007) competence framework included the category 'ability to make use of supervision', which specified a capacity for active learning (e.g., acting on the supervisor's reading suggestions), and an ability to take the initiative, in relation to their learning (e.g., by incorporating reading material into their clinical practice). Counter-balancing these responsibilities, Ellis et al. (2017) also noted some supervisees' rights, including being respected and treated as an individual, addressing and resolving conflicts, and being treated ethically.

While expert consensus statements are common, there is far less research on the supervisees' role. To quote Watkins and Scaturo (2013, p. 88), 'Research on preparing supervisees for the supervision experience is virtually non-existent'. In one of the rare studies, Rieck et al. (2015) found positive associations between learning styles (being open to new experiences), extraversion, and supervisory alliances. They conjectured that appropriate levels of openness and extraversion were desirable supervisee characteristics, and likely to facilitate their smooth professional development. They referred to such supervisees as 'supervision ready'. One especially powerful and fascinating example of participation is the supervisee's use of their 'learning expertise' (Bransford & Schwartz, 2009), which has been described qualitatively (Green et al., 2014). This refers to supervisees drawing on their experience as

Resolving Critical Issues in Clinical Supervision: A Practical, Evidence-based Approach, First Edition.
Derek L. Milne and Robert P. Reiser.
© 2023 John Wiley & Sons Ltd. Published 2023 by John Wiley & Sons Ltd.

learners to optimise their supervision. We return to learning expertise later, but for now we note that the first basic skill in dealing with challenging supervisees is to value their strengths, engaging them collaboratively to resolve any critical issues.

Supervisees have also been surveyed for their opinions on their roles and responsibilities. Drawing on samples of final year undergraduate health students (e.g., those in nursing, medical radiation science, occupational therapy, physiotherapy, and medicine), O'Brien et al. (2019) used focus groups and semi-structured interviews to clarify the mutual responsibilities, but the supervisees' narratives were mainly concerned with their supervisors' behaviours, rather than their own. O'Brien et al. (2019) interpreted these data as indicating that these supervisees did not view their contributions as essential, undervaluing their part in the supervision process and outcomes, and generally externalising both successes and failures in their experiences of supervision. A survey involving 22 medical residents by LaDonna et al. (2017) also indicated supervisees' ambivalence about sharing responsibility for learning, related to the use of direct observation, As O'Brien et al. (2019) pointed out, this perspective suggests that supervisees position themselves as passive partners, failing to reciprocate their supervisors' efforts or take some ownership of the supervision processes and outcomes. This can feed into a common collusive reaction from supervisors (and authors), one that 'infantalises' supervisees (i.e., treating supervisees as if they were children, for example, by under-estimating their competence and maturity).

Challenging Supervisees

As suggested by O'Brien et al. (2019), although the policy is to treat supervisees as partners in supervision, actual practice is much less heartening. In Chapter 1 we outlined the negative role played by supervisees' behaviour, especially those individual characteristics that fundamentally undermined their ability to benefit from supervision. Technically, we classified this as a case of 'faulty receipt', which interferes with supervisees' professional development, and in turn compromises their clinical work. General concerns are that there is a failure to engage properly with supervision (e.g., avoiding experiential learning), or such supervisee behaviours slow competence development (a failure to thrive). This may be due to low self-esteem or morale, or to adverse health (physical or mental, such as burnout). There may also be complications concerning cultural competencies, or worrying theoretical or philosophical beliefs, which may undermine the way that they are supervised. As a result, our Chapter 1 conclusion was that such supervisees were unfit for their clinical purpose (or for an academic award).

On the other hand, supervisors should do their best to resolve challenging behaviour. Supervisees will inevitably present some critical issues within supervision, as novices struggling to cope with novel techniques, adopting a professional role, and operating in complex healthcare environments. For example, tensions and disagreements in supervision are to be expected, arising from the pressure on the pre-licensure supervisee to succeed in a context where there are often competing demands, in addition to differing personnel, policies, and procedures. Most naturally, there are challenges surrounding the development of the supervisees' clinical competence, which entails uncomfortable learning episodes, featuring events such as de-skilling and the loss of self-confidence.

Chapter Plan

We next summarise the five main types of exceptionally challenging supervisee behaviours, ones that go beyond the normal adjustment and developmental struggles. In keeping with our understanding of the transactional nature of behaviour, we first define 'challenging', then offer some ways of understanding these issues. The heart of the chapter is again devoted to guidelines on the supervision skills you might use to cope with your supervisee's challenging behaviours. But these guidelines also include ways in which the supervisee can contribute to the resolution of critical issues, in the spirit of co-construction.

Definition of 'Challenging' Behaviour

What do we mean when we refer to supervisees' behaviour as 'challenging'? We mean the same thing as we do when referring to any other critical issue (stressor): a challenging supervisee is someone who is behaving in ways that are perceived by the supervisor (or other involved person) as requiring a coping response (i.e., a personal adjustment to the stressor). As per the earlier examples, this is usually regarded as undesirable behaviour (e.g., alliance ruptures; ignoring feedback). But consistent with the coping model (see Figure 1.1 in Chapter 1), we also include desirable behaviour that positively challenges the supervisor in ways that are beneficial (e.g., presenting clinical material that creates 'teachable moments'; posing searching questions). And we similarly assume that the supervisor and others may play a significant role in the creation and management of challenging episodes. This is also broadly consistent with the more familiar definition of challenging behaviour in patients, in that it represents behaviour that may create the risk of harm, or reduce their quality of life, by eliciting controlling responses from those who are supposedly trying to help them. This is illustrated in the narratives of harm in supervision (Ellis et al., 2017), where supervisees may be perceived as not communicating effectively, leading to unethical controlling responses from their supervisors (Reiser & Milne, 2017).

In short, we again apply the coping model to account for the fluid, transactional, and complex ways in which a supervisee may be perceived as challenging by their supervisor. Table 8.1 provides a breakdown of the main types of challenging supervisee behaviours that have been defined in the literature, drawn from competence frameworks, surveys, the measurement of supervisory relationships, and the perspectives of 'wise' supervisors (Beinart, 2014; Ellis et al., 2014; Grant et al., 2012; Kemer & Borders, 2017; Ladany et al., 2016; Milne, 2020; Molloy et al., 2020; Nelson et al., 2008; Rieck et al., 2015; Roth & Pilling, 2007; Watkins & Scaturo, 2013; Wilcoxon et al., 2018). Table 8.1 is another of our novel and preliminary classification efforts in this book, a logically driven attempt to clarify matters, as once again no suitable framework could be located in the literature, nor any definitive summary. Note too, that this table is largely theoretical, being based almost entirely on experts' opinions and self-report surveys. Therefore, it is also 'preliminary' in terms of awaiting empirical evaluation.

Table 8.1 A preliminary classification of challenging supervisee behaviours, together with the supervisee and supervisor skills that have helped to resolve them.

Challenging supervisee behaviours	Supervisee skills (prevention or resolution)	Supervisor skills
1. Adverse personal characteristics (e.g., poor health, personality and attitude problems, character weaknesses, dependence and diffidence, rejection of protocols/procedures, dogmatism, inappropriately high self-image, unethical conduct).	Self-care, heightened self-awareness, constructive attitudes. Consider roles and responsibilities in relation to shared objectives, actively question evidence-base, check and adjust value-base.	Facilitate reflection and awareness, offer empathy and emotional support. Adopt an explicitly 'normative' stance, to clarify and ensure professionalism, challenge faulty thinking, while fostering open-mindedness and gratitude.
2. Low motivation (e.g., lack of preparation, avoidance behaviours, such as persistent lateness).	Invest in supervision: take responsibility and make the effort; be more open, trusting, and resilient. Develop humility.	Encourage the use of learning expertise, especially over experiential learning; foster collaboration and co-construction.
3. Incompetence (e.g., limited background experience or general intelligence, slowing or preventing learning, not ready for supervision).	Commit to deliberate practice for skills development, reflect more deeply, and study more effectively.	Support and guide deliberate practice, support intellectual capability and key 'literacy' skills.
4. Inadequate self-regulation (e.g., insufficient self-awareness, resistance to ideas or guidance, poor insight into personal competence limits).	Improve self-appraisal ability, manage emotional reactions productively.	Provide extensive structure and 'scaffolding', ensure effective alliance, draw on self-disclosure and professional norms.
5. Interpersonally ineffective (e.g., regular alliance ruptures, consistently poor engagement with staff, problematic interactions within the organisation such as unassertiveness or non-disclosure).	Develop relationship skills (e.g., negotiating agenda); engage in relational work with supervisor (e.g., assimilation of a problematic experience). Improve communication skills.	Address as appropriate any emotional barriers (through managing corrective relational experiences); promote relational skills (e.g., interpersonal process recall technique).

Descriptions of Challenging Supervisee Behaviours

A colourful account of the kinds of behaviours with which supervisees' challenge their supervisors was provided in their marvellous book by Kadushin and Harkness (2002, p. 124): 'Supervisors face situations in which (supervisees) consistently fail to get work done on time; are consistently late or absent; fail to turn in reports; complete forms carelessly; conspicuously loaf on the job; disrupt the work of others by excessive gossiping; are careless with agency cars or equipment; are inconsiderate, insulting, or disrespectful to clients; or fail to keep appointments with personnel of cooperating agencies and services'. When other expert or 'wise' supervisors are asked for their perspective, they have added yet more irritating personal characteristics, such as being unprepared, unmotivated, and uncooperative in the supervision process (e.g., adopting the attitude that they had little to learn: Grant et al., 2012; Nelson et al., 2008; Wilcoxon et al., 2018). These experts also listed challenges noted by several authors, such as excessive incompetence or disabling personal distress, as touched on in Chapter 1 (e.g., Beddoe & Davys, 2016; Haarman, 2013; Ladany et al., 2016).

These expert opinions are firmly supported by the small amount of available research, which indicates that the most common problems concern clinical incompetence (including difficulty in developing skills), negative attitudes, and challenging behaviours (ethical, professional, and interpersonal (Shen-Miller et al., 2014)). From their review of the literature, these authors estimated that up to 95% of supervisees experience a clinical competence problem during their professional training, with recurring concerns over their professionalism, mental health, interpersonal, and academic skills. Kadushin and Harkness (2002) reported a survey of 469 social workers, which used a 16-item questionnaire containing only one item directly concerning supervisees' performance: 'Dissatisfaction with having to work with supervisees who are resistive or hostile or dependent or slow learners'. This was perceived to be a 'strong source of dissatisfaction' by 39% of these respondents.

In a qualitative study, Kemer and Borders (2017) invited those they identified as expert counselling supervisors in the USA to participate in a concept mapping study. Sixteen expert supervisors were asked to identify two of their recent supervisees, one with whom they worked well, and one who had challenged them. The experts then described the supervisee factors that contributed to their response to supervision, and their replies were subjected to a content analysis. For both 'easy' and 'challenging' supervisees, the analysis indicated that the experts effectively utilised seven categories to construe their supervisees. Expressed in terms of the challenging supervisees, their supervisees were generally regarded as having hindering personal traits and background (e.g., difficult to connect with); lacking investment and desirable behaviours toward supervision (e.g., unprepared and uncooperative); clinically incompetent; deficient in self-awareness and self-reflection skills (e.g., unwilling to hear feedback); having negative supervisory relationship characteristics (defensive and rigid in their thinking); displaying negative attitudes towards their clients (e.g., resisting taking the client's perspective), clinic, and/or the supervisor (e.g., belief that could not learn anything from the supervisor); and lastly, on a personal level they were perceived negatively by their supervisors (e.g., not liked, due to incompatible beliefs). In essence, these experts concluded that the challenging supervisees did not collaborate with them to make supervision work. This conclusion was endorsed by Kangos et al. (2018, p. 18), who considered that most often the critical issues are not so much about competence, but rather '(the supervisees') inability to benefit from supervision, demonstrate progress in remediation, and/or maintain a professional attitude'.

We summarise these diverse types of challenging supervisee behaviours in Table 8.1. Note that these five categories of challenging behaviour are presented in Table 8.1 entirely as undesirable actions (column 1), reflecting the angle taken in most of the theoretical and empirical literature. But in order to be constructive we also use this breakdown as a way of clarifying how supervisees can contribute to resolutions (or prevent problems from arising); and as a convenient, user-friendly way to summarise the kinds of skills that supervisors in particular have used to resolve these critical issues (i.e., the most evidence-based techniques of supervision). Within the text we will note some of the supporting evidence for these skills, but also note strengths and desirable episodes, aiming in part to counterbalance the general message that supervisees are solely responsible for challenging behaviours. We provide an explanation of Table 8.1 as we proceed through our suggestions for resolving the five types of challenging supervisee behaviour. But one other preliminary point: we do not assume that these categories are discrete, but rather that they combine in different causal pathways (e.g., that adverse personal characteristics, such as negative attitudes to authority figures like supervisors, may undermine motivation, and/or disrupt interpersonal effectiveness). In this sense, the classification is intended to tease apart factors that in real life will tend to be far more inter-twined. Nonetheless, we hope that you find this a helpful way of defining challenging behaviours, one that can contribute to understanding and resolving critical issues.

Formulation

Challenging supervisee behaviours may be irritating, but they are not necessarily irrational: they can potentially be understood in the light of various motivational factors. To illustrate, LaDonna et al. (2017) drew on interviews with a wide range of medical supervisees (residents), suggesting how they became ambivalent about direct observation because it was perceived as a threatening form of assessment, having the effect of reducing proficiency and thereby of lowering the perceived accuracy of any subsequent feedback. As we have stressed in previous chapters, this kind of formulation helps us to better understand why supervisees' behave as they do, and so is the best route to resolution: it enables you to identify the forces at work, and to intervene in a better-tailored and more empathic manner. Here we focus on the transactional power differential as a motivating factor.

Power Imbalance

It has been suggested that the inherent power differential between supervisor and supervisee may contribute to supervisees being generally uninformed and uninvolved in their clinical supervision, rather than active participants and collaborators (Falender & Shafranske, 2012). In addition to that status difference, supervisees may also have little or no training about supervision, their role, and in particular how proactive they should be in supervision (Ellis et al., 2014). This includes limited role inductions at the start of placements, and the absence of detailed or signed supervision contracts in the majority of cases (Kangos et al., 2018). For example, in psychiatry Parker et al. (2017) noted that the purpose and processes of supervision are often poorly defined, with limited guidance available for trainees about their role in making supervision work. The implication for training programmes is to prepare supervisees properly; supervisors should establish a detailed learning contract.

Alternatively, supervisees who are challenging may be active in managing their supervision through the subtle use of transactional 'games'. The role and nature of power games in supervision has been amusingly caricatured by Kadushin and Harkness (2002), who understood them as a form of counter-control, which they termed 'countervailing power'. This account recognised with grudging admiration the imaginative ways that social work supervisees used 'counter-measures' to reduce the power imbalance and so manage their supervisors. The serious point behind these amusing accounts is that supervisees are not powerless by virtue of their low status: supervisory power and even authority are transactional in nature. Kadushin and Harkness (2002) point out that the supervisee has to grant the authority of the supervisor and respond to the power the supervisor has the ability to exercise: 'Authority can be rejected, and power can be resisted' (p. 106). They pointed out the nature of this transaction, which is one that surely affects all healthcare disciplines: supervisees depend on supervisors for guidance and support; but supervisors in turn depend on their supervisees to do the supervised work to the required standard, so that they do not suffer adverse consequences (e.g., vicarious liability). Either party can make life difficult for the other, using different kinds of interpersonal power (veto, reward, social, informational, etc.).

Guidelines

In Table 8.1 we classified five types of challenging supervisee behaviour. Now we take each of these types in turn, offering suggestions that reflect our co-constructive approach to resolving these issues. We introduce each type of challenging behaviour in relation to a relevant supervision method, an example of a general strategy that could be taken by the supervisor, such as adopting a restorative approach to adverse personal characteristics (i.e., row one of Table 8.1). After outlining these general methods, we provide procedural examples of some more specific techniques, intended for the benefit of both supervisors and supervisees.

Respond to Adverse Personal Characteristics with a Restorative Supervision Strategy

There are some supervisee characteristics which may prove impossible to resolve through supervision, such as personality disorders and ingrained unethical practices. However, these may respond to personal therapy, and where appropriate you should encourage supervisees to consider that option, part of taking care to ensure that supervision does not itself become therapy. This does not mean that personal issues are completely off the agenda, as ignoring issues such as personal distress may alienate the supervisee and further damage your alliance. As illustrated in a vignette outlined by Enlow et al. (2019), it is generally better to acknowledge distress and related personal issues, validating them as part and parcel of professional life, and to offer some basic forms of social support. Provided that this help is clearly concerned with coping at work and does not feel like therapy (to you or the supervisee), then you may well be able to help your supervisee with their general adjustment and self-care (e.g., Emelianchik-Key et al., 2021). The heart of this help is to guide their personal coping strategies at work. This is the caring or 'restorative' aspect of supervision, which can be highly effective in boosting your supervisee's well-being. In our book on restorative supervision, we offered this definition: *Supportive supervision addresses supervisees' emotional experience of their workplace, and their personal functioning in that context. It is a formal, case-focussed, and intensive relational process, conducted with due authority by a trained, suitably experienced, and appropriate supervisor. Specific supervision techniques include problem formulation, coping strategy enhancement, facilitating peer support, empathic debriefing, and efforts to prevent or manage workplace stressors. The primary mechanisms within supervision that enable these outcomes to be achieved are experiential learning, the supervision alliance, personal coping strategies, and social support. The main intended outcomes for supervisees are reductions in personal distress and enhanced well-being* (Milne & Reiser, 2020, p. 6). That book provided detailed guidance on these and related techniques. For instance, in relation to coping strategy enhancement, we encouraged supervisors to use careful questioning, to encourage self-awareness in the supervisee. Because self-awareness is also a promising way to resolve some personal issues, we offer two procedural guidelines:

- **Encourage adaptive coping:** Efforts at dealing with workplace stressors are often based on avoidance behaviours, such as emotional detachment and blaming others. Step one in developing self-awareness of such coping patterns is for the supervisee to notice what is happening. Recognising such patterns helps the supervisee to realise why certain interpersonal problems keep occurring with colleagues (for example), such as being on the defensive or being passive. The supervisor should also encourage adaptive coping in the supervisee, especially by supporting the use of logical analysis to consider the optimal coping strategies (e.g., positive appraisal of stressors that cannot be avoided or postponed as an opportunity to develop a skill). Supervisors can encourage reflection and offer feedback to pinpoint promising improvements and demonstrate and reinforce the key coping strategies.
- **Use awareness-raising questions:** One way to encourage the supervisee's use of logical analysis is by posing questions that encourage deeper reflection. A popular and often powerful technique is 'Socratic questioning'. This is also termed 'guided discovery' as it involves the supervisor raising a sequence of open-ended questions to encourage a fresh episode of reflection by the supervisee, drawing out their fundamental assumptions about a distressing topic. For example, if the troubling issue is one of coping with a critical colleague, the supervisor might ask: 'Why do you think you are being criticised?' The supervisee will tend to harbour some irrational or exaggerated reasons, such as: 'They think I'm useless, and shouldn't be in training'. The supervisor might then probe into these assumptions, such as getting the supervisee to set out examples where they are not useless, and reasons why they merit training. In this way, the supervisor helps the supervisee to discover their assumptions and irrational tendencies and can demonstrate ways to encourage a more logical approach to coping with distressing events. Note that such questioning is conducted in a curious non-directive way, to clarify what the supervisee alone knows, so the process is fundamentally collaborative and empowering. Another benefit is that the answers to questions are a useful guide to the supervisee's developmental level (see Table 8.2), which should help to ensure that supervision is pitched at the right level.

Table 8.2 The extended Dreyfus scale, a popular classification of skill proficiency. (Dreyfus, 2004; SAGE: Milne et al., 2011)

Incompetent	0	Absence of feature, or highly inappropriate performance. Unable to complete techniques; working slowly and falteringly, with multiple errors and a failure to achieve the intended outcome.
Novice	1	Inappropriate performance, with major problems evident. Non-adherence. Errors of omission (underuse), or errors of commission (overuse). Rigid or inflexible manner, showing inability to take account of situational factors or apply discretionary judgement.
Advanced beginner	2	Evidence of competence, but numerous problems and lack of consistency. Signs of competence, including evidence of adopting a situational perspective.
Competent	3	Competent, but some problems and/or inconsistencies. Rare evidence of incompetence, which is insignificant.
Proficient	4	Good features, but minor problems and/or inconsistencies. Rare or no evidence of incompetence.
Expert	5	Very good features, minimal problems and/or inconsistencies. National star.
Elite	6	Excellent performance, or very good even in the face of difficulties. Features: automaticity; fast pattern recognition; more speed, smoothness, and accuracy; fewer errors; greater success when completing a technique (e.g., better outcomes); superior self-awareness, understanding of the key principles, and self-monitoring (greater metacognitive ability). Can troubleshoot to solve problems, and be creative. International star.

Respond to Low Motivation with a Collaboration-building Strategy

The second row in Table 8.1 concerns low motivation, and major examples are the supervisee's lack of preparation, or their avoidance of effortful work. On the face of it, these are problems residing in the supervisee, and guidelines produced by professional bodies (e.g., Association of State and Provincial Psychology Boards (ASPPB), 2019) and by experts (e.g., Kangos et al., 2018), without exception urge supervisees to play their full part. For instance, the latter group stated that supervisees should develop a sense of their strengths and weaknesses, to help to identify the issues they would like to work on in supervision. Similarly, in developing guidelines for both supervisees and supervisors on the use of direct observation in medical education, Kogan et al. (2017) included suggestions on creating the right learning culture (e.g., 'observe longitudinally to facilitate learners' integration of feedback'). But many aspects of supervision can also motivate a supervisee. For example, supervisors who use positive feedback and collaborate with their supervisee will tend to boost their supervisee's motivation (Enlow et al., 2019). Therefore, consistent with co-construction, we now consider how both parties can build collaboration and motivation.

The example we now consider is especially relevant, involving 'learning expertise', a resource that the supervisee brings to supervision, which can boost their motivation (and greatly aid the supervisor). Learning expertise concerns one's expertise as a learner. It is the capacity to learn from and draw on past experiences of learning. This includes beliefs such as the need to work hard and persist, despite setbacks: 'Learning expertise involved the degree to which would-be experts continually attempt to refine their skills and attitudes to learning – skills and attitudes that include practicing, self-monitoring and finding ways to avoid plateaus and move to the next level.' (Bransford & Schwartz, 2009, p. 433). This makes learning expertise a valuable personal resource of the supervisee, something to be highlighted and strengthened in supervision. Indeed, since we all have some degree of learning expertise, the supervisor should also draw on their own learning expertise to facilitate the process. To again quote Bransford and Schwartz (2009), 'it takes expertise to make expertise' (p. 432). They reasoned that both sources of expertise are necessary, and hence that both parties play complementary roles. Therefore, in fostering learning expertise, supervisees should draw on the ways of developing their clinical skills that work best for them (e.g., reading books, self-monitoring, trial-and-error experimentation, problem-based learning, or information from patients or peers). We can think of this as a form of 'self-supervision', a way of acquiring a specific competency without any help from their supervisor. But along with Bransford and Schwartz (2009), we believe that the best results come from combining the respective expertise of supervisor and supervisee. Collaborating in this way will involve the supervisor supporting and guiding the supervisee, and part of the motivational effect of so doing is the credit accorded to the supervisee. At times it will also involve the supervisor learning from the supervisee, as in when the supervisee describes their personal learning expertise or provides feedback on supervision.

An example of learning expertise in supervision was provided by Green et al. (2014), in a study of the contribution that individual therapists made to clinical outcomes ('therapist effects'). There were significant differences between these therapists, and Green et al. (2014) used qualitative methods to try to clarify the explanation for the different success rates (i.e., interviews and ratings, involving both supervisees and their supervisors). They found that the more effective practitioners drew on their learning expertise, to be more proactive. They did this through being better prepared, assembling key material to present within supervision, by raising specific patients for review, by clarifying what they sought from the discussion, through conducting online research, by observing other clinicians, by showing a readiness to discuss difficulties, and by virtue of greater activity within supervision. For their part, supervisors offered the more effective clinicians greater procedural knowledge, and worked in a more experiential way. This example illustrates excellent collaboration, which will surely motivate supervisees. To summarise, we offer these procedural guidelines:

- **Supervisees: draw on your learning expertise and be proactive.** Supervisees should reflect on how they can get the best out of themselves as learners, sharing this personal approach with their supervisor in order to personalise and maximise supervision. This may include planning ahead, ensuring that they come to supervision with a prioritised agenda, some suggestions on suitable experiential learning methods, valuable materials properly organised (e.g., video clips, outcome data), and an eagerness to acquire procedural knowledge of direct relevance to the problems that they face in their current casework.
- **Supervisors: use your learning expertise.** Taking time to understand how best to collaborate with your supervisee will provide benefits in terms of accelerated learning

(through personalising the supervision approach) and boosting the supervisee's motivation. But using your learning expertise also means drawing on your expertise as a supervisor, such as ensuring that learning goals are appropriately challenging, and that you demonstrate the competent performance of skills. 'Deliberate practice' is an approach that clarifies such techniques, which we discuss next.

Improve Competence with a 'Deliberate Practice' Strategy

In the last chapter we considered incompetence in the supervisor, defining it as deficiencies in proficiency, adherence, appropriateness, and/or effectiveness. Supervisees may also be deficient in these respects, though the benchmark needs to be lowered to reflect what is often pre-licensure supervision. Therefore, we define supervisee incompetence as *the inability to perform relevant techniques or competencies with sufficient proficiency, adherence, appropriateness, or effectiveness, and falling below the standard that is expected of a comparably experienced supervisee within the context of professional supervision. The incompetent supervisee may also lack the necessary qualifications, lack basic understanding, and behave inappropriately (i.e., inconsistent with relevant standards, guidelines, professional values, and ethical practice). As a consequence, incompetent supervisees are likely to harm their patients.* As per the last chapter, this definition is based on the integration of US and UK definitions of competence (e.g., Watkins & Milne, 2014; ten Cate et al., 2010).

One of the best-known ways of defining incompetence is by reference to the Dreyfus scale (Dreyfus, 2004), a taxonomy that describes five stages of skill development, ranging from 'incompetent' to 'expert'. In evaluating supervision with the observational instrument SAGE (Milne et al., 2011), we have extended this to a seven-point rating scale, as shown in Table 8.2. This extension was to allow ratings to cover the full range of what we actually observed in our samples of supervision (i.e., some supervision contained skills that were performed in a highly incompetent manner; some skills were outstanding, despite difficult circumstances). Other popular approaches include using Bloom's competence taxonomies, covering thoughts, feelings, and behaviours (e.g., Bloom et al., 1956).

An example of a supervision strategy that focusses on skill development is 'deliberate practice' (Ericsson, 2009; Rousmaniere et al., 2017), which we summarised in the last chapter in relation to supervisor incompetence. Now we consider how deliberate practice can help to identify the complementary roles that can be played by the supervisor and the supervisee in tackling supervisee incompetence. Table 8.3 provides a breakdown of the seven elements of deliberate practice. In the left-hand column we indicate what supervisors might do to help to build supervisee competence. In the right-hand column we match these to the supervisee's role. For example, in row one we start with the first element of deliberate practice, creating a highly structured context. In column one we suggest that the supervisor does this by arranging effortful tasks, linked to challenging performance objectives, encouraging high motivation within a supportive environment. In column two we relate this to the supervisee's role, which includes responding as an 'adult learner', by doing things like negotiating and clarifying tasks, while also seeking regular feedback and welcoming the supportive environment.

Table 8.3 A summary of deliberate practice (Ericsson, 2009), setting out the recommended complementary roles of the supervisor and the supervisee in tackling incompetent supervisees.

Supervisor skills in applying deliberate practice	Supervisee skills in benefitting from deliberate practice
Highly structured context: Supervisor arranges effortful tasks, such as simulations and structured learning opportunities (e.g., carefully designed experiential learning exercises); these include challenging performance objectives (competence standards); aim for high motivation and a supportive environment.	Supervisee responds as an 'adult learner', negotiating and clarifying tasks, while ensuring a clear link to the collaboratively agreed learning contract (avoiding 'mission creep'); also seeks regular feedback and welcomes motivating and supportive environment.
Task analysis: Specific elements of performance are delineated by the supervisor, to better pinpoint incompetence. These elements are then reconstructed to create realistic 'task chunks' and eventually 'whole tasks'. To be practised in carefully designed situations.	Task analysis benefits from the supervisee's perceptions of the elements and their difficulty. Aim to build on existing competencies, and to demonstrate them within supervision (drawing on material from the supervisee's clinical practice).
Hierarchical: Supervisor arranges progressively more difficult challenges (i.e., graded practice to build up competence). Most difficult tasks to be practiced most. Activate prior learning (i.e., learning expertise) and provide progressively less 'scaffolding'.	Supervisee ensures that developmental challenges reflect their strengths and weaknesses, clarifying the required performance standards (e.g., competence objectives). Cooperate in working towards increasing autonomy, and tolerate or reframe the inevitable setbacks.
Repetition and sustained practise: Supervisor encourages intense periods of skill practise, suggesting refinements and helping to eliminate errors. This guidance includes explicit advice, pinpointing of errors, demonstrations of competence, and modelling sustained practice.	Supervisee engages and invests in the practice, making a significant effort and showing commitment (e.g., through affirmative comments, like 'no pain, no gain'). Reads guidelines and views recordings of competent performance.
Feedback: Supervisor observes the supervisee's performance, and immediately provides feedback; attention given to critical aspects of performance (processes), relative to objectives (outcomes), followed by demonstration, repetition, and ongoing correction. Precision, timeliness, and objectivity are essential. Request feedback.	Supervisee encourages feedback, being receptive responsive, offers feedback to the supervisor, completes rating scales or self-evaluates against performance standards, identifying own strengths and areas for development. Listens actively, restating or clarifying the feedback, and drawing out the action implications; requesting a demonstration.
Problem-solving: Supervisor encourages learning from errors; teaches essential concepts and procedural information (ensuring supervisee truly grasps what constitutes competent action). Focusses on developing in supervisee a highly structured mental representation of the required competencies or tasks.	Supervisee draws attention to their errors, in order to progress quickly. Studies problems to develop a deep understanding of how they arise, and the solutions that may prove effective (e.g., through computer simulations). Presents summaries of progress in supervision and seeks guidance.

(Continued)

Table 8.3 (Continued)

Supervisor skills in applying deliberate practice	Supervisee skills in benefitting from deliberate practice
Coaching: Supervisor needs to play a central and highly active leadership role (e.g., structuring, managing, goal-setting, monitoring, providing feedback, motivating). Provides plentiful support and guidance, steering the supervisee towards competence.	Supervisee should assume a follower role, acknowledging the supervisor's status and expertise. As a successful follower, the supervisee will engage fully in experiential learning (i.e., reflecting, conceptualising, planning, experiencing, and experimenting).

Overcome Inadequate Self-regulation by Developing Metacognitive Skills

Metacognition is the ability to monitor and adjust our own thinking, which in turn can guide our efforts at managing ourselves (self-regulation). As noted in Table 8.1, when self-regulation goes awry we can exhibit poor self-awareness, as in having difficulty judging the limits of our personal competence. This may link to negative emotions, such as defensiveness (e.g., resistance to ideas or guidance). A vicious cycle may ensue, as helpers abandon their efforts to help, and instead start blaming individuals for their challenging behaviours.

Various strategies have been found to be valuable in resolving self-regulation issues, including providing extensive structure (strengthen the 'scaffolding' within supervision, to increase the sense of support and confidence); ensuring that you have an effective alliance (e.g., manage emotional reactions more productively); and drawing on self-disclosure and professional norms as reference points. We will address the alliance in the next section, but next we outline the strategy of improving the supervisee's metacognition within supervision. According to Schraw (1998), this improvement begins with raising the supervisee's awareness of the nature and role of metacognition. Group supervision is another useful vehicle (peer support), and Buus et al. (2011) described how groups of supervisees reflected together on the personal and organisational barriers to their regular supervision, following action learning principles. This is associated with improved problem-solving strategies, to address the identified barriers and to enhance the benefits of supervision. In the Schraw (1998) example, a range of training methods were used, including modelling, reflection and group activities (e.g., sharing knowledge about cognitions). Part of this training was the use of a 'regulatory checklist', which prompted participants to go through the steps in developing metacognitive thinking. This starts with planning (e.g., 'What is the nature of the problem?' 'What kind of information do I need?'), then moves on to implementation and monitoring (e.g., 'Does this action make sense?', 'Do I need to make changes?'). The concluding step is evaluation (e.g., 'What worked?', 'What would I do differently?'). Schraw (1998) argued that such training can improve metacognitive knowledge and self-regulation, building the foundations for effective and self-sufficient problem-solving.

Our procedural guidelines summarise the detect-articulate-respond approach (DAR: Dunn et al., 2017), which can be applied to a supervisee's beliefs and values, when these disrupt self-regulation:

- **Detect** a value conflict: Notice instances where there is a difference in beliefs between yourself and your supervisee, regarding the desirability of certain ways of behaving. Inform the supervisee that you will use the DAR approach to try to resolve conflicts in a mutually beneficial and respectful way.
- **Articulate** the conflict: clarify and understand the supervisee's reactions, aiming to normalise these. Explain that the reason for the discussion is to try and resolve the conflict, to aid their development and to ensure patient safety. Differences and tensions between the respective values should be identified and discussed, ensuring that the supervisee has the power to stop the discussion if it becomes too uncomfortable. This is important, since many values are gut feelings based on some unquestioned moral intuition, making discomfort likely and discussion inherently difficult.
- **Respond:** Determine the best course of action: decide whether the DAR approach needs some escalation (e.g., self-control education, therapy), or can probably be managed through such techniques as educational role-plays, or by observing work samples. The DAR approach may indicate that the supervisor is actually adopting a particularly biased value and may hence need to engage in their own personal values, exploration, and examination. There is also a recognition that sincerely held values that are a matter of personal conscience, and that have been discussed appropriately (e.g., in supervision) in order to determine the proper course of action (to avoid harming the client), should not be challenged. Dunn et al. (2017) note that this reflects legislation in the USA that has limited the ability of professional training programmes to require supervisees to attain competence when working with clients whose values conflict with their own conscience.

Raise Inter-personal Effectiveness with an Alliance-building Strategy

Parker et al. (2017) have also urged psychiatry supervisees to contribute to their supervision experience by demonstrating respect for the supervisory relationship, to try to enhance the supervisor's investment in the process. They suggest that supervisees might also be wise to follow up on supervisor recommendations, advice, and homework; and to demonstrate their learning in their day-to-day work. They may also ask about their supervisor's professional interests and skills (e.g., to explore why they became a psychiatrist and how they came to work in their current role). In return, supervisees can try to communicate what they want from the supervisory relationship, actively contributing towards a constructive alliance.

In this final category of challenging supervisee behaviour, we address critical issues concerned with interpersonal functioning. This might appear within supervision, in terms of regular alliance ruptures, or a general lack of collaboration. For instance, in this chapter's illustration (Table 8.4), the supervisor feels that the supervisee is being 'manipulative' (e.g., non-disclosure), and avoids asking his seniors for guidance when he should have done so. Interpersonal issues may also emerge in the supervisee's interactions with other staff, such as consistently poor engagement with staff (e.g., recurring communication breakdowns, unassertiveness). As supervisor, your role is to be aware of any issues, and in general to develop the supervisee's relationship skills in the normal, constructive way (i.e., developing relationship skills is a routine part of ongoing professional development for all in healthcare).

Table 8.4 Examples of one supervisee's challenging behaviour.

Challenging supervisee behaviours	Illustrations of supervisee behaviours	Consequences for supervisor and others
1. Adverse personal characteristics	Erratic adherence to department protocols, such as a failure to ask his seniors when he should have done so (e.g., high risk cases, or when protocol states: 'ask senior'). When confronted, supervisee threatened to resign (viewed as 'manipulative' by supervisor).	Attempts by supervisor to educate and impress on supervisee the importance of adherence to protocols, and of the need to ask a senior before finalising treatment. Supervisee's reactions effected the supervisor ('probably what he was wanting'), who started to feel differently about the supervisee ('I then felt sorry for him, and tried to protect him from other supervisors, and convince him that he was not that bad').
2. Low motivation	'Sloppy at his job' (other trainees had no trouble following protocols).	'Massive hassle, a lot of supervisor time taken up'.
3. Incompetence	Resulted in a few cases where sub-optimal treatment was given.	Other staff of his grade had to cover a lot of his workload.
4. Inadequate self-regulation	Less pressure on supervisee, who was able to complete placement and progress (albeit with only partial time credit, and with thoroughly documented record of these difficulties passed on to training programme).	Trainee taken off clinical rota, placed on shadowing shifts (i.e., as supernumerary), and not permitted to see patients without senior involvement (i.e., closely supervised, requiring more consultant time, but patient safety assured).
5. Interpersonally ineffective	Trainee escalates situation by starting to play role of victim, initially reporting mental health issues and feeling picked on, as he was a foreign graduate. Later he escalated further, with claim he was being victimised due to his ethnic origin.	Increasingly became focus of concerns and discussions among seniors, as pattern of errors was repeated, in spite of above interventions. Clinical supervisor involved GP training programme supervisor and learnt for first time of history of similar problems (unfortunate that clinical supervisor not informed sooner, as: 'would have made us more alert to issues before they got as far as they did').

One of most frequently and strongly recommended methods for developing relationship skills is to build on your supervisory alliance, usually conceived as an emotional bond (the 'safe base'), agreement over the goals of supervision, and collaboration over the tasks listed in the supervision contract. Relevant supervision competencies are: 'Ability to structure supervision sessions in a professional manner'; and 'Ability to help the supervisee reflect on their work and on their supervision' (Roth & Pilling, 2007). Our own guideline on the supervision alliance recommends specific ways of performing these competencies, with video demonstrations of competent practice (Milne & Reiser, 2017). Here we summarise two parts of that guideline, concerning relationship skills, and experiencing.

- **Relating:** The way we relate to our supervisee carries subtle but important messages. If you are able to provide what counsellors call the 'core conditions' of relating, then your supervisee will probably respond positively (e.g., by being less defensive and more involved). These relational conditions are genuineness, warmth, empathy, honesty, and openness (e.g., acknowledging negative feelings and sharing positive emotions). This may be a new level of openness, so may create some initial difficulties for the supervisee. Part of being genuine is to discuss such issues freely, which could include you describing some of the difficulties that you have faced in the past ('self-disclosure'). Specific actions that tend to boost relationship skills are providing reassurance, encouragement, validation, praise, and emotional support (i.e., social belonging and acceptance).
- **Experiencing:** Experiencing includes dealing with troublesome feelings, through mechanisms such as 'assimilation' or 'resolution' (Greenburg & Malcolm, 2002; Stiles et al., 1990). The essential steps are to heighten awareness of relevant thoughts and feelings (especially irrational thoughts or exaggerated reactions); develop a greater recognition and understanding of the associated feeling reactions (e.g., that they do not have to follow from our thoughts); use some awareness-raising questions (e.g., 'What is your most intrusive or upsetting thought just now?'); seek a clear description of the key event that triggered the thought or emotion (especially why the supervisee finds it so troubling, e.g., clarifying the role that your supervisee felt that they played in the incident); consider other ways of thinking or feeling about the incident (or re-enact some important aspect through a role-play); this should lead into a resolution phase, signalled by relief, catharsis, insight, or some constructive planning.

Another popular technique is 'interpersonal process recall' (IPR: Kagan & Kagan, 1997), which is especially valuable in tackling relationship issues. IPR involves the supervisor and supervisee viewing video clips of work together, but with the supervisee in control of what is viewed (e.g., to reduce anxiety). The supervisor poses a series of questions about the clip, to encourage the supervisee's reflections (e.g., 'What were you feeling at this point?', 'Do you wish you'd done something different?'). Although dated, IPR remains a valuable tool, and has been used latterly to improve medical practice (Larsen et al., 2019).

Illustration

Our illustration is drawn from the supervision of a physician on the three-year Junior Hospital Doctor training programme in a UK hospital's Accident and Emergency (A&E) department. This illustration shows how one individual may to some extent display all five of the challenging behaviours that we have addressed in this chapter (see Table 8.1). Note that the left-hand column of Table 8.1 remains unchanged in Table 8.4, but that we have altered the middle and right-hand columns to try and capture the variety of these behaviours (column 2: 'Illustrations of supervisee behaviours'), alongside the 'Consequences for the supervisor and others' (right-hand column). The words in inverted commas are quotes from the supervisor. Table 8.4 therefore indicates a wide range of challenging behaviours, featuring attitudinal issues (non-compliance with protocols), mental health concerns, and cultural challenges, which together were judged by the supervisor to result in 'sub-optimal treatment' to patients. This illustration also identifies several 'knock-on' or systemic impacts of these behaviours, resulting in extra clinical work for his peers, 'massive hassle' for the supervisor, and the involvement of a representative of the training programme. Although these challenging behaviours were managed, and the risk of patient harm was reduced, this illustration shows their wide-ranging impact, and the several critical issues that are raised for the supervisor.

Conclusions

Supervisees may position themselves as passive partners in supervision, reflecting much of the professional literature, but we believe that this tends to infantilise them. It leads to lowered expectations, under-estimates their competence, and devalues their maturity and fundamental contribution to high-quality supervision. This is not to deny that supervisees can exhibit challenging behaviours, and indeed we have detailed five major examples. These are united by problems in supervisees 'receipt' of supervision (a general inability to benefit from supervision) that also compromises their clinical work.

In this chapter we have challenged the prevailing view of supervisee passivity, partly by trying to understand why supervisees might behave this way. The most common explanation is that the inherent power differential between supervisor and supervisee leads to supervisees being generally uninformed and uninvolved in their clinical supervision (Falender & Shafranske, 2012). In addition to that status difference, supervisees may also have little or no training about supervision, their role, and about how proactive they should be in supervision (Ellis et al., 2014). This includes limited role inductions at the start of placements, and the absence of detailed or signed supervision contracts in the majority of cases (Kangos et al., 2018). Similarly, in psychiatry, Parker et al. (2017) noted that the purpose and processes of supervision are often poorly defined, with limited guidance available for trainees about their role in making supervision work. In short, supervisees may be socialised into passivity.

But supervisees are not powerless by virtue of their low status since supervisory power and even authority are transactional in nature. As pointed out by Kadushin and Harkness (2002), the supervisee has to grant the authority of the supervisor and respond to the power the supervisor has the ability to exercise: 'Authority can be rejected, and power can be resisted' (p. 106). Personally, we have no difficulty recalling many supervisees who very effectively exercised their power and played a full and constructive role in making supervision work. So, with Kangos et al. (2018), our conclusion is that supervisees can play an active role in empowering themselves, and supervisors should contribute directly to that uplifting process. We hope that our guidelines are empowering for supervisors and supervisees, enabling supervisees to play their role as essential and valued partners in the pursuit of effective supervision.

References

American Psychological Association. (2015). Guidelines for clinical supervision in health service psychology. *The American Psychologist*, *70*(1), 33–46. https://doi.org/10.1037/a0038112

Association of State and Provincial Psychology Boards (ASPPB). (2019). *ASPPB disciplinary data system: Historical discipline report reported disciplinary actions for psychologists: 1974 – 2019*. https://cdn.ymaws.com/www.asppb.net/resource/resmgr/dds/dds_historical_report_2019.pdf. Accessed on 20 November 2020.

Beddoe, L., & Davys, A. (2016). *Challenges in Professional Supervision*. Jessica Kingsley Publishers.

Beinart, H. (2014). Building and sustaining the supervisory relationship. In C. E. Watkins & D. L. Milne (Eds.), *The Wiley International Handbook of Clinical Supervision* (pp. 257–281). Wiley.

Bloom, B. S., Englehart, M. D., Furst, E. J., Hill, W. H., & Krathwohl, D. R. (1956). *Taxonomy of educational objectives, handbook I: Cognitive domain*. McKay.

Bransford, J. D., & Schwartz, D. L. (2009). It takes expertise to make expertise: Some thoughts about why and how and reflections on the themes in chapters 15–18. In K. A. Ericsson (Ed.), *Development of professional expertise* (pp. 432–448). Cambridge University Press.

Buus, N., Angel, S., Traynor, M., & Gonge, H. (2011). Psychiatric nursing staff members' reflections on participating in group-based clinical supervision: A semistructured interview study. *International Journal of Mental Health Nursing*, *20*(2), 95–101. https://doi.org/10.1111/j.1447-0349.2010.00709.x

Dreyfus, S. E. (2004). The five-stage model of adult skill acquisition. *Bulletin of Science, Technology & Society*, *24*(3), 177–181. https://doi.org/10.1177/0270467604264992

Dunn, R., Callahan, J. L., Farnsworth, J. K., & Watkins, C. E. (2017). A proposed framework for addressing supervisee-supervisor value conflict. *The Clinical Supervisor*, *36*(2), 203–222. https://doi.org/10.1080/07325223.2016.1246395

Ellis, M. V., Berger, L., Hanus, A. E., Ayala, E. E., Swords, B. A., & Siembor, M. (2014). Inadequate and harmful clinical supervision: Testing a revised framework and assessing occurrence. *The Counseling Psychologist*, *42*(4), 434–472. https://doi.org/10.1177/0011000013508656

Ellis, M. V., Taylor, E. J., Corp, D. A., Hutman, H., & Kangos, K. A. (2017). Narratives of harmful clinical supervision: Introduction to the Special Issue. *The Clinical Supervisor*, *36*(1), 4–19. https://doi.org/10.1080/07325223.2017.1297753

Emelianchik-Key, K., Labarta, A., & Glass, B. (2021). Infusing dialectical behaviour therapy skills into supervision to address challenges and enhance performance. *Journal of Creativity in Mental Health*. https://doi.org/10.1080/15401383.2020.1870599

Enlow, P. T., McWhorter, L. G., Genuario, K., & Davis, A. (2019). Supervisor-supervisee interactions: The importance of the supervisory working alliance. *Training and Education in Professional Psychology*, *13*(3), 206–211. https://doi.org/10.1037/tep0000243

Ericsson, K. A. (2009). *Development of Professional Expertise*. Cambridge University Press.

Falender, C. A., & Shafranske, E. P. (2012). *Getting the most out of clinical training and supervision: A guide for practicum students and interns*. American Psychological Association.

Grant, J., Schofield, M. J., & Crawford, S. (2012). Managing difficulties in supervision: Supervisors' perspectives. *Journal of Counselling Psychology, 59*(4), 528–541. https://psycnet.apa.org/doi/10.1037/a0030000

Green, H., Barkham, M., Kellett, S., & Saxon, D. (2014). Therapist effects and IAPT psychological wellbeing practitioners (PWP's): A multi-level modelling and mixed methods analysis. *Behavior Research and Therapy, 63*, 43–54. https://doi.org/10.1016/j.brat.2014.08.009

Greenburg, L. S., & Malcolm, W. (2002). Resolving unfinished business: Relating process to outcome. *Journal of Consulting and Clinical Psychology, 70*(2), 406–416. https://psycnet.apa.org/doi/10.1037/0022-006X.70.2.406

Haarman, G. B. (2013). *Clinical supervision: Legal, ethical and risk management issues*. Foundations: Education & Consultation.

Kadushin, A., & Harkness, D. (2002). *Supervision in social work* (4th ed.). Columbia University Press.

Kagan, H., & Kagan, N. I. (1997). Interpersonal process recall: Influencing human interaction. In C. E. Watkins (Ed.), *Handbook of psychotherapy supervision* (pp. 296–309). Wiley.

Kangos, K. A., Ellis, M. V., Berger, L., Corp, D. A., Hutman, H., Gibson, A., & Nicolas, A. I. (2018). American psychological association guidelines for clinical supervision: Competency-based implications for supervisees. *The Counseling Psychologist, 46*(7), 821–845. https://doi.org/10.1177/0011000018807128

Kemer, G., & Borders, L. (2017). Expert clinical supervisors' descriptions of easy and challenging supervisees. *The Journal of Counselor Preparation and Supervision, 9*(1), 1–25. http://dx.doi.org/10.7729/91.1151

Kogan, J. R., Hatala, R., Hauer, K. E., & Holmboe, E. (2017). Guidelines: The do's, don'ts and don't knows of direct observation of clinical skills in medical education. *Perspectives in Medical Education, 6*(5), 286–305. https://doi.org/10.1007/s40037-017-0376-7

Ladany, N., Friedlander, M. L., & Nelson, M. L. (2016). *Supervision essentials for the critical events in psychotherapy supervision model*. American Psychological Association.

LaDonna, K. A., Hatala, R., Lingard, L., Voyer, S., & Watling, C. (2017). Staging a performance: Learners' perceptions about direct observation during residency. *Medical Education, 51*(5), 498–510. https://doi.org/10.1111/medu.13232

Larsen, J. H., Nordgren, G., Ahlkvist, J., & Grafstrom, J. (2019). Helping doctors to improve the 'patient's part' of consultation using the 'macro-micro' supervision teaching method. *Education for Primary Care, 30*(2), 117–121. https://doi.org/10.1080/14739879.2019.1565926

Milne, D., & Reiser, R. P. (2020). *Supportive Clinical Supervision: From burnout to well-being, through restorative leadership*. Pavilion.

Milne, D. L. (2020). Preventing harm related to CBT supervision: A theoretical review and preliminary framework. *The Cognitive Behaviour Therapist, 13*(e54). https://doi.org/10.1017/S1754470X20000550

Milne, D. L., & Reiser, R. P. (2017). *A Manual for Evidence-based CBT Supervision*. Wiley-Blackwell.

Milne, D. L., Reiser, R. P., Cliffe, T., & Raine, R. (2011). SAGE: Preliminary evaluation of an instrument for observing CBT supervision. *The Cognitive Behaviour Therapist, 4*(4), 123–138. https://psycnet.apa.org/doi/10.1017/S1754470X11000079

Molloy, E., Ajjawi, R., Bearman, M., Noble, C., Rudland, J., Ryan, A. (2020). Challenging feedback myths: Values, learner involvement and promoting effects beyond the immediate task. *Medical Education*, *54*, 33–39. https://doi.org/10.1111/medu.13802

Nelson, M. L., Barnes, K. L., Evans, A. L., & Triggiano, P. J. (2008). Working with conflict in clinical supervision: Wise supervisors' perspectives. *Journal of Counseling Psychology*, *55*(2), 172–184. https://psycnet.apa.org/doi/10.1037/0022-0167.55.2.172

O'Brien, A., McNeil, K., & Dawson, A. (2019). The student experience of clinical supervision across health disciplines – Perspectives and remedies to enhance clinical placement. *Nurse Education in Practice*, *34*, 48–55. https://doi.org/10.1016/j.nepr.2018.11.006

Parker, S., Suetani, S., & Motamarri, B. (2017). On being supervised: Getting value from a clinical supervisor and making the relationship work when it is not. *Australasian Psychiatry*, *25*(6), 625–629. https://doi.org/10.1177/1039856217734668

Reiser, R. P., & Milne, D. L. (2017). A CBT formulation of supervisees' narratives about unethical and harmful supervision. *The Clinical Supervisor*, *36*(1), 102–115. https://psycnet.apa.org/doi/10.1080/07325223.2017.1295895

Rieck, T., Callahan, J. L., & Watkins, C. E. (2015). Clinical supervision: An exploration of possible mechanisms of action. *Training and Education in Professional Psychology*, *9*(2), 187–194. https://psycnet.apa.org/doi/10.1037/tep0000080

Roth, A. D., & Pilling, S. (2007). *A competence framework for the supervision of psychological therapies*. University College London. The full set of competences referred to in this document are available for downloading from the CORE website: www.ucl.ac.uk/CORE

Rousmaniere, T., Goodyear, R. K., Miller, S. D., & Wampold, B. E. (2017). *The Cycle of Excellence: Using deliberate practice to improve supervision and training*. Wiley-Blackwell.

Schraw, G. (1998). Promoting general metacognitive awareness. *Instructional Science*, *26*(1-2), 113–125. https://psycnet.apa.org/doi/10.1023/A:1003044231033

Shen-Miller, D. S., Schwartz-Mette, R., Sickle, K. S. V., Jacobs, S. C., Grus, C. L., Hunter, E. A., & Forrest, L. (2014). Professional competence problems in training: A qualitative investigation of trainee perspectives. *Training and Education in Professional Psychology*, *9*(2), 161–169. Advance online publication. http://dx.doi.org/10.1037/tep0000072

Stiles, W. B., Elliott, R., Llewelyn, S., Firth-Cozens, J., Margison, F. R., Shapiro, D. A., & Hardy, G. (1990). Assimilation of problematic experiences by clients in psychotherapy. *Psychotherapy*, *27*(3), 411–420. https://psycnet.apa.org/doi/10.1037/0033-3204.27.3.411

ten Cate, O., Snell, L., & Carraccio, C. (2010). Medical competence: The interplay between individual ability and the health care environment. *Medical Teacher*, *32*(8), 669–675. https://doi.org/10.3109/0142159X.2010.500897

Watkins, C. E., & Milne, D. L. (Eds.). (2014). *The Wiley International Handbook of Clinical Supervision*. Wiley-Blackwell.

Watkins, C. E., Jr., & Scaturo, D. J. (2013). Toward an integrative, learning-based model of psychotherapy supervision: Supervisory alliance, educational interventions, and supervisee learning/relearning. *Journal of Psychotherapy Integration*, *23*, 75–95. http://dx.doi.org/10.1037/a0031330

Wilcoxon, S. A., Norem, K., & Magnuson, S. (2018). Supervisees' contributions to lousy supervision outcomes. *Journal of Professional Counseling: Practice, Theory, and Research*, *33*(2), 31–49. https://doi.org/10.1080/15566382.2005.12033816

9

Resolving Other Supervisee Challenges: Ineffective Treatment

Introduction

According to most experts, the effectiveness of supervision should be judged by the supervisees' clinical success: 'The impact of clinical supervision on client outcome is considered by many to be the acid test of the efficacy of supervision' (Ellis & Ladany, 1997, p. 485). The definition of client outcome or clinical effectiveness will depend on the nature of the healthcare intervention, but generally a successful outcome is measured in terms of improvements to desired patient health outcomes (e.g., enhanced physical functioning, symptomatic relief, improved quality of life), and/or reductions in undesirable patient outcomes (e.g., harm, mortality (Snowdon et al., 2017)). In this chapter, adherence to treatment protocols (or best practice guidelines or quality of care indicators in general) will be considered a precondition or proxy for clinical effectiveness. However, we do not include as clinical outcomes, patients' experiences or expressions of satisfaction with their care. Therefore, in this chapter we regard supervisee ineffectiveness as a failure to adhere to protocols, or to achieve successful outcomes. This is consistent with the 'acid test' criterion, and in agreement with this book's guiding logic, the fidelity framework (Borrelli, 2011), which defines the final test of an intervention like supervision as the 'enactment' phase. According to this framework, if the treatment enactment has high fidelity (high adherence), then supervision leads to the correct treatment being applied correctly, with the anticipated benefits for patients.

Research on the acid test has helped to illuminate why supervisees may sometimes be clinically ineffective, despite receiving well-designed supervision (i.e., which is also implemented in a professional and competent manner, and which successfully develops competence in the supervisee). Among other things, research suggests that perfectly competent supervisees may have their work compromised primarily by their own self-defeating behaviours, by difficult patients, or by unsupportive working conditions. Supervisors need to be alert to the possibility that their supervisees may experience these kinds of enactment difficulties as set out in Table 1.1 (Chapter 1). Indeed, the list of difficulties could go on (e.g., see Chapter 8). So, to make these factors manageable, and to ensure that they complement our earlier chapters, we now focus on these three most-commonly identified critical issues related to supervisees' ineffectiveness:

- **Personal factors that lead the supervisee to implement the wrong treatment**: In theory, the wrong treatment may be implemented because the diagnosis may be inaccurate or incomplete, by choosing a contra-indicated procedure, by complications, by incorrect clinician performance, or by applying the treatment to the wrong patient (Chang et al., 2005). These various errors may take the form of misapplying treatment protocols (e.g., rigid adherence), or an over-enthusiastic commitment to a preferred treatment (e.g., the excessive use of 'natural childbirth' by midwives). Contributory reasons include supervisees' own self-defeating behaviour (e.g., the non-disclosure of vital information in supervision: Ladany et al., 1996); disabling emotions and poor self-regulation skills (e.g., anxiety and burnout (Sewell et al., 2021)); cultural incompetence (e.g., Thomas, 2014); non-adherence to guidelines, and/or a drift away from evidence-based practice (EBP: e.g., Simpson-Southward et al., 2017); as well as attitudinal complications, such as a lack of humility (i.e., inability to recognise one's own errors or limits: Watkins, 2020).
- **Patient factors cause the treatment to be applied ineffectively**: Ineffective treatment by supervisees may also in theory be due to failures linked to patient characteristics or actions that are beyond the supervisees' control (Chang et al., 2005). Patient factors according to Chang's taxonomy include patients' risk-taking behaviours, and the cultural diversity challenges that some patients present to the supervisee (e.g., unfamiliar presentations, incompatible beliefs or practices). Patient actions that compromise treatment include non-compliance and ruptures in the therapeutic alliance. Other patient factors not included in the Chang taxonomy might include avoidance, low motivation for treatment, and secondary gains that affect the uptake of treatment recommendations.
- **Environmental factors that undermine the treatment**: Thirdly, supervisees may prove ineffective due to other social or environmental factors that mediate treatment and so undermine the desired clinical outcomes. Social factors include a lack of social support, or hostile reactions by staff, patients, or others (e.g., drop-outs due to the negative reactions of family members to patients' treatment). Environmental factors include an adverse workplace, such as excessive or inappropriate workloads, or inadequate resources. This may cause the supervisee to 'drift' away from following the correct procedures (Simpson-Southward et al., 2017), limiting their clinical effectiveness. There may also be various logistical impediments (e.g., limited time, money, or other organisational resources).

Although there are other ways of categorising these reasons for ineffective treatment, these three reasons are consistent with reviews within the supervision literature (Snowdon et al., 2017), agree with the types of problems reported by clinicians (Currell et al., 2015; Kjoge et al., 2015), fit with the reasons thought to influence the transfer of professionals' training to the healthcare workplace (Bluestone et al., 2013), and accord with other frameworks used to understand enactment issues (e.g., implementation science: Bearman et al., 2019), including healthcare accidents (Chang et al., 2005).

Plan

Therefore, we will now use these three main reasons for supervisee ineffectiveness to organise this chapter. Although some topics overlap with those in earlier chapters, such as therapist drift (treatment non-adherence), we aim to complement the earlier material by now focussing on the supervisee's ineffective clinical work, concentrating on the interface between the supervisee and the patient. As in earlier chapters, we will define and describe these reasons, consider some ways of formulating them, then present some supervision guidelines. Also, we will again provide an illustration before offering some concluding thoughts.

Personal Factors that Lead Supervisees to Implement the Wrong Treatment

According to the classification system of Chang et al. (2005), problematic supervisee factors include communication breakdowns with the patient or with other staff; errors in patient management (e.g., improper referral, consultation, delegation, or follow-up); and faulty clinical performance (failures during interventions, such as those due to incompetence or distractions). The most dramatic example of the latter is 'wrong-site surgery', in which the patient's operation is performed on the wrong body part, or even on the wrong patient.

To take the example of poor communication, this is defined as the failure to exchange meaningful and relevant information, or to ensure that the information exchanged has been understood, or to acknowledge or take into account patients' views (Campbell et al., 2018). These authors conducted a review of the literature related to communication breakdowns in nursing, midwifery, and allied health professions, examining the reasons for patient harm. Based on the review of 139 studies, Campbell et al. (2018) developed a 17-category healthcare miscommunication taxonomy. According to this taxonomy, ineffective treatment may be due to communication problems involving colleagues and others, but here we take the example of 'Communicate ineffectively with patients'. This includes the sub-categories: 'Fail to listen to patient'; 'Fail to meet communication needs'; and 'Fail to share appropriate information' (e.g., 'The clinician has not actively listened to the patient or taken account of the patient's views. This can also include responding dishonestly to any questions that they ask'). Campbell et al. (2018) concluded that communication failures were common, and that the most frequently reported communication failures linked to patient harm were these: a failure to provide the patient with appropriate and timely information, a failure to keep colleagues informed, a failure to listen to the patient, and a failure to work collaboratively with patients, family, or carers. Their evidence indicated that 'individual factors' were among the most frequent contributing factors for all four of these types of communication failure followed by 'patient factors', 'staff workload', 'communication systems', and 'team factors'. Individual factors include a clinician's inexperience, stress reactions, personality issues, or problematic attitudes (e.g., a lack of humility).

Formulation

One reason for faulty clinical performance is that the supervisee has also suffered from a communication breakdown in supervision and is unclear about what exactly is entailed in a clinical procedure. Snowdon et al. (2017) pointed out that a more detailed representation of clinical performance may be essential to improving supervisees' treatment processes.

Unfortunately, this lack of procedural clarity is not surprising, given the general finding (as described in Chapter 7) that supervision tends to lack the necessary kind of active experiential activity, such as practical demonstrations by the supervisor, or corrective feedback (e.g., Bailin et al., 2018; Schriger et al., 2020) that aim to develop procedural competence. In turn, supervisees may impair supervision through a reluctance to discuss their difficulties in being effective ('non-disclosure'). This reluctance may be influenced by the supervisee's lack of confidence and anxiety, in the context of a weak supervisory alliance (Mehr et al., 2015).

In addition to non-disclosure, a major factor influencing effectiveness is impaired self-regulation: the clinician's inability to regulate their emotions effectively. This factor was covered extensively in the last chapter under the topic of helping manage problematic supervisees and so we don't intend to recapitulate all our recommendations and guidelines here. High levels of anxiety or depression are particularly likely to disrupt clinical performance, exacerbated by an associated lack of insight (Ellis et al., 2015; Johnson et al., 2013). Supervisors can contribute to improved supervisee self-regulation by guiding their reflections on their working relationships (using interpersonal process recall: IPR (Hill et al., 2015)); and by ensuring that they are properly orientated to their role (Role induction: Ellis et al., 2015). In their study of IPR in Australia, Hill et al. (2015) enlisted seven clinical psychology supervisors and their supervisees. A manual was provided to guide the IPR procedure, and the participants were subsequently invited to comment on the experience. Six of these seven dyads reported discussing supervisee anxiety, the most frequently mentioned theme, and they felt that IPR had increased their discussion of anxiety including the problem of the non-disclosure of this anxiety. IPR was felt to have been valuable in developing better ways of addressing anxiety in supervision by discussing it more frequently; by reducing the didactic content of supervision; and by reducing the supervisors' use of excessive reassurance. Other benefits reported were enhanced reflection on practice, improvements in the supervision alliance, and the clarification of concerns.

Negative emotions such as anxiety can also be triggered by irrational thinking, such as excessive self-criticism. Watkins (2020) used the term 'humility' to capture a personal virtue in clinicians that includes accurate self-assessment acknowledging professional limitations; openness to new ideas (e.g., accepting challenges to one's professional practices); and a facilitating orientation towards others (e.g., being humble in collegial relationships). When humility is a characteristic of the supervisee, it would be expected to benefit their clinical effectiveness (e.g., recognition of errors, willingness to change). Conversely, an absence of humility raises problems of poor self-assessment, dogmatism, and a reluctance to correct mistakes.

Guidelines

- **Ensure that the procedure is clear,** by attending to procedurally oriented active experiential strategies, including modelling and role play with corrective feedback in supervision, to assist with procedural knowledge. To provide a more detailed representation of clinical performance (Snowdon et al., 2017), supervisors and supervisees can draw on procedural guidelines or measurement instruments. These both clarify in detail how a procedure should be performed and can also provide precise corrective feedback. For example, discussing CBT procedures, Roth (2016) noted that supervisors need some way of monitoring the development and maintenance of competence, and recommended the use of structured observation scales for the task. His own instrument included these specific items: 'Agenda setting and structuring sessions: Does the therapist share responsibility for session structure and content with the client, by negotiating an explicit agenda?' And: 'Did the therapist consistently foster collaborative working i.e., encouraging the client to take an active role in the therapy, such that the client and therapist work as a team?'

- **Communicate clearly**: by structuring supervision and clinical training in an explicit manner, including clear goals and explicit learning objectives, supervisors model the process of clear communication and appropriate collaboration with patients. The structuring of supervision and setting appropriate learning goals has been presented as a key procedural guideline in our supervision manual (Milne & Reiser, 2017). We have also mentioned the use of interpersonal process recall (IPR: Hill et al., 2015) and role induction (Ellis et al., 2015) in facilitating communication. Role induction is appropriate when clinician anxiety is partly due to the supervisee's lack of information about the roles, rights, responsibilities, and procedures for supervision. Anxiety is typically best managed with suitable clarifications and discussion. The role induction procedure used by Ellis et al. (2015) followed a workshop training format, including explanations and interactive exercises (e.g., identifying roles from videotaped supervision sessions and role plays). Participants also discussed their fears and concerns about supervision regarding evaluation and feedback, role-playing how they would seek to influence the supervision that they received. Ellis et al. (2015) reported reductions in anxiety for their small sample of counsellor trainees, especially the more junior participants.

Patient Factors that Cause the Treatment to Be Applied Ineffectively

Patient-related factors have been defined as the resources, knowledge, attitudes, beliefs, perceptions and expectations of the patient (WHO: World Health Organisation, 2003, p. 30). According to this source, the range of such factors with known impact on treatment effectiveness is huge, including anxieties about possible side effects, low motivation, inadequate knowledge, lack of self-perceived need for treatment, negative beliefs about effectiveness, misunderstanding treatment instructions, frustration with healthcare providers, and a fear of treatment dependence.

One of the most-studied factors bearing on clinical effectiveness is the patients' adherence to treatment. Adherence is 'the extent to which a person's behaviour – taking medication, following a diet, and/or executing lifestyle changes- corresponds with agreed recommendations from a health care provider' (World Health Organisation, 2003, p. 3). Medical research has indicated that adherence is influenced by a number of issues, including side effects and the cost of treatment (e.g., medication). But patients' beliefs, demographics, physical and mental function, disease, family history, and education levels have also been implicated. Some of these factors are modifiable. For example, Cornelissen et al. (2020) reported a review of studies concerned with patients' adherence to medication for osteoporosis, which has been shown to be effective in fracture risk reduction. But adherence to the medication ranges from 34% to 75% in the first year of treatment, declining to between 18 and 75% after one year. Because of this patient factor there are worse health outcomes (e.g., more subsequent fractures, lower quality of life). Cornelissen et al. (2020) concluded that the most effective approaches were based on collaboration between the patient and the clinician, combining patient involvement, counselling, and shared decision-making.

The importance of patients' characteristics has long been stressed in psychological therapies, especially active patient involvement. In CBT, for example, this is indicated by the inclusion of patient factors within instruments designed to assess the therapist's competence, such as the revised cognitive therapy scale (CTS-R: Blackburn et al., 2001). The key idea was that, in order to succeed, therapists and patients had to collaborate: 'The patient should be encouraged to be active in the session. There must be clear evidence of productive teamwork, with the therapist skilfully encouraging the patient to participate fully (e.g., through questioning techniques, shared problem solving and decision making) and take responsibility'. A distinctive feature of CBT and a particular test of collaboration is clinical 'homework', where the patient is expected to work on achieving symptomatic relief in between therapy sessions (e.g., by exposing themselves to objects or situations that trigger panic attacks). According to the CTS(R) manual, this means that the patient should: 'test out ideas, try new experiences, predict and deal with potential obstacles, and experiment with new ways of responding'. Subsequent CBT research based on clinicians' perceptions also acknowledges the importance of other patient factors, such as the ability to recognise and report relevant thoughts; to identify problems; to pursue goals collaboratively; and to concentrate, understand, and retain information between sessions (Currell et al., 2015). By contrast, these clinicians believed that other patient characteristics would hamper therapy, such as thought disorder, cognitive biases, sleep deprivation, and symptom severity.

Formulation

Within the broader context of problems in communication and collaboration with patients, we have selected 'cultural issues' as one component within patient factors that we are especially interested in formulating. One major explanation for ineffective treatment is a failure to bridge cultural divisions between clinician and patient. This can result in profound misunderstandings on both sides, greatly hampering collaboration. Systematic reviews of racial disparities in healthcare delivery focus on the role of patient–provider communication, shared decision-making and collaboration as important factors in systemic care outcomes (Saha et al., 2008). There is an extensive literature addressing the importance of cultural competence in clinical care, and it is also a competency within the domain of clinical supervision (APA, 2015). Unfortunately, the results of systematic literature reviews of culturally focused interventions that produce positive clinical outcomes suggest a cautious approach should be taken (Bhui et al., 2007; Truong et al., 2014). For example, Truong et al. (2014) concluded; 'there is some evidence that interventions to improve cultural competency can improve patient/client health outcomes. However, a lack of methodological rigor is common among the studies included in reviews and many of the studies rely on self-report, which is subject to a range of biases, while objective evidence of intervention effectiveness was rare.' (p. 1).

Guidelines

- **Boost clinicians' cultural competence:** One of the most interesting aspects of attempting to reduce disparities in healthcare delivery by improving clinician's cultural competence concerns the hypothesised presence of implicit or unconscious bias in healthcare decision-making. Gopal et al. (2021) reviewed the role of cognitive errors and implicit bias in healthcare decision-making. By definition, practitioners are unaware of these factors operating in their clinical decision-making. Gopal et al. (2021) pointed out that decision-making processes are comprised of two elements – Type I – a fast, unconscious, intuitive decision-making process that requires little effort; and Type II processes – a slower conscious and analytic reasoning process that is more resource intensive. Type I processing is especially prone to cognitive biases and implicit bias. The review notes 'Despite the critique of implicit bias, such automatic decisions are necessary for human function' (p. 41) and that specifically this type of mental heuristic is an essential element in efficient and rapid clinical decision-making. So how do we reduce these types of implicit cognitive biases? Gopal et al. (2021) do conclude that 'decreasing bias through a single faceted intervention may be very difficult as bias is a "wicked" or multi-faceted problem.' (p.43.). However, they pointed to several specific interventions that seem promising, including a cultural awareness checklist (see Gopal et al., Box 1, p. 45), and 'health equity rounds' training, incorporating case-based discussions and evidence-based exercises (Perdomo et al., 2019). They suggested a single salient question that presumably could be imbedded in the clinical record, hence available at the time of the assessment: 'If this person were different in terms of race, age, gender, etc., would we treat them the same?' (p. 43).

    One of the longest-established supervision techniques for addressing issues surrounding a clinician's self-awareness and clinical interactions is 'interpersonal process recall', as mentioned earlier (IPR; Hill et al., 2015; Kagan & Kagan, 1997). IPR aims to heighten the supervisee's awareness of thoughts, emotional reactions, and interpersonal processes that are usually not noticed or mentioned, in order to aid reflections on critical issues and to develop skills in discussing and tackling such reactions. The key steps are for supervisor and supervisee to jointly review a recording of the supervisee's clinical activity, pausing at points where cultural issues may arise (e.g., thoughts or feeling reactions to the material). The supervisor plays an enquiring role, posing relevant questions to encourage re-experiencing or heightened awareness. There may also be opportunities to practise more effective ways of managing cross-cultural concerns. Ivers et al. (2017) provide a powerful case study, and a wide range of questions that can facilitate IPR.
- **Increase collaboration with patients:** According to a literature review related to radiation therapy by Morley and Cashell (2017), collaboration with patients aids their treatment adherence by engaging them in their own care. Vital elements include coordination

(working to achieve shared goals), cooperation (understanding and valuing the contributions of patients), shared decision-making (relying on negotiation, openness, and trust), and establishing partnerships (open, respectful relationships cultivated over time). More specific actions that supervisees can take include informing and educating patients, increasing their involvement in self-care, thinking through clinical decisions together (e.g., agreeing on goals and prioritising the methods to be used), making communication as respectful and inclusive as possible, and developing trust and mutual accountability, so acknowledging their mutual dependence.

Environmental Factors that Undermine the Treatment

According to the classification system of Chang et al. (2005), problematic supervisee factors include the questionable use of resources, negative reactions to treatment by patients' families, and the impact of adverse workplaces on treatment adherence. A review of the negative effects of treatment on family members noted that family relationships tended to suffer (Golics et al., 2013). This effect can be quite prominent and detrimental to effective treatment. For instance, these authors reported that 38% of adolescents with dermatological conditions felt that their family relationships had been adversely affected because of their treatment. In another example, family members of patients with multiple sclerosis reported negative effects on their relationships with one an other, leading to arguments and tension. Relatives reported struggling to cope with patients whose beliefs, outlook, and behaviour have altered because of their disease. There may also be little time for relationships between other members of the family. Golics et al. (2013, p. 405) concluded that 'The impact of disease on families of patients is often unrecognised and underestimated'. In addition, perhaps arising from these kinds of adverse effects, family members or patients themselves may impede or sabotage treatment, sometimes with the intention of aggravating their condition. According to Sansone et al. (2008), a significant minority of patients actively sabotage or intentionally impair their medical care in covert ways, often related to borderline personality disorder (BPD).

In terms of the impact of adverse workplaces on treatment adherence, one relevant instance is the relationship between the organisational pressure to implement evidence-based practices (EBP's) and the common phenomenon of clinician 'drift' away from EBP's (Waller, 2009). Drift away from adherence to EBP's can be driven by an avoidance of the more distressing or challenging treatments (e.g., exposure to feared situations in CBT). This makes it important for supervisors to monitor the supervisees' use of EBPs to correct any such drift. However, it is also possible that supervisors can themselves drift away from such monitoring, partly as a result of their supervisees' characteristics. In one study, anxious female supervisees were guided away from technical adherence towards alliance-strengthening methods by their supervisors (Simpson-Southward et al., 2017).

Formulation

In a qualitative study, involving 76 practitioners from six professions working in a large urban centre for addiction and mental health (Bogo et al., 2011), three inter-related environmental factors were judged critical to their professional competence, performance, and job satisfaction. These were the availability of supervision (best from experts who validated practitioners' work experiences and provided knowledge for effective interventions); teams that provided support through positive interpersonal relations, collaboration and informal feedback; and organisations and managers who helped by providing assistance and training, while clarifying quality performance and productivity requirements. These factors were deemed essential in correcting the adverse effects of the recent organisational changes that were seen as eliminating profession-based departments, replacing them with general management structures. The next chapter is devoted to the organisational context.

A similar emphasis on the role of peer support was advocated by Johnson et al. (2013, p. 345), who challenged 'the assumption that most professionals are self-contained, perpetually rational, and nearly always competent'. Instead, they recommended a more preventative, communitarian perspective on maintaining competence based on theories of social support and the ethics of care. Johnson et al. (2013) detailed the kinds of collegial competencies that might help to create a 'communitarian constellation', a supportive group and ethos. These included 'authenticity and self-awareness' (expressing one's thoughts and feelings), 'vulnerability and non-defensiveness' (admitting to one's limitations, an openness to help), and 'collegial assertiveness' (having difficult conversations, to promote self and colleague competence). These authors predicted that the creation of such a collegial ethos with a cluster of professional relationships would help to prevent problems of incompetence, which could be especially valuable if there was no supervisor available.

Within supervision the sense of being supported is most readily associated with the 'restorative' function, a balanced approach to supervision with a caring style that is intended to help supervisees to cope with the personal and professional demands of their role. However, it appears that supervisees rarely receive such care, which in turn reduces their motivation to care for their patients (Milne & Reiser, 2020). In a survey completed by 56 supervisors and 207 clinicians from community mental health organisations in the USA (Dorsey et al., 2017), only 13% of the supervision were regarded as restorative. This finding is consistent with an earlier survey (Accurso et al., 2011), where participants' self-reports indicated that the most restorative aspect of their supervision occurred on only 4% of occasions and was not even explicitly restorative (the item was labelled: 'supervisory relationship/process'). In a more positive finding, Dorsey et al. (2018) subsequently collected observational data from 28 supervisors and 70 supervisees, using an observational instrument including 13 items, only one of which was restorative in nature: 'supportive listening'. However, this sole restorative item was observed in 99% of supervision session samples, defined as explicit support, validation, or praise. This finding was based on audio recordings of supervision, which were sampled at five-minute intervals (the frequency of items was derived from the number of intervals in which they occurred). In addition, supportive listening occurred at a high level of intensity in 29% of instances, at a comparatively higher intensity than information gathering, didactic instruction, providing clinical suggestions, and several other 'formative' methods were also almost always present in the sampled supervision. Milne and Westerman (2001) also directly observed supervision with an instrument that only included one item that was explicitly supportive in nature (within a 16-item tool). In this intensive n = 1 analysis, the supervisor's support to his three supervisees averaged 20% of all observed interactions. This 'supporting' item was defined in a similar way to 'supportive listening'. The results of this observational study suggest that the restorative function still remains a secondary element within supervision. Limited or absent restorative supervision could provoke several types of challenging supervisee behaviour (e.g., low motivation and impaired social interactions; see Table 8.1), and undermine clinical effectiveness.

Guidelines

- **Create a support system**: If professional competence fluctuates with changing personal and workplace factors (Johnson et al., 2013), then clinicians should employ social support strategies for consistently checking and strengthening their competence. This includes training supervisees for the role of being supportive colleagues (e.g., how to express concern and provide advice to colleagues in a caring and constructive manner). Clinicians should maintain regular engagement with their colleagues, during their routine work and by participating in consultation groups, continuing professional development, and professional organisations. When they sense that a colleague is experiencing problems that may compromise their effectiveness, they should offer care and support (e.g., by working together to assess the need to limit their duties). More suggestions on social support and the 'restorative' approach to supervision can be found in Chapter 8, and in Milne and Reiser (2020).
- **Manage professional role transitions with extra care**: According to Kjoge et al. (2015), many clinicians feel that the transition from training to routine practice is especially challenging. Helpful factors reported were: regular supervision, routines and opportunities to maintain skills, enough time to learn about the new environment, and enough time for each patient, and time to keep up-to-date.

Illustration

The supervisor became aware of a critical issue when routine patient contact data indicated that a new supervisee was seeing fewer patients per shift than his peers. This supervisee was on a 6-month placement as part of his GP training programme. The placement was a stressful one, in an A&E department of a UK hospital where workload pressures can quickly become extreme. Naturally, the situation is aggravated if one member of the medical team is slow. Consequences can include increasing waiting times, complaints, pressure on staff, and delays in commencing medical care (which can lead to increased morbidity/mortality, greater costs, etc.).

During supervision, the supervisor raised the slowness issue with the supervisee, who grudgingly acknowledged a lack of confidence due to his inexperience and admitted feeling 'out of my depth' and 'afraid of getting into trouble'. It became apparent that he coped with his confidence issue by being extra careful, for example, by excessively referring to written guidelines, and by repeatedly asking his peers for guidance. This would often result in him changing his course of treatment and repeating some steps. His fear of getting into trouble was leading to another coping strategy: hiding his struggles from the supervisor. The supervisor thanked the supervisee for explaining his situation and emphasised that it would be much better to be up front about being out of his depth, instead of hiding it. In addition to preventing harm to patients, an open approach would have got the supervisor on his side and resulted in closer support.

A second type of critical incident emerged: on closer examination, the supervisee was also making poor clinical decisions, which appeared to be due to sticking too rigidly to departmental protocols, rather than using some common sense and clinical judgement about their use. While this was in keeping with feeling low in confidence, it resulted in what the supervisor regarded as sub-optimal treatment for his patients. In addition, a particularly tricky issue was that other staff were complaining that he had not actually followed the protocols correctly. For example, when a patient was transferred from A & E to another ward, the ward doctors receiving the patient would point out that the protocol had not been correctly followed (compounded by other factors, such as poor nurse handover). When the supervisor raised an example of this decision-making issue, the supervisee protested and pointed out that the protocol did not apply to the patient, he had used his judgement, and he had done the right thing. The supervisor had to explain that the protocol did actually apply to that patient. Moreover, if the patient had not fitted the protocol, then this was not straightforward and he should therefore have asked the supervisor for guidance.

Reflections

The treatment provided by this junior doctor in this example was faulty. He had been shown the protocol alongside his peer group, and they were not making these errors. The reasons appeared to the supervisor to be personal failings in the supervisee: low confidence, faulty clinical reasoning, and inappropriate coping strategies (e.g., non-disclosure). Thankfully, after repeating the cycle of error and correction several more times, the supervisee did eventually respond to the supervisor's training on his use of protocols, and on how and when to ask for advice. It was also heartening that the supervisee became generally more willing to engage with the supervisor, an attitude change indicating that he had learnt the value of supervision, which would hopefully be enduring.

It could have been worse: there had not been any significant harm done to patients, and the faulty treatment was restricted to delays and occasional non-adherence to protocols. As explained in Chapter 7, faulty treatment could also have included inappropriate behaviour (e.g., unethical conduct), a lack of proficiency (e.g., making mistakes and causing accidents), or general ineffectiveness (e.g., not obtaining clinical outcomes comparable with peers). Thankfully, there were no signs of these more serious issues.

One hypothetical explanation for the supervisee's initial avoidance of supervision is the 'impostor syndrome'. This is a common experience among healthcare supervisees, reported at some stage in their career by over 70% of respondents in some surveys (Young, 2011), based on a persistent fear of being exposed as the fraud that they believe themselves to be. This sense of inadequacy and self-doubt may continue throughout their careers, despite objective success, or plentiful praise. Supervisors can help by discussing and challenging these self-defeating thoughts, recognising and praising clinical successes while modelling a healthy reaction to the inevitable errors that come within healthcare. 'Self-disclosure' is an example, where a supervisor can recount their own feelings of being an impostor, aiming to normalise the self-doubting thoughts, and to offer emotional support (e.g., by empathising with the associated feelings). This could also be done proactively with all trainees, for example, during induction. The supervisor provided an example of the use of this supportive approach, which he had used to help a foreign graduate trainee some years before. The trainee had been strongly criticised by the nurses and reported to the supervisor for not providing enough pain-killing injection to a patient. In discussion with the supervisor, the trainee disclosed how difficult he was finding it to gain acceptance into a foreign medical system, feeling that he was an outsider. The supervisor was able to reveal that he too had been through this same situation, having worked abroad himself. In particular, he disclosed that he had been helped by telling his hosts that he was finding it hard fitting in, and also by acknowledging the limitations to his competence during the adaptation period. This self-disclosure by the supervisor helped the supervisee to feel understood, and empowered him to deal with this issue, which was evidently central to his difficulties.

Another complementary explanation provided by the supervisor for the supervisee's avoidance behaviour was environmental: that the exceptionally challenging culture and stressful atmosphere in the emergency department could have contributed to the trainees feeling inadequate. The culture within medicine at the time of this example could be considered exceptionally harsh, with a 'sink or swim' message to members of the profession. This encourages concealment of any self-doubt. The implications for supervisors are to be alert to signs of self-doubt (e.g., avoidance behaviours, low self-confidence), so as to detect problems earlier, and to then proactively reach out to those who appear to be struggling.

Conclusions

According to the fidelity framework (Borrelli, 2011), the final test of an intervention like supervision is the 'enactment' phase, the topic of this chapter. If the treatment enactment has high fidelity, then supervision leads to the correct treatment being applied effectively, with the anticipated benefits for patients. In this chapter we have explained why supervisees (the clinicians) often struggle with enacting their competencies, particularly due to poor self-regulation, difficult patients, or because of challenging workplaces. We drew on a diverse range of research findings to illuminate these enactment challenges, and to tease out guidelines for resolving the various critical issues.

Reflecting on this struggle to enact competencies in the 'swampy lowlands' (Schon, 1984) of everyday clinical practice, we note that training programmes for healthcare professionals assume significant enactment, but that sadly the evidence suggests that the successful transfer of training is actually surprisingly difficult to achieve (Beidas & Kendall, 2010; Rakovshik & McManus, 2010). This is thoroughly documented in the more general efforts to implement evidence-based practice (EBP), where an 'implementation cliff' has been recognised (Weisz et al., 2014, p. 59). This cliff separates the well-resourced and systematic analyses conducted in research studies from the poorly resourced and unsystematic efforts at implementation under naturalistic clinical circumstances. In the latter, there is typically low fidelity to EBP treatments, accompanied by low-fidelity supervision, leading to poor enactment (Bearman et al., 2019a). Therefore, to boost treatment enactment, there is a need to supplement systematic training with support arrangements, such as high-fidelity supervision (Milne & Reiser, 2017). This view is indicated by the impressive but rare demonstrations of the supervision-related enactment of EBP (e.g., Clark, 2018; Schoenwald, 2016). Therefore, the implementation cliff highlights why supervisees may struggle with enactment and fail to pass the 'acid test'. We should not find this surprising, as enactment (implementation) is well-established as the biggest challenge in achieving high-fidelity healthcare, and can only be achieved through well-organised care systems (Bearman et al., 2017; Schoenwald, 2016). We detail what such a system would look like in the next chapter.

References

Accurso, E. C., Taylor, R. M., & Garland, A. F. (2011). Evidence-based practices addressed in community-based children's mental health clinical supervision. *Training and Education in Professional Psychology*, 5(2), 88–96. https://doi.org/10.1037/a0023537

American Psychological Association. (2015). Guidelines for clinical supervision in health service psychology. *American Psychologist*, 70(1), 33–46. https://doi.org/10.1037/a0038112

Bailin, A., Bearman, S. K., & Sal, R. (2018). Clinical supervision of mental health professionals serving youth: Format and micro-skills. *Administration and Policy in Mental Health and Mental Health Services Research*. https://doi.org/10.1007/s10488-018-0865-y

Bearman, S. K., Bailin, A., & Sale, R. (2019). Graduate school training in CBT supervision to develop knowledge and competencies. *The Clinical Supervisor*. https://doi.org/10.1080/07325223.2019.1663459

Bearman, S. K., Bailin, A., Terry, R., & Weisz, J. R. (2019a, Advance online publication). After the study ends: A qualitative study of factors influencing intervention sustainability. *Professional Psychology: Research and Practice*. http://dx.doi.org/10.1037/pro0000258

Bearman, S. K., Schneiderman, R. L., & Zoloth, E. (2017). Building an evidence base for effective supervision practices: An analogue experiment of supervision to increase EBT fidelity. *Administration and Policy in Mental Health and Mental Health Services Research*. https://doi.org/10.1007/s10488-016-0723-8

Beidas, R. S., & Kendall, P. C. (2010). Training therapists in evidence-based practice: A critical review of studies from a systems-contextual perspective. *Clinical Psychology: Science & Practice*, 17, 1–30.

Bhui, K., Warfa, N., Edonya, P., McKenzie, K., & Bhugra, D. (2007). Cultural competence in mental health care: a review of model evaluations. *BMC Health Services Research*, 7(1), 1-10. https://doi.org/10.1186%2F1472-6963-7-15

Blackburn, I-M., James, I.A., Milne, D.L., Baker, C., Standart, S.H., Garland, A., & Reichelt, F.K. (2001). The revised Cognitive Therapy Scale (CTS-R): Psychometric properties *Behavioural & Cognitive Psychotherapy*, 29, 431–446. doi:10.1017/S1352465801004040

Bluestone, J., Johnson, P., Judith Fullerton, J., Carr, C., Alderman, J., & BonTempo, J. (2013). Effective in-service training design and delivery: Evidence from an integrative literature review. *Human Resources for Health*, 11. https://doi.org/10.1186/1478-4491-11-51

Bogo, M., Paterson, J., Tufford, L., & King, R. (2011). Supporting front-line practitioners' professional development and job satisfaction in mental health and addiction. *Journal of Interprofessional Care*, 25, 209–214. https://doi.org/10.3109/13561820.2011.554240

References

Borrelli, B. (2011). The assessment, monitoring, and enhancement of treatment fidelity in public health clinical trials. *Journal of Public Health Dentistry, 71*, S52–S63. https://doi.org/10.1111/j.1752-7325.2011.00233.x

Campbell, P., Torrens, C., Pollock, A., & Maxwell, M. (2018). *A scoping review of evidence relating to communication failures that lead to patient harm*. Nursing, midwifery & allied health professions research unit.

Chang, A., Schyve, P. M., Croteau, R. J., O'Leary, D. S., & Loeb, J. M. (2005, December 8). The JCAHO patient safety event taxonomy: A standardized terminology and classification schema for near misses and adverse events. *International Journal for Quality in Health Care*. https://doi.org/10.1093/intqhc/mzi021

Clark, D. M. (2018). Realising the mass public benefit of evidence-based psychological therapies: The IAPT programme. *Annual Review of Clinical Psychology, 14*, 159–183. https://doi.org/10.1146/annurev-clinpsy-050817-084833

Cornelissen, D., de Kunder, S., Si, L., Reginster, J.-Y., Evers, S., Boonen, A., & Hiligsmann, M. (2020). Interventions to improve adherence to anti-osteoporosis medications: An updated systematic review. *Osteoporosis International*. https://doi.org/10.1007/s00198-020-05378-0

Currell, S., Christodoulides, T., Siitarinen, J., & Dudley, R. (2015). Patient factors that impact upon cognitive behavioural therapy for psychosis: Therapists' perspectives. *Behavioural and CognitivePsychotherapy*. https://doi.org/10.1017/S1352465815000260

Dorsey, S., Kerns, S. E. U., Lucid, L., Pullmann, M. D., Harrison, J. P., Berliner, L., Thompson, K., & Deblinger, E. (2018). Objective coding of content and techniques in workplace-based supervision of an EBT in public mental health. *Implementation Science, 13*, 1–12. https://doi.org/10.1186/s13012-017-0708-3

Dorsey, S., Pullmann, M. D., Kerns, S. U., Jungbluth, N., Meza, R., Thompson, K., & Berliner, L. (2017). The juggling act of supervision in community mental health: Implications for supporting evidence-based treatment. *Administration and Policy in Mental Health and Mental Health Services Research*. https://doi.org/10.1007/s10488-017-0796-z

Ellis, M., & Ladany, N. (1997). Inferences concerning supervisees and clients in clinical supervision. An integrative review. In C. E. Watkins (Ed.), *Handbook of psychotherapy supervision* (pp. 447–507). Wiley.

Ellis, M. V., Hutman, H., & Chapin, J. (2015). Reducing supervisee anxiety: Effects of a role induction intervention for clinical supervision. *Journal of Counseling Psychology, 62*, 608–620.

Golics, C. J., Khurshid, M., Basra, A., Finlay, A. Y., & Salek, S. (2013). The impact of disease on family members: A critical aspect of medical care. *Journal of the Royal Society of Medicine, 106*, 399–407. https://doi.org/10.1177/0141076812472616

Gopal, R., Singh, V., & Aggarwal, A. (2021). Impact of online classes on the satisfaction and performance of students during the pandemic period of COVID 19. *Education and Information Technologies, 26*(6), 6923-6947. https://doi.org/10.1007/s10639-021-10523-1

Hill, C. E., Baumann, E., Shafran, N., Gupta, S., Morrison, A., Rojas, A. E. P., Spangler, P. T., Griffin, S., Pappa, L., & Gelso, C. J. (2015). Is training effective? A study of counselling psychology doctoral trainees in a psychodynamic/interpersonal training clinic. *Journal of Counseling Psychology, 62*, 184–201.

Ivers, N. N., Rogers, J. L., Borders, L. D., & Turner, A. (2017). Using interpersonal process recall in clinical supervision to enhance supervisees' multicultural awareness. *The Clinical Supervisor, 36*, 282–303. https://doi.org/10.1080/07325223.2017.1320253

Johnson, W. B., Barnett, J. E., Elman, N. S., Forrest, L., & Kaslow, N. J. (2013). The competence constellation model: A communitarian approach to support professional competence. *Professional Psychology: Research and Practice, 44,* 343–354. https://doi.org/10.1037/a0033131

Kagan, H., & Kagan, N. I. (1997). Interpersonal process recall: Influencing human interaction. In C. E. Watkins (Ed.), *Handbook of psychotherapy supervision* (pp. 296–309). Wiley.

Kjøge, K., Turtumøygard, T., Berge, T., & Ogden, T. (2015). From training to practice: a survey study of clinical challenge in implementing cognitive behavioural therapy in Norway. *The Cognitive Behaviour Therapist, 8.* doi:10.1017/S1754470X15000471

Ladany, N., Hill, C. E., Corbett, M. M., & Nutt, E. A. (1996). Nature, extent, and importance of what psychotherapy trainees do not disclose to their supervisors. *Journal of Counselling Psychology, 43,* 10–24.

Mehr, K. E., Ladany, N., & Caskie, G. I. L. (2015). Factors influencing trainee willingness to disclose in supervision. *Training and Education in Professional Psychology, 9,* 44–51. http://dx.doi.org/10.1037/tep0000028

Milne, D., & Reiser, R. P. (2020). *Supportive Clinical Supervision: From burnout to well-being, through restorative leadership.* Pavilion.

Milne, D. L., & Reiser, R. P. (2017). *A Manual for Evidence-based CBT Supervision.* Wiley-Blackwell.

Milne, D. L., & Westerman, C. (2001). Evidence-based clinical supervision: Rationale and illustration. *Clinical Psychology and Psychotherapy, 8,* 444–445.

Morley, L., & Cashell, A. (2017). Collaboration in Health Care. *Journal of Medical Imaging and Radiation Sciences, 48,* 207–216. https://doi.org/10.1016/j.jmir.2017.02.071

Perdomo, J., Tolliver, D., Hsu, H., He, Y., Nash, K. A., Donatelli, S., ... & Michelson, C. D. (2019). Health equity rounds: An interdisciplinary case conference to address implicit bias and structural racism for faculty and trainees. *MedEdPORTAL, 15,* 10858. doi:10.15766/mep_2374-8265.10858.

Rakovshik, S. G., & McManus, F. (2010). Establishing evidence-based training in CBT: A review of current empirical findings and theoretical guidance. *Clinical Psychology Review, 30,* 496–516.

Roth, A. D. (2016). A new scale for the assessment of competences in cognitive and behavioural therapy. *Behavioural and Cognitive Psychotherapy, 44,* 1–5. http://dx.doi.org/10.1017/S1352465816000011

Saha, S., Freeman, M., Toure, J., Tippens, K. M., Weeks, C., & Ibrahim, S. (2008). Racial and ethnic disparities in the VA health care system: A systematic review. *Journal of general internal medicine, 23*(5), 654–671. https://doi.org/10.1007%2Fs11606-008-0521-4

Sansone, R. A., McLean, J. S., & Wiederman, M. W. (2008). The relationship between medically self-sabotaging behaviors and borderline personality among psychiatric inpatients. *Primary Care Companion Journal of Clinical Psychiatry, 10,* 448–452.

Schoenwald, S. K. (2016). Clinical supervision in a quality assurance/quality improvement system: Multisystemic Therapy® as an Example. *The Cognitive Behaviour Therapist, 9,* e21. https://doi.org/10.1017/S1754470X15000604

Schon, D. (1984). *The reflective practitioner: How professionals think in action.* Basic Books. http://dx.doi.org/10.1016/0738-3991(84)90022-3

Schriger, S. H., Becker-Haimes, E. M., Skriner, L., & Beidas, R. S. (2020). Clinical supervision in community mental health: Characterizing supervision as usual and exploring predictors of supervision content and process. *Community Mental Health Journal.* https://doi.org/10.1007/s10597-020-00681-w

Sewell, K. M., Kao, D., & Asakura, K. (2021): Clinical supervision in frontline health care: A survey of social workers in Ontario, Canada, *Social Work in Health Care, 60*(3), 282–299. https://doi.org/10.1080/00981389.2021.1880532

Simpson-Southward, C., Waller, G., & Hardy, G. E. (2017). How do we know what makes for 'best practice' in clinical supervision for psychological therapists? A content analysis of supervisory models and approaches. *Clinical Psychology & Psychotherapy, 24*(6), 1228–1245. https://doi.org/10.1002/cpp.2084

Snowdon, D. A., Leggat, S. G., & Taylor, N. F. (2017). Does clinical supervision of healthcare professionals improve effectiveness of care and patient experience? A systematic review. *BMC Health Services Research, 17*(1–11). https://doi.org/10.1186/s12913-017-2739-5

Thomas, J. T. (2014). Disciplinary supervision following ethics complaints: Goals, tasks, and ethical dimensions. *Journal of Clinical Supervision: In Session, 70*(11), 1104–1114. https://doi.org/10.1002/jclp.22131

Truong, M., Paradies, Y., & Priest, N. (2014). Interventions to improve cultural competency in healthcare: a systematic review of reviews. *BMC Health Services Research, 14*(1), 1-17. https://doi.org/10.1186%2F1472-6963-14-99

Waller, G. (2009). Evidence-based treatment and therapist drift. *Behaviour Research and Therapy, 47*(2), 119–127. https://doi.org/10.1016/j.brat.2008.10.018

Watkins, C. E. (2020). Relational humility and clinical supervision: On hypotheses, method, and measurement. *The Clinical Supervisor, 9*(2), 209–228. https://doi.org/10.1080/07325223.2020.1744056

Weisz, J. R., Ng, M. Y., & Bearman, S. K. (2014). Odd couple? Re-envisioning the relation between science and practice in the dissemination-implementation era. *Clinical Psychological Science, 2*(1), 58–74. http://dx.doi.org/10.1177/2167702613501307

World Health Organisation. (2003). *Adherence to long-term therapies: Evidence for action.* Switzerland.

Young, V. (2011). *The Secret Thoughts of Successful Women: Why capable people suffer from the impostor syndrome and how to thrive in spite of it.* Random House.

10

Placing Supervision in Context: How the Organizational System Affects the Quality of Supervision

Introduction

We introduced the idea of 'context' in Chapter 1, defining it as the environment that surrounds and moderates the workplace or organisational system, as illustrated by Figure 1.1 (we use 'workplace' and 'organisation' interchangeably). Context is therefore a broad notion, and might most simply be thought of as 'society'. It is most commonly visible in terms of such things as the ways that national politics affects healthcare budgets (e.g., financial issues), the influence of distal societal, health, and cultural factors (e.g., pandemics), and the impact of professional bodies' practice standards on our clinical practice (e.g., encouraging evidence-based practice). If we aim to understand and resolve critical issues related to the organisations that we work within, then we must take the wider context into account: everything happens in a context. 'Context is key … critical supervisory events do not occur in a vacuum' (Ladany et al., 2016, p. 35). One of the most prominent systems thinkers within the supervision field has been Holloway (2016), who defined context as including the patients (problems, ethnicity, diagnoses), the supervisees and supervisors (experience, theoretical orientation, learning needs, cultural characteristics), and the host institution (an organisation's standards, structure, and climate). While there is little dispute regarding the important role of contexts and organisations as settings for supervision, she pointed out that their influence had rarely been discussed or investigated. To illustrate the importance of context, Maslach et al. (2001) described how changing national financial policies can impact the way that organisations function, creating the conditions for mergers, downsizing, and the weakening of trade/labour unions. In turn, this changing work context can make employees feel insecure about their jobs, leading to them investing greater time, flexibility, and effort, but with an increased cost, in terms of risking occupational burnout (Milne & Reiser, 2020). As this example indicates, these contextual factors are usually national or international factors, which technically act as moderators, affecting the speed, strength, or direction of the embedded workplace factors. A sobering example can be found in a report on a healthcare disaster within the NHS (Francis, 2013, p. 3): 'appalling suffering of many patients … was primarily caused by a serious failure on the part of a (healthcare) provider … It did not listen sufficiently to its patients and staff or ensure the correction of deficiencies brought to (its) attention. Above all, it failed to tackle an insidious negative

Resolving Critical Issues in Clinical Supervision: A Practical, Evidence-based Approach, First Edition.
Derek L. Milne and Robert P. Reiser.
© 2023 John Wiley & Sons Ltd. Published 2023 by John Wiley & Sons Ltd.

culture involving a tolerance of poor standards and a disengagement from managerial and leadership responsibilities. This failure was in part the consequence of allowing a focus on reaching national access targets, achieving financial balance ... at the cost of delivering acceptable standards of care'. Support for this association comes from surveys of supervision in social work, where 'results lend credence to concerns that declining resources and cost-containment measures have resulted in decreased staff supervision, with a greater focus on the administrative function – oversight and accountability at the cost of reflection and professional growth' (Sewell et al., 2021, p. 11). These systemic issues have not gone away (Ockenden, 2022), and seem to occur internationally (Molina, 2018), underlining the importance of working to better understand and resolve them, as we do in this chapter.

The more proximal environment for supervision is the workplace site, the place where we conduct our clinical practice and treat our patients (e.g., a hospital or community service setting). We define the workplace as an organisational bureaucracy, a traditional Western system made up of facilities (e.g., equipment and the built environment), the people who use those facilities (e.g., patients and staff), and the departments or personnel that support them (e.g., clinical managers, Occupational Health). In turn, workplaces can have distinctive and powerful influences on these sub-systems, including supervision arrangements, and can be thought of as cascading down on the individual members of staff within these systems. This can be for better or for worse, and healthcare disasters indicate how even the most well-intentioned clinicians can be 'crushed' by a flawed workplace (Tomlinson, 2015, p. 4). Seeking to learn the lessons from excess deaths at an NHS hospital in England, (Berwick, 2013, p. 8) noted that: 'NHS staff are not to blame: neither at Mid Staffordshire, nor more widely, is it scientifically justifiable to blame the staff of the NHS or label them as uncaring, unskilled, or culpable. A very few may be exceptions, but the vast majority of staff wish to do a good job, to reduce suffering and to be proud of their work. Good people can fail to meet patients' needs when their working conditions do not provide them with the conditions for success'. We share this systemic view of staff behaviour, which is one reason why we advocate for supervision. As set out in Chapter 1 and indicated in Figure 1.1, we regard the context and the workplace as systems which interact with the other factors in the model, such as social support and coping. If we are to understand and resolve critical issues in supervision, we need to take account of these linked systems. Therefore, this chapter addresses these systems, moving our focus to the critical issues that they raise, and to the related systemic resolutions.

An example of how the context and the workplace interact comes from a survey of 239 therapists and 40 supervisors from community health clinics providing services for young people in the USA (Maxwell et al., 2021). Considering the role of financial resources, Maxwell et al. (2021, p. 2) stated that: 'variables related to the (context) ... (e.g., funding policies, financial characteristics of service system), often indirectly influence implementation via mediating variables related to the organisational environment (e.g., leadership, organisational climate). Thus, policy efforts must be coordinated'. The organisational climate includes the ways that leaders communicate to staff about what is expected, rewarded, and supported, through both formal policies and informal practices. We follow this advice in this chapter, by considering the contextual and the workplace systems together.

However, given the endless factors that can exert an influence within these two systems, we need a way to focus our attention. In Chapter 1 we summarised research findings concerning the main workplace stressors. These were long working hours, work overload and pressure, lack of control over work, lack of participation in decision-making, inadequate social support, and unclear and conflicting job roles. We then reduced these many and varied contextual and organisational factors to three themes (see Table 1.1):

- **Faulty workplaces:** Structural problems, arising from inadequate resources: Faulty local management (e.g., leaders fail to remove barriers to supervision). Service managers unfit for practice (e.g., fail to monitor and detect resource issues, or to use supervision standards/guidelines as a benchmark). May be compounded by work overload, and inadequate social support. May lead to the loss of staff morale and impaired resourcefulness.
- **Dysfunctional organisational systems:** Problems arising from faulty workplace processes. Flawed feedback systems (i.e., belated or inaccurate information); dysfunctional human systems (e.g., communication breakdowns; multi-disciplinary team dynamics; role conflicts). Worst case scenario: healthcare disasters.
- **Ineffective quality improvement systems:** Problems related to unacceptable outcomes. Flawed attempts to improve healthcare. Organisational systems unfit for purpose (e.g., poor quality control over supervision, such as inappropriate supervision standards and inadequate audits); national leaders unfit for practice (e.g., policy failings regarding supervision, under-funding of improvement efforts, governance failures, whole system violations, or ineffectuality). Loss of public trust (e.g., reduced governmental support or private donations).

These three themes represent the most common sources of critical issues that affect supervision, as indicated by the major textbooks of most relevance to normative supervision (e.g., Beddoe & Davys, 2016; Haarman, 2013), and by recent reviews (e.g., Bearman et al., 2019; Rothwell et al., 2021; Snowdon et al., 2017). This summary slightly rearranges some of the examples in Chapter 1, to provide greater clarity to these three themes, based on the well-established elements of healthcare quality: structure, process, and outcome (Donabedian, [1966] 2005). The logic is that, in order to operate an effective system, we need to know not only whether something works (the outcome criterion), but also what processes led to that outcome (i.e., the healthcare activities). Thirdly, it is of little value to know that certain processes yield certain outcomes if we know nothing about the input or resources on which this was based (e.g., staffing, equipment, facilities). Therefore, effective healthcare systems will take account of their key structures, processes, and outcomes.

When healthcare quality is poor then patients can be harmed, together with many other adverse consequences (Milne, 2020). This is most dramatically illustrated in healthcare disasters, which typically feature a systemic failure to manage the quality of care (Francis, 2013; Kirkup, 2015; Ockenden, 2022; Vaughn et al., 2019). The antidote is to apply a 'human factors' approach in healthcare, as endorsed in Ockenden (2022). This entails 'Enhancing clinical performance through an understanding of the effects of teamwork, tasks, equipment, workspace, culture and organisation on human behaviour and abilities and application of that knowledge in clinical settings' (National Quality Board, 2013, p. 3). Clinical supervision is gaining recognition as a valuable mechanism within this ergonomic strategy, providing one of the means of better matching up clinicians and their workplaces, and so preventing disasters (Tomlinson, 2015). Although Tomlinson (2015) specifically encourages his medical colleagues to embrace supervision as a mechanism for improving the quality and safety of patient care, his specification of supervision is rare. More often, reviews of the relevant literature and the reports on healthcare disasters are more general in their recommendations. For instance, Berwick (2013, p. 16) embraced a wider range of related options, which could readily subsume supervision: 'All NHS leaders and managers should actively address poor teamwork and poor practices of individuals, using approaches founded on learning, support, listening and continual improvement, as well as effective appraisals, retraining and, where appropriate, revalidation'.

Plan

In response to Berwick (2013), we will therefore use this chapter to indicate how these three contextual themes undermine supervision, and threaten to reduce healthcare quality. We build on Chapter 6 in addressing the critical issues also related to the provision of supervision training. For each theme, we will describe the kinds of critical issues that can occur, then provide a typical example. Our objective is to develop an understanding of how the selected critical issues arise within the contextual and organisational systems, such as flawed information systems that undermine feedback. We then offer some suggestions for resolving these issues, based on the best-available evidence. To do justice to the wide range of critical issues that can arise within healthcare systems, we will also include two illustrative vignettes. Our aim is to outline a firm foundation for ensuring that normative supervision is successful.

Faulty Workplace Issues

We start our workplace analysis with those critical issues that arise primarily from inadequate resources. As touched on in the introduction, this issue most commonly features work overload, ineffective leadership, inadequate social support, and the absence of sufficient supervision. These and other factors will often influence one another, compounding the critical issues (e.g., Pullman et al., 2018). Our first illustration brings this possibility to life, in that a consultant physician was faced with excessive work demands ('not enough hours in the day'), together with a line manager who avoided dealing with the problem, followed by a senior manager who decided (without any joint analysis of the situation) that it was all the fault of the consultant. To make matters worse, the consultant did not even receive social support from his peers. One of the consequences was that the excessive workload squeezed out the consultant's provision of supervision, to the detriment of the supervisees' training, and possibly to the quality and safety of their care.

Illustration: 'It's All Your Fault'

A critical issue arose when I took up my first post as a consultant physician. It was a new post, and everyone had differing and conflicting expectations of what I should be spending my time doing. There were not enough hours in the day to meet all of these expectations. Indeed, some of the aspects of the job exceeded a full-time job, such as the clinical work. Another role was to supervise the junior trainees. As the situation worsened, I advised my immediate boss, a senior consultant, that I did not have time to properly supervise these young doctors. This was noted, but no actions or solutions were agreed. Instead, to my annoyance, I later found out that the matter had been referred to the Medical Superintendent of the hospital, as a short time later I was called to his office.

The Superintendent told me that I was to properly supervise these trainee doctors. When I tried to explain, he did not acknowledge my workload dilemma, but simply told me that I was to attend a course on supervision. I asked the Superintendent if I was therefore being blamed for the situation. He replied 'I wouldn't put it that way'. Unhappy with this conversation, I left the office without committing to go on a course. I never did attend a supervision course, nor did the situation change, as there was no further discussion of the workload dilemma with my boss, or with anyone from hospital management. I had no support, even from my peers, as I struggled to manage the excessive work demands. I felt as if my concerns and difficulties had simply been dealt with by blaming me. The message that I got was: 'get on with it, and if you can't do it, it's your fault'.

Feeling cornered, and without any other choice except to resign from my post, I learnt to accept that the expectation was to simply muddle on as best I could, while trying to conceal the inevitable results of being grossly overburdened with work, and completely without support. I also learnt to try and strictly ration my time between the various aspects of my role, but doing this mostly based on others expectations, to appease my critics. During the first year or so, I was up front with my trainees about not having enough time to supervise them properly. However, I soon gave up on this explanation, as the culture of blame that was pervasive at the time viewed this as an excuse or weakness. During their time under my supervision, the trainees therefore had insufficient training or supervision from me, and I felt bad about that. But at a personal level I grew to accept that I could never keep everyone happy. At least the supervisees received frequent informal training, with a variety of peers and seniors, but most of the trainees did not receive any other supervision from anyone else during their six-month tenure with me. However, as the years passed, better organised training posts started to appear, which meant that a second external supervisor oversaw their whole training programme. Although this did improve the situation for the trainees, it added to my woes as this external supervisor would occasionally confront me, for example, accusing me of not providing adequate support for a struggling supervisee. This further added to my feeling of injustice: I was being blamed, but lacked the necessary time and support to be able to respond. Another consideration was that my own training as junior was very rudimentary, in that I received little supervision, and there was little overall governance. This experience probably affected my attitude to my own supervisees, in that I assumed that they would manage somehow.

Reflections

This illustration was based on something that happened some years ago, at a time when supervisors were not required to have any training, and annual appraisal had not yet been introduced in medicine in the UK. Nowadays postgraduate medical training has become increasingly formalised as continuing medical education (CME), including clinical oversight, and training arrangements are routinely reviewed as part of hospital governance procedures. Nonetheless, this illustration still carries a sense of enduring injustice, and highlights an absence of support, which is only magnified by the ineffective hospital management (e.g., work overload, role conflicts ignored, communication unclear). It also presents a classic faulty workplace scenario, with none of these leaders willing to help the new consultant come to terms with the inherent dilemmas of this new post (arising from their errors in designing the post). This stance was consistent with the prevailing view that consultants are expert enough to be able to sort out these kinds of dilemmas for themselves. Therefore, the clinical managers were passive, and failed to acknowledge a problem, or to ensure that supervision standards were achieved. In effect, they played their part in what was a cascade of uncaring indifference: The Superintendent and senior consultant did not help the consultant (supervisor), who was then unable to help the supervisees, and the hospital managers did not help anyone. No-one cared for the carers, and 'what went around, came around'. That was the culture and the way things were in this hospital, at that time. There was no effective leadership, so the hospital system was allowed to carry on being dysfunctional.

To fully accept this new 'indifference norm' took the consultant several years. He learnt that the accepted approach to coping was to adopt strategies that most effectively concealed shortcomings, rather than to do what would previously have felt to him like the morally right course of action. He also learnt to contain his concerns, and to replace the ineffective formal support system (the Superintendent, hospital managers, et al.) with an informal mutual support and advice network, made up of other consultants in the hospital. Now retired, the consultant looks back on this as a truly 'sink or swim' experience, an episode when he was put to the test without any support, in spite of explicitly requesting it. He is saddened that he and his supposed supervisees were made to suffer, but feels proud that he struggled on, and found a way to cope. As far as he is aware, his approach did not cause his supervisees any harm, and he believed that his dedication to his own clinical work ensured that patients received the best possible care.

Example of a Faulty Workplace Issue: Ineffective Leadership

As highlighted by the illustration, ineffective leadership may well be associated with work overload, inadequate social support, and the absence of sufficient supervision (e.g., failing to detect resource issues that drive supervision below the required standard). By contrast, effective leadership 'is about mobilising the attention, resources and practices of others towards particular goals, values or outcomes ... continual improvement comes from what leaders do, through their commitment, encouragement, compassion and modelling of appropriate behaviours' (Berwick, 2013, p. 15). To be more specific, empirical analyses of high performing healthcare organisations (e.g., Keroack et al., 2007), reviews of the literature on implementing EBP (e.g., Williams & Beidas, 2019), and case studies (e.g., Schilling et al., 2011) indicate that effective strategic leaders in healthcare guide and direct the work of clinicians, take a systemic approach, clarify what is expected of clinicians, inspire and motivate them (e.g., through their expertise), implement performance monitoring and feedback systems, and also use the data to help solve problems. These characteristics are reflected in the Implementation Leadership Scale (Aarons et al., 2014), which boils down the key behaviours to four factors: 'proactive', 'supportive', 'knowledgeable', and 'perseverant' leadership. Example items are, respectively 'removed obstacles', 'recognizes and appreciates employee efforts', 'knows what he/she is taking about', and 'reacts to critical issues'.

The consequences of ineffective leadership can include an organisation in which there is insufficient supervision. Supervision is a required component of initial professional training internationally, part of essential continuing professional development in some countries (Watkins & Milne, 2014), and integral to clinical trials (Roth et al., 2010). But the quantity and quality of supervision has been found to vary widely, within and between professions, and across service settings (e.g., Choy-Brown & Stanhope, 2018; Dorsey et al., 2017). For example, a survey of 666 qualified Canadian social workers within the healthcare sector indicated that only 52% received clinical supervision, though slightly larger proportions received administrative (79%) or supportive supervision (64%), Sewell et al. (2021). A small minority (8%) of these social workers reported receiving no supervision whatsoever. A regression analysis indicated that males and relatively junior staff were significantly more likely to receive clinical supervision, as were those respondents working in primary care settings (as opposed to acute or long-stay care settings), 'demonstrating the importance of context' (p. 10). However, other surveys have indicated that 40% of early career social workers have reported receiving no clinical supervision at all during a key period of their professional development (Carpenter et al., 2015), related to declining resources and cost-containment measures that reduced or eliminated supervision for many social workers (Bogo et al., 2011).

Similar data were reported from a survey of Danish nurses, even when supervision was enshrined by one employing organisation's policy. Gonge and Buus (2010) reported that 47% of the nurses in their study did not participate in supervision at all during the three-month study period, all of them being based in the hospital wards. Furthermore, less than 10% of those who did participate had more than one supervision session per month (the authors' criterion for 'regular' supervision). The quality of supervision was unknown. By contrast, all staff based in the community centres participated, and 79% of them had received regular supervision. In addition to working in a community team, the authors found that being offered supervision during working hours during the day shift (for the hospital staff), and that being a registered nurse (rather than an auxiliary nurse) boosted participation in clinical supervision, as did social support. The organisational barriers included the unavailability of supervision (staff working evening and night shifts were expected to attend supervision when they were off duty), inconsistent management support, and the excessive demands of the job. In a subsequent study, based on interviewing 24 of those staff who did not have supervision (Buus et al., 2017), managers were regarded as uncommitted, failing to create an environment for staff to participate on a regular, sufficient basis. By contrast, a review of 43 studies undertaken in rural and remote settings indicated that management commitment could lead to culture changes and effective supervision systems (e.g., the senior management team forming a committee to oversee implementation and evaluation of the supervision programme (Moran et al., 2014)).

Dysfunctional Organisational System Issues

As we noted in the introduction, there are many ways in which a healthcare organisation can create dysfunctional supervisory systems. A fundamental concern is the under-resourcing of supervision, a lack of 'structure' which results in issues insufficient supervisors, facilities, materials, equipment, (etc.,). It includes a lack of management support. To illustrate, Moran et al. (2014) indicated that middle managers had been hostile and resistant to the provision of supervision, while White and Winstanley (2011) described how some managers 'thwarted' the supervision arrangements. Other examples of supervision-adverse workplaces are not hard to find (e.g., Dorsey et al., 2017; Gonge & Buus, 2014).

Clinical managers might be more willing to resource and support supervision if it is a cost-effective approach, especially in relation to the retention of motivated staff, or avoiding the highly costly and damaging litigation that is often related to patient harm (Milne & Reiser, 2020). An example comes from Weigl et al. (2016), who conducted a survey of work overload and supervisor support in a sample of over 300 nurses working in general hospitals and day-care homes in Germany, finding that those nurses who received supervisor support appeared to be protected from occupational burnout. Unfortunately, there are few relevant studies of the cost-effectiveness of supervision, and the findings are inconsistent. For example, Martino et al. (2016) studied outpatient substance abuse programmes in the USA, demonstrating that evidence-based supervision significantly out-performed SAU on treatment adherence and competence. But they found no advantage in relation to patient retention or clinical outcomes (i.e., substance abstinence). By contrast, significantly improved clinical outcomes were obtained in a study that utilised a much cheaper intervention – live video coaching by an external consultant (Funderburk et al., 2015).

Example of a Dysfunctional Organisational System Issue: Peer Group Supervision

A clear instance of an under-resourced approach to supervision is peer group supervision. According to the review by Martin et al. (2017b), peer group supervision is intended to provide supportive collegial assistance in relation to group members' clinical and professional concerns, on a reciprocal basis, with the aim of fostering self-care, together with safe and effective clinical practice. The emphasis is on restorative topics, such as professional isolation and burnout, and the dominant if not exclusive method used is discussion. Leadership is based on turn-taking, reflecting a non-hierarchical structure in which no one individual has formal authority over the other group members. In addition to the collegial and professionally non-threatening method, peer supervision is easier to organise and fund than clinical supervision. It is also supported by most professional and governmental bodies, which generally endorse peer supervision (1:1 or in groups) as an acceptable alternative to clinical supervision. These features help to make it a popular arrangement within healthcare organisations, with surveys indicating that approximately half of those sampled participated in peer supervision (e.g., Martin et al., 2017a).

Although popular, peer group supervision illustrates several of the problems that can arise when systems are dysfunctional (Martin et al., 2017b), and has led to tragic consequences for patients (Kirkup, 2015). As reflected in the 'peer supervision' illustration that follows, this includes unrealistic objectives, inappropriate methods, communication breakdowns, damaging multi-disciplinary team dynamics, and misleading feedback systems. Part of the miscommunication is that 'peer supervision' is a misnomer, since the absence of an authorised leader mean that it is better described as peer group discussion, reflection, or consultation, depending on the objectives. This is not to devalue these activities, which can of course serve valuable functions, such as providing social support. Peer supervision is also inappropriate, in that it is not designed to provide the oversight and guidance of supervision. It is therefore a great concern that some organisational leaders and clinicians appear to regard it as equating to supervision (Kirkup, 2015). As stated in Chapter 1, supervision is defined as: 'The formal provision, by approved supervisors, of a relationship-based education and training that is work-focused and which manages, supports, develops and evaluates the work of designated supervisees' (Milne, 2007). The critical differences are therefore that clinical supervision entails hierarchical leadership providing systematic training and formal evaluation. These distinctively normative functions include the role of supervision as a fundamental process in managing the organisational system (Kadushin & Harkness, 2002), with the supervisor positioned as the clear leader, by virtue of greater experience, expertise, and fundamentally through the formal authorisation of the supervision role (including accountability arrangements). Similarly, participation is mandatory. A further clear distinction is that a supervisor has the right to ask a supervisee to alter their clinical practice (e.g., to stop using a particular technique, because of concerns over harming patients). In terms of training, supervision that is conducted in accord with evidence-based methods will be highly structured and include experiential learning techniques, such as behavioural rehearsal and feedback (i.e., akin to 'deliberate practice'; see Chapter 8). These enactive methods are chosen because they are best-suited to developing clinical proficiency and raising the quality of care, unlike symbolic techniques, such as discussion. In terms of evaluation, supervision entails the routine oversight of the supervisee, in order to monitor the development and application of clinical skills, to provide direction where necessary, and to enable the supervisor to assume clinical responsibility for the supervisee (see Chapter 2). Further distinctions are that clinical supervision has a contractual basis (ensuring informed consent, etc.), a sound research base, trains supervisors for their role, and includes evaluation of supervision, linked to an organisation's quality-enhancement processes.

In summary, peer supervision is pseudo-supervision, a classic instance of a dysfunctional healthcare system. Indeed, it is perhaps the single most worrying example of a critical issue in supervision, exemplifying multiple problems embracing healthcare structures, processes and outcomes. Consequently, it is possibly the issue most likely to deprive supervisees of proper supervision. To begin to resolve matters, it is best labelled more accurately (e.g., 'peer support'), and supplemented by proper supervision, so that staff receive the support and guidance to which they are entitled, and patients receive the high quality care that they deserve. We note some additional suggestions below, starting with some now, in our second illustration.

Illustration: 'Peer Supervision'

This supervisee was on a six-month placement as part of his three year GP training programme. The placement was in an A&E department of a UK hospital. This is widely recognised as being more difficult than most other placements, having a fast-moving, stressful atmosphere, with more time pressure due to the unpredictable surges in patient numbers, and because of the occasional lack of supervision (due to night shifts, or seniors being overburdened with other cases). This results in greater demands on supervisees, including raising their clinical responsibility.

In trying to cope with these challenges, the supervisee made extensive use of his peer group to guide him in deciding how to treat individual patients. He persisted with this despite having been told on several occasions to always ask his supervisor (or other seniors) if he needed any guidance. It was emphasised to him that doing so was routine and normal procedure, that all the other trainees were doing this, and that it would not reflect badly on him. This trainee's wife was working in the same department at the time, also being a junior doctor at a slightly more advanced stage of training. A pattern emerged where the supervisee would routinely ask his wife for advice, and on one occasion he was even spotted phoning his wife for advice when she was off duty, at home. This 'horrified' the supervisor, as (not least) the wife was not yet very competent herself.

Because of this recurring and obstinate pattern, the supervisee's behaviour became a focus of discussion at the weekly meeting of supervisors. It became apparent that he probably asked for peer advice on all of his clinical cases, but was attempting to do so without any senior colleagues noticing. A related concern was that his peers felt pressured to help him, becoming drawn into potentially poor treatment and vicarious responsibility (or alternatively would feel guilty about not helping him). Additionally, this upset the normal balance in the peer group, limiting its value as a source of broader mutual support for all of them.

The supervisor decided to introduce closer supervision, with the trainee instructed to discuss every case with his supervisor, and prohibiting him from consulting his peers. However, this had the unintended effect of slowing his work rate still further, as he was taking extra time to thoroughly prepare before discussing a case (e.g., by referring to extensive written guidance). Consequently, his pace of work was now so slow that a locum doctor was required to provide additional cover for his shifts. However, this helped to ensure patient safety and limited waiting times while providing the supervisee with the extra supervision that he required.

Unfortunately, following this intervention the supervisee now started conspicuously missing shifts, on the grounds of a variety of minor health problems. The supervisor therefore initiated a review meeting with the trainee, which began by asking how the increased support was working for him. During this meeting the trainee became angry and blamed the supervisor for not providing better training and supervision from the outset of his placement, pointing out that the post was supposed to be training and not simply seeing patients. He produced material printed from various websites which he cited as proof. The supervisor acknowledged that it was indeed a training post, and also that additional support should be provided as needed. However, he pointed out that there was a limit to the support that can reasonably be provided, in the context of a resource-limited and highly stretched service, which has the primary purpose of providing safe treatment for sick patients. The trainee did not appear to take these points on board. In closing, the supervisor nonetheless expressed a desire to continue to try and help the trainee as much as possible, within these limits. As part of this extra effort, he invited the trainee to choose an additional supervisor as a mentor. In this way, a mentor subsequently provided significant additional support to the trainee, partially in a counselling role.

To further help improve his self-confidence, another supervision technique which was used with some success was to respond to his requests for guidance by first asking the trainee for his thinking about the case (e.g., 'what would you do with this patient. if you had to decide yourself?'). This allowed the supervisor to praise the trainee with regard to the aspects of his assessment which were correct (e.g., 'Good, that's basically what I would do'), and using encouraging phrases to boost his confidence (e.g., 'Well done: you seem to be growing in self-belief').

Although these extra efforts were enough to see the supervisee through his placement, the supervisor judged that he had not achieved the required level of experience and competence, and so he was signed off for only four of the six months worked. The supervisee came to the supervisor's office to appeal this judgement, arguing that his progress has been limited by the lack of help, and by the inadequacy of the training and supervision. He emphasised how difficult it had been for him, and that failing him would therefore be unfair and lacking in empathy. He did not accept, or appear to understand, what the supervisor told him: 'There is a competence standard for this placement, and it is what it is ... I can't simply change the standard for you, in relation to how difficult you found it.' The supervisor acknowledged that he had faced significant challenges and added that others often find this placement the most difficult on their three-year rotation. The supervisee left the meeting feeling aggrieved and misunderstood. He subsequently appealed unsuccessfully to the overall supervisor of his three-year training programme, and ultimately had to make up the two months in another A&E department two years later, as an extension to his training programme. By this stage, due to the subsequent experience since his first A&E placement, his competence and self-confidence had thankfully improved, and he successfully completed his training.

Reflections

Trainees are usually eager to take guidance on board, as they are naturally keen not to repeat errors. In this instance, the trainee was exceptionally unreceptive, despite the supervisor taking care to use gentle reasoning (rather than apportioning blame). He also pointed out ways in which the supervisee could overcome his over-reliance on peer support, make better use of supervision, and avoid similar errors in the future. Unfortunately, this supervisee remained unreceptive to guidance, and angry that he was the victim of inadequate supervision within a highly stretched service, which had training as a secondary purpose. The extra efforts and costs that the service had committed to helping him succeed were dismissed as ineffective, since he had to repeat part of his training.

In this systemic sense, this illustration carries implications for the selection and induction of trainees by the training programme (e.g., might it increase attention to stress-management techniques, while ensuring that trainees hold realistic expectations of training). In particular, the role of peer-support merits attention. There is no question about the importance of emotional and informational support from peers, but there are boundaries that should be highlighted and avoided (e.g., not calling peers at home for advice on a patient; not using 'peer supervision' as a substitute for supervision). Secondly, the healthcare organisation might advantageously review its commitment to training, since the supervisor appears over-stretched by the clinical workload and so is unable to commit fully to supervision. The attendant risk to patient care is high, not least as supervisees may feel pressured to rely on peer supervision in this context. Satisfaction with training and its effectiveness will presumably also suffer, and the value of supervision may be undermined, alongside perceptions of the organisation (which may affect future recruitment). We next offer a complementary example of how the organisational context can also damage patients.

Example: The 2014 Veterans Administration Waiting List Scandal

The Veterans' Administration (VA) is the largest integrated healthcare system in the United States, comprised of 1,298 healthcare facilities with a 2023 budget request totalling $301 billion dollars serving 9 million enrolled veterans (retired military personnel) annually. In 2014, a hospital in Phoenix, Arizona was accused of keeping secret waiting lists of veterans seeking care and grossly underreporting actual waiting and access times. For example, patients had to wait an average of 115 days to be seen by a primary care provider, and as many as 40 veterans died while on the waiting list (Lopez, 2015). An official investigation determined that the waiting list directly contributed to patient deaths. Among the most egregious findings in another review of the scandal, Molina (2018) concluded: 'The role-modelling behaviours of VA supervisors was also a key factor in the scandal. The use of work-arounds to manipulate waitlist data was widespread and routinely accepted as standard operating procedure. Even though many of the schedulers involved sensed that what they were doing was somehow unethical, the vast majority went along with the directives of their immediate supervisors.' (Molina, 2018, p. 9). According to the Report of the Office of Inspector General, 'Staff continued to enter the wrong date in the scheduling system primarily because facility management did not ensure staff consistently implemented VA's scheduling requirements.' (VA Office of Inspector General, 2018, p.iv). In trying to formulate this corrupt culture, we should note that veterans seen within 14 days of their desired appointment date yielded significant financial incentives for managerial staff. As Molina (2018, p. 10) concludes in his summary, 'First, organizational leaders should take care to communicate expected norms of behavior in a clear and unambiguous manner, which includes communicating those expectations through their own role-modelling behaviour. In addition, careful attention should be paid to the ways in which unrealistic performance goals may provide incentives for organizational members to take ethical shortcuts.'

This example captures many essential features of a dysfunctional organisational system driven badly off course by unrealistic performance standards developed from the top, without regard to economic realities or conditions on the ground. This dysfunctional top-down approach was then amplified by the collusion of line management and supervisory staff, who disregarded and presumably encouraged cheating by lower-level administrative staff, in order to benefit from financial incentives. The shocking result was that clinical care took a back seat to meeting standards and patients died. The unethical behavior of individuals in this case was embedded within a systemically dysfunctional organisation and, as Molina (2018, p. 2) notes, this individual unethical conduct occurred within 'the wider organizational and social systems, such as legal institutions, organizational culture, leadership, and compliance programs'.

But it wasn't just Phoenix that cheated on waiting time standards. A follow-up VA audit (VA Office of Inspector General (2020). later determined that facilities around the country were also falsifying waiting list data and that 'At 24 locations, respondents said they even felt threatened or coerced by superiors to manipulate the scheduling records.' (Lopez, 2014). As a result, '7.3 million appointments (were) cancelled from March 15 through May 1, 2020, (and) about 2.3 million (32 percent) had no indication of follow-up or tracking at the time of the review.' (VA Office of Inspector General, 2020, p. ii).

Ineffective Quality Improvement Systems

In the preceding sections we have considered the resource ('structure') and 'process' dimensions of the quality of a clinical service. We now address 'outcome', the third and final dimension (Donabedian, [1966] 2005). Our focus is on critical contextual issues in supervision that are related to unacceptable outcomes, such as the poor quality control over supervision (e.g., inappropriate supervision standards and inadequate audits). In essence, we ask: What are the outcomes of 'good enough' supervision, and what does a healthcare organisation need to do to ensure them?

Quality is a notoriously elusive concept, but it is a vital issue to address. In our supervision workshops we have asked the participants to do this by working in small groups, each group allocated a particular perspective on quality (e.g., structure, process, or outcome). We then show a video clip of supervision and invite the participants to judge the quality of this sample, from their delegated perspective. In the ensuing large-group discussion this invariably raises critical issues, such as how one can best judge quality, our subjective biases, and the goals or standards that we should have for supervision. It is clear that these issues can readily generate considerable debate, and that resolutions are not immediately obvious, or shared by one and all. Of course, this kind of debate is common in healthcare generally, where it is also at best only partly resolved. For example, Donabedian ([1966] 2005) himself defined a health outcome as a change that resulted from antecedent healthcare, in terms of recovery, restoration of function, or survival. In supervision, Wampold and Holloway (1997) defined an outcome as 'any phenomena representing a change or state that persists beyond the actual supervision session' (p. 16). Thus, outcomes may refer to beneficial or harmful changes related to an intervention like supervision, and are traditionally regarded as the paramount measure of healthcare.

Example of Ineffective Quality Improvement Systems: Poor Quality Control

For supervision to be 'good enough', it follows that it must produce beneficial outcomes. A long-standing debate about quality within the supervision literature is this so-called acid test, as already mentioned (e.g., Chapter 8). This test itself invites criticism, as, thanks in large part to the inherent difficulty of studying supervision, it remains unclear whether supervision is truly effective. As noted by Rousmaniere et al. (2014) and by Whipple et al. (2020), both clinician and supervisor effectiveness are compromised by a wide range of confounding factors. To have an effect on patient outcomes, supervisors' interventions have to be strong enough to overcome barriers within supervision (e.g., only using didactic methods), then barriers within supervisees (e.g., non-disclosure; weak working alliance), then barriers within patients (e.g., weak compliance, symptom severity, adverse treatment history), then moderating barriers within their respective contexts (e.g., lack of peer support). To further emphasise the challenging causal pathway from supervision to clinical benefit, each of these types of barrier have multiple moderators. To illustrate, in our review of 24 studies, 35 different moderating factors were identified, alongside 26 different kinds of supervisory intervention, associated with 28 different kinds of outcome (Milne et al., 2008). Furthermore, the interactional complexity of these variables and barriers serve to weaken the observable links between supervision and clinical effectiveness (i.e., some variables weaken or strengthen other variables, altering their effects unpredictably in some contexts). When combined with the many methodological weaknesses, this situation can readily explain why regression studies and other research analyses indicate that supervision does not consistently pass the acid test.

On the other hand, some studies do indicate how supervision can pass the acid test, and clarify what represents 'good enough' supervision outcomes. For example, Snowdon et al. (2017) reviewed 14 studies drawn from a range of healthcare professions (medicine, nursing, and allied health) that investigated the impact of supervision. They found a positive outcome in terms of the process of care, when there was what they termed 'direct supervision' of this care. This was defined as the personal presence of the supervisor during the clinical activity (face-to-face, or through a communication device), with the potential to influence patient care (i.e., what is usually termed 'clinical oversight'). Examples of improved processes of care included greater compliance with guidelines for the management of patients requiring emergency care by medical residents, and improved post-partum nursing care. However, not all of these direct supervision-related improvements in the process of care resulted in significantly improved clinical outcomes, when compared to those managed by unsupervised professionals. Snowdon et al. (2017, p. 9) concluded that 'supervision of health professionals is associated with effectiveness of care. The review found significant improvement in the process of care that may improve compliance with processes that are associated with enhanced patient health outcomes'. In summary, although the acid test is only passed on some occasions, many other valuable outcomes are often achieved, or at least patient harm is prevented (Milne, 2020). An optimistic interpretation is that supervision that is done properly (e.g., 'directly') is clinically effective, and 'good enough' by that outcome criterion. A wide range of outcomes have been attributed to supervision, ranging from benefits for the supervisees (e.g., competence development and confidence enhancement (Wheeler & Richards, 2007)), benefits for the supervisors (e.g., validation and collegial support (Milne & Reiser, 2020)), benefits for the patients (e.g., improved care processes and outcomes (Snowdon et al., 2017)), and benefits for the host organisations (e.g., job satisfaction, job retention and ability to manage workload (Watkins, 2019)). If these are representative of the outcomes of 'good enough' supervision, we should next ask what healthcare organisations need to do to ensure them.

In our third bulleted theme earlier, we noted that organisational systems that are unfit for purpose fail to ensure adequate quality control over supervision, including a failure to define and communicate the competencies or standards for supervision. There can also be a related failure to support and guide supervisors, so that they can achieve the required standards (e.g., through providing training in supervision; see Chapter 6). This may well be compounded by related failings in the relevant national organisations (e.g., underfunding of health services; lack of effective professional body leadership on supervisor training standards). Again, healthcare disasters provide painfully detailed accounts of these interwoven systemic failings (e.g., Berwick, 2013). Peer group supervision is a clear example of the institutional and professional body's acceptance of a poorly defined and unregulated pseudo-supervisory practice (Kirkup, 2015). What is the alternative?

'Good enough' supervision systems succeed in ensuring that supervision leads to the benefits just enumerated, particularly to improved clinical care by supervisees, associated with enhanced patient outcomes (including reduced harm (Milne, 2020)). Working backwards up the fidelity framework (see Table 1.2, Chapter 1), this entails that supervisory guidance is properly enacted by the supervisee during their clinical activities, that this draws on the supervisee having developed competence within supervision, that supervision is itself conducted effectively (e.g., supervisor had been trained to supervise), and that there is an appropriate and professional approach to supervision. Each of these steps in the fidelity framework imply how the workplace can facilitate a 'good-enough' system of support and guidance for supervisors, as discussed in previous chapters (e.g., resolving unprofessional supervision practices, Chapter 5). Here we want to again highlight the key role of organisational leadership. On the one hand, this means ensuring that supervision is provided with due attention to the normative, formative, and restorative functions. When line managers provide supervision there is a risk of role conflicts that undermine its effectiveness. Specifically, normative issues will tend to dominate, and supervisees will not feel able to seek restorative support, or to talk freely about their clinical work (Hawkins & McMahon, 2020; Tomlinson, 2015). Surveys suggest that up to a quarter of supervisees are supervised by their line managers (Nicholas & Goodyear, 2020), so this is a significant issue. Strategic leadership should result in the right people providing supervision, with the right training and support (Milne & Reiser, 2020). Such leadership should also encourage a systems approach to improvement, including organisational learning through research and development activity (e.g., Schilling et al., 2011). Examples from the supervision field include the systems developed to encourage evidence-based clinical practice on a wide scale by Schoenwald (2016) and by Clark (2018); and the local action-research work undertaken to overcome barriers and strengthen boosters to supervision (e.g., Buus et al., 2016; Lynch & Happel, 2008).

Formulation

In the absence of a definitive conceptual framework for making sense of organisational systems, our preferred approach is 'force-field analysis' (Lewin, 1953). Force-field analysis is a dynamic perspective, based on identifying opposing contextual or organisational forces, some 'driving' and others 'restraining' change within a system (e.g., the introduction of supervision within a profession). Although the model is dated, this logic is still useful and popular, including within supervision research (e.g., Gonge & Buus, 2010) and implementation science (e.g., Flottorp et al., 2013), though latterly the terms have changed to organisational 'barriers' and 'boosters', or similar. This kind of force-field analysis represents a formulation, indicating how the identified boosters and barriers within an organisational and societal context combine to provide an understanding of the critical issues, such as inaccessible or ineffective supervision. We prefer this approach because it can indicate more precisely the relative force of the different boosters and barriers, and provides an accessible and practical summary of the outcome of these forces at any particular point in time. These features help to complete a formulation, as they indicate what might best describe a problem, which interventions might best fix it, and it incorporates a simple means of measuring progress. We provide a diagrammatic illustration in Figure 10.1, where these opposing forces are represented by a weighted see-saw. Strategic leaders could utilise this kind of force-field analysis to understand and resolve supervision issues, ideally working collaboratively with other stakeholders, such as supervisors and supervisees (e.g., see Lynch & Happel, 2008).

On the left-hand side of the see-saw in Figure 10.1 are the barriers, which are opposed by the boosters, positioned to the right. The size of the boxes surrounding each barrier or booster represents their relative importance or 'weight', so creating an analysis of the opposing forces on the see-saw. We have inserted examples of the boosters and barriers

Workplace barriers **Workplace boosters**

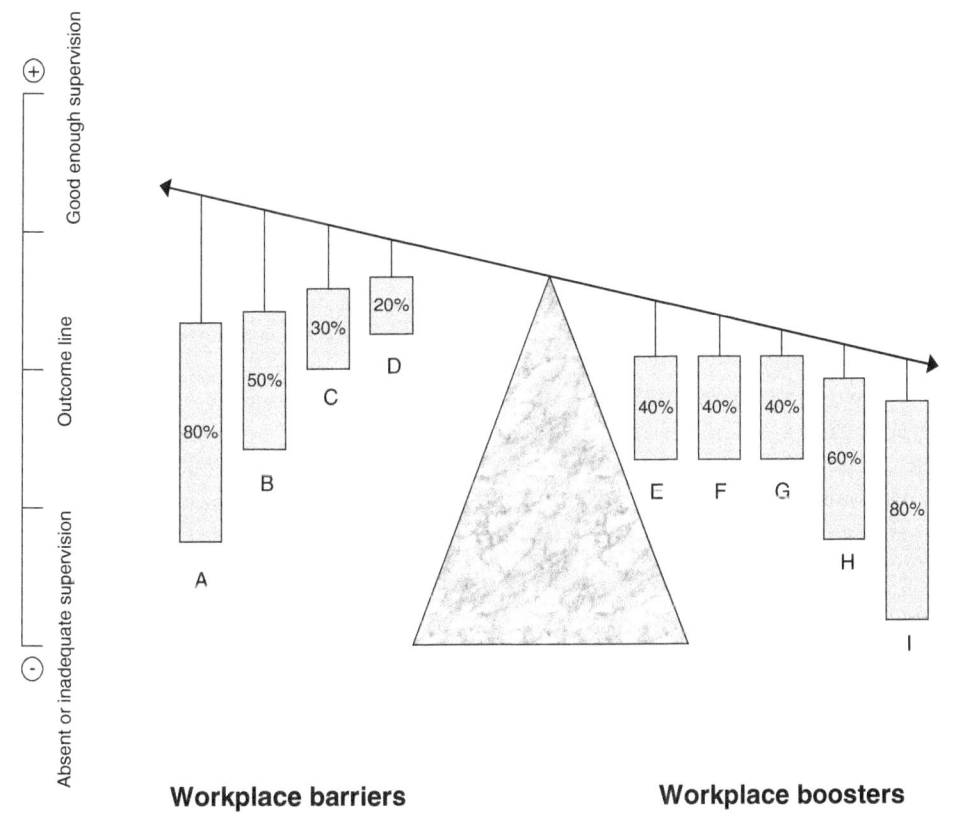

Figure 10.1 A hypothetical formulation of the barriers and boosters affecting supervision within a healthcare system. **Key:** A = Inconsistent management support; B = Insufficient resources; C = Work overload; D = Peer group supervision; E = Social support from colleagues; F = Positive organisational climate; G = Performance monitoring and feedback; H = Supervisor training; I = Supervision guidelines and achievable standards.

that we have discussed in this chapter, for illustrative purposes. In practice, a force-field analysis would use relevant data from the workplace under study, such as supervisees' ratings of the various factors perceived to be influencing their supervision. This could provide an average percent rating for all participants in relation to each main factor identified (Figure 10.1 suggests what percent of participants rated each listed factor as important). Reflecting the dynamic nature of the organisational context, slight shifts in the relative weight of the barriers and boosters (or the emergence of new factors) will take the see-saw to a new tipping point. The outcome of the balance of these forces is indicated by the position of the see-saw relative to the outcome line on the left of Figure 10.1. In this example the see-saw is mostly tilted upwards by boosters, indicating that the overall organisational context is having a positive effect. This hypothetical example would help to explain why certain critical issues are prominent, and which barriers or boosters might afford the best prospect of resolution.

Suggestions

As the scope for suggestions is vast in this exceptionally wide-ranging chapter, we will restrict ourselves to one suggestion for each of the factors in Figure 10.1, all phrased positively this time.

- **Provide consistent management support**: The executive and strategic leaders within healthcare organisations must strive to establish a workplace environment where supervision is a routine and valued part of the job. Joint problem-solving efforts can be especially effective (including reviewing and defining clinical problems; shared decision-making over selected actions; and co-working to resolve problems: Kadushin & Harkness, 2002).
- **Ensure that there are sufficient resources:** National health services and professional groups usually ensure that adequate funding streams exist to support supervision, and that quality control agencies exist to monitor whether or not supervision is provided routinely, and to a 'good-enough' standard. But nonetheless surveys of practitioners indicate that significant problems do still occur, so that effective leadership also needs to ensure the adequate resourcing of supervision. Management can form a project steering group to oversee implementation and evaluation of a suitable supervision enhancement programme (Moran et al., 2014). This may include drawing attention to the cost-effectiveness of supervision (Funderburk et al., 2015), or developing supervisor training to increase capacity and confidence (alongside some of the other suggestions in this section). Managers can seek the best value for money and sustainability, for instance, by developing internal supervisors to gradually replace external supervisors (Weisz et al., 2018). Improving access to other resources can also be a great help (e.g., implementing policies that ensure that staff have the time to participate in supervision; organising suitable rooms and IT equipment).
- **Review and manage workloads:** Identify specific and essential duties and tasks, create a system for effective re-prioritisation on a regular basis (e.g., based on feedback), ensure that goal-setting leads to challenging but achievable objectives, make mutual

action-planning part of this problem-solving cycle, work towards optimal coordination and appropriate delegation, manage the overall system more effectively, such as waiting lists and caseloads (Kadushin & Harkness, 2002).
- **Re-label and replace 'peer group supervision':** There is much to be said for peer group activities, as long as they do not masquerade as supervision. Especially valuable are mutual support groups, as they tend to be formed among colleagues with common issues, and they tend to feature peer support. But these activities need to be labelled accurately, and clearly distinguished from supervision. Group supervision is a perfectly suitable format, provided that the supervisor meets the definition of a supervisor (e.g., carrying authority, ensuring that experiential learning occurs, providing feedback). Many helpful descriptions of group supervision exist (e.g., Beddoe & Davys, 2016; Hawkins & McMahon, 2020).
- **Foster social support from colleagues:** Supervision should enable clinicians to provide safe care and help them to feel supported and respected while learning from a senior colleague (e.g., providing feedback related to personal progress, to boost self-confidence: Gregory & Demartini, 2017); supervisors can also advantageously guide supervisees to strengthen their social support systems (Milne & Reiser, 2020).
- **Develop a positive organisational climate:** Develop hands-on, engaged leadership in a collaborative workplace climate; adopt team-based approaches to problems; enhance communication, including efforts to secure more resources to overcome issues with challenging patient (e.g., have well-integrated IT systems); strengthen external relationships (Vaughn et al., 2019).
- **Provide performance monitoring and feedback:** Key competencies should be defined and competence development efforts related to quality control (e.g., collecting, and acting on audit data); institute a system for evaluation, monitoring and feedback, to facilitate quality improvements. Clear assessments need to be established, ones which link supervision to the quality of care across the service, to allow norms to be established, and so that poor performance can be identified and resolved (Francis, 2013). Do not rely on self-report, but verify through direct observation that supervision is being conducted competently (Wilkins et al., 2018).
- **Train and support supervisors:** As per Chapter 6, supervision should be treated as a professional sub-specialisation, entailing continuing professional development (CPD/CME: e.g., initial workshop training in groups, followed by supervision-of-supervision or consultancy for supervisors); this CPD should include the occasional direct observation of supervision, and related assessments of the supervision and training environment, sufficient to enable detection and remediation of poor practice (e.g., by training providers or professional bodies), from which both patients and supervisees should be sheltered (Francis, 2013).
- **Utilise supervision guidelines and agree achievable standards:** collaborate with professional bodies and others to specify the desired supervision profile, including the competencies and methods that represent 'good enough' supervision; address common issues (e.g., clinical responsibilities, the ethical and legal context, professional practice guidelines).

Conclusions

Our focus throughout this chapter has been on how the workplace system, embedded in the wider societal context, creates critical issues in supervision, and what can be done to resolve them. As we stated at the start of this chapter, our reasoning is that we must take the wider context into account in order to understand and resolve critical issues, including those in our healthcare organisations. This reflects the truism that everything happens in a context.

To manage the large number of issues that we could have discussed, we made extensive use of illustrations, and focussed on three broad themes. Reflecting the most common sources of critical issues that affect supervision, these themes were: structural problems within workplaces, such as ineffective leadership, problems relating to dysfunctional systems or processes such as peer group supervision, and ineffective quality improvement methods, where the desired outcomes of supervision are unclear or ignored. These themes can combine within supervision, as indicated by surveys in social work (Sewell et al., 2021). In turn, such inadequate supervision can ultimately lead to healthcare disasters (e.g., Kirkup, 2015; Ockenden, 2022), because even the most well-intentioned clinicians can be 'crushed' by a flawed workplace environment (Tomlinson, 2015). As summarised in Figure 10.1, our force-field formulation of these kinds of factors included the barriers of inconsistent management support for supervision (e.g., inadequate funding or commitment), work overload, insufficient social support, and the implementation of misguided methods (e.g., peer group supervision). Such issues can be countered through various boosters to supervision, such as effective leadership that takes a systemic perspective, including performance monitoring and feedback systems. By formulating our workplaces in this kind of way, we take a 'human factors' approach, seeking to resolve critical issues in healthcare. This is also the recommended approach noted in the enquiry into a healthcare disaster within English maternity services (Ockenden, 2022), including improved staffing levels, systematic staff training, and more effective leadership arrangements. Implementation science provides related suggestions, based on evidence-based resolutions (Powell et al., 2015). Clinical supervision is gaining recognition as a valuable mechanism within this ergonomic, evidence-based strategy, providing one of the means of better matching up clinicians and their workplaces, and ensuring that supervision is 'good-enough', so helping to resolve critical issues and prevent disasters (Tomlinson, 2015).

References

Aarons, G. A., Ehrhart, M. G., & Farahnak, L. R. (2014). The Implementation Leadership Scale (ILS): Development of a brief measure of unit level implementation leadership. *Implementation Science, 9*(1), 45. https://doi.org/10.1186/1748-5908-9-45 (PubMed: 24731295).

Bearman, S. K., Bailin, A., & Sale, R. (2019). Graduate school training in CBT supervision to develop knowledge and competencies. *The Clinical Supervisor, 39*(1), 66–84. https://doi.org/10.1080/07325223.2019.1663459

References

Beddoe, L., & Davys, A. (2016). *Challenges in professional supervision*. Jessica Kingsley Publishers.

Berwick. (2013). *A promise to learn – A commitment to act improving the safety of patients in England*. Crown Publishing.

Bogo, M., Paterson, J., Tufford, L., & King, R. (2011). Supporting front-line practitioners' professional development and job satisfaction in mental health and addiction. *Journal of Interprofessional Care, 25*(3), 209–214. https://doi.org/10.3109/13561820.2011.554240

Buus, N., Delgado, C., Traynor, M., & Gonge, H. (2017). Resistance to group clinical supervision: A semi-structured interview study of non-participating mental health nursing staff members. *International Journal of Mental Health Nursing, 27*(2), 783–793. https://doi.org/10.1111/inm.12365

Buus, N., Lisa Lynch, L., & Gonge, H. (2016). Developing and implementing 'meta-supervision' for mental health nursing staff supervisees: Opportunities and challenges. *The Cognitive Behaviour Therapist, 9*, e22. https://doi.org/10.1017/S1754470X15000434

Carpenter, J., Shardlow, S. M., Patsios, D., & Wood, M. (2015). Developing the confidence and competence of newly qualified child and family social workers in England: Outcomes of a national programme. *British Journal of Social Work, 45*(1), 153–176. https://doi.org/10.1093/bjsw/bct106

Choy-Brown, M., & Stanhope, V. (2018). The availability of supervision in routine mental health care. *Clinical Social Work Journal, 46*(4), 271–280. https://doi.org/10.1007/s10615-018-0687-0

Clark, D. M. (2018). Realising the mass public benefit of evidence-based psychological therapies: The IAPT programme. *Annual Review of Clinical Psychology, 14*(1), 159–183. https://doi.org/10.1146/annurev-clinpsy-050817-084833

Donabedian, A. ([1966] 2005). Evaluating the quality of care. *The Milbank Quarterly, 83*(4), 691–729. doi:10.1111/j.1468-0009.2005.00397.x (Reprinted from *The Milbank Memorial Fund Quarterly*, 1966, *44*, 166–203).

Dorsey, S., Pullmann, M. D., Kerns, S. U., Jungbluth, N., Meza, R., Thompson, K., & Berliner, L. (2017). The juggling act of supervision in community mental health: Implications for supporting evidence-based treatment. *Administration and Policy in Mental Health and Mental Health Services Research, 44*(6), 838–852. https://doi.org/10.1007/s10488-017-0796-z

Flottorp, S. A., Oxman, A. D., Krause, J., Musila, N. R., Wensing, M., Godycki-Cwirko, M., & Eccles, M. P. (2013). A checklist for identifying determinants of practice: A systematic review and synthesis of frameworks and taxonomies of factors that prevent or enable improvements in healthcare professional practice. *Implementation Science, 8*, 35. https://doi.org/10.1186/1748-5908-8-35

Francis, R. (2013). *Report of the Mid Staffordshire NHS foundation trust public inquiry*. The Stationery Office.

Funderburk, B., Chaffin, M., Bard, E., Shanley, J., Bard, D., & Berliner, L. (2015). Comparing client outcomes for two evidence-based treatment consultation strategies. *Journal of Clinical Child & Adolescent Psychology, 44*(5), 730–741. https://doi.org/10.1080/15374416.2014.910790

Gonge, H., & Buus, N. (2010). Individual and workplace factors that influence psychiatric nursing staff's participation in clinical supervision: A survey study and prospective longitudinal registration. *Issues in Mental Health Nursing, 31*(5), 345–354. https://doi.org/10.3109/01612840903427849

Gonge, H., & Buus, N. (2014). Is it possible to strengthen psychiatric nursing staff's clinical supervision? RCT of a meta-supervision intervention. *Journal of Advanced Nursing, 71*(4), 909–921. https://doi.org/10:1111/jan.12569

Gregory, S., & Demartini, C. (2017). Satisfaction of doctors with their training: Evidence from UK. *BMC Health Services Research, 17*, 851. https://doi.org/10.1186/s12913-017-2792-0

Haarman, G. B. (2013). *Clinical Supervision: Legal, ethical and risk management issues*. Foundations: Education & Consultation.

Hawkins, P., & McMahon, A. (2020). *Supervision in the Helping Professions*. Open University Press.

Holloway, E. L. (2016). *Supervision Essentials for a Systems Approach to Supervision*. American Psychological Society.

Kadushin, A., & Harkness, D. (2002). *Supervision in Social Work* (4th ed.). Columbia University Press.

Keroack, M. A., Youngberg, B. J., Cerese, J. L., Krsek, C., Prellwitz, L. W., & Trevelyan, E. W. (2007). Organizational factors associated with high performance in quality and safety in Academic Medical Centres. *Academic Medicine, 82*(12), 1178–1186. https://doi.org/10.1097/ACM.0b013e318159e1ff

Kirkup, B. (2015). *Morecambe Bay Investigation*. This publication is available at https://www.gov.uk/government/publications. ISBN 9780108561306

Ladany, N., Friedlander, M. L., & Nelson, M. L. (2016). *Supervision essentials for the critical events in psychotherapy supervision model*. American Psychological Association.

Lewin, K. (1953). *Field theory in social science: Selected theoretical papers*. Tavistock.

Lopez, G. (2014). Audit: 76 percent of VA facilities report at least one instance of schedulers potentiallyfalsifyingrecordshttps://www.vox.com/2014/6/9/5793794/full-va-audit-highlights-perverse-incentive

Lopez, G. (2015). The VA scandal of 2014, explained. https://www.vox.com/2014/9/26/18080592/va-scandal-explained.

Lynch, L., & Happel, B. (2008). Implementation of clinical supervision in action: Part 2: Implementation and beyond. *International Journal of Mental Health Nursing, 17*(1), 65–72. https://doi.org/10.1111/j.1447-0349.2007.00512.x

Martin, P., Kumar, S., & Lizarondo, L. (2017a). When I say clinical supervision. *Medical Education, 51*(9), 890–891. https://doi.org/10.1111/medu.13258

Martin, P., Reiser, R., & Milne, D. (2017b). Peer supervision: International problems and prospects. *Journal of Advanced Nursing, 74*(5), 998–999. https://doi.org/10.1111/jan.13413

Martino, S., Paris, M., Añez, L., Nich, C., Canning-Ball, M., Hunkele, K., Carroll, K.M., & Olmstead, T.A. (2016). The effectiveness and cost of clinical supervision for motivational interviewing: A randomized controlled trial. *Journal of Substance Abuse & Treatment, 68*, 11–23. https://doi.org/10.1016%2Fj.jsat.2016.04.005

Maslach, C., Schaufeli, W. B., & Leiter, M. P. (2001). Job burnout. *Annual Review of Psychology, 52*, 397–422. https://doi.org/10.1146/annurev.psych.52.1.397

Maxwell, C. A., Ehrhart, M. G., Williams, N. J., Moore, T. M., Kendall, P. C., & Beidas, R. S. (2021). The organizational financial context of publicly-funded mental health clinics: Development and preliminary psychometric evaluation of the Agency Financial Status Scales. *Administration* and *Policy in Mental Health and Mental Health Services Research, 48*(5), 780–792. https://doi.org/10.1007/s10488-021-01128-4

Milne, D., & Reiser, R. P. (2020). *Supportive Clinical Supervision: From burnout to well-being, through restorative leadership*. Pavilion.

Milne, D. L. (2007). Developing clinical supervision through reasoned analogies with therapy. *Clinical Psychology and Psychotherapy, 13*(3), 215–222. https://doi.org/10.1002/cpp.489

Milne, D. L. (2020). Preventing harm related to CBT supervision: A theoretical review and preliminary framework. *The Cognitive Behaviour Therapist, 13*. https://doi.org/10.1017/S1754470X20000550

Milne, D. L., Aylott, H., Fitzpatrick, H., & Ellis, M. V. (2008). How does clinical supervision work? Using a best evidence synthesis approach to construct a basic model of supervision. *The Clinical Supervisor, 27*(2), 170–190. http://dx.doi.org/10.1080/07325220802487915

Molina, A. D. (2018). A systems approach to managing organizational integrity risks: Lessons from the 2014 veterans affairs waitlist scandal. *American Review of Public Administration, 48*(8), 1–14. https://doi.org/10.1177/0275074018755006

Moran, A. M., Coyle, J., Boxall, D., Nancrow, S. A., & Young, J. (2014). Supervision, support & mentoring interventions for health practitioners in rural and remote contexts: An integrative review and thematic synthesis of the literature to identify mechanisms for successful outcomes. *Human Resources for Health, 12*(1). http://www.human-resources-health.com/content/12/1/10

National Quality Board. (2013). *Human factors in healthcare. A concordat from the National Quality Board*. National Health Service.

Nicholas, H., & Goodyear, R. (2020). Supervision of a sample of clinical and counselling psychologists in the UK: A descriptive study of their practices, processes and perceived benefits. *The European Journal of Counselling Psychology, 9*(1), 39–48. http://dx.doi.org/10.46853/001c.22014

Ockenden, D. (2022). *Findings, conclusions and essential actions from the independent review of maternity services at The Shrewsbury and Telford Hospital NHS Trust*. Crown publications.

Powell, B. J., Waltz, T. J., Chinman, M. J., Damschroder, L. J., Smith, J. L., Matthieu, M. M., ... Kirchner, J. E. (2015). A refined compilation of implementation strategies: Results from the Expert Recommendations for Implementing Change (ERIC) project. *Implementation Science, 10*, 21. https://doi.org/10.1186/s13012-015-0209-1

Pullman, M. D., Lucid, L., Harrison, J. P., Martin, P., Deblinger, E., Benjamin, K. S., & Dorsey, S. (2018). Implementation climate and time predict intensity of supervision content related to evidence-based treatment. *Frontiers in Public Health, 6*, 280 www.frontiersin.org/articles/10.3389/fpubh.2018.00280

Roth, A. D., Pilling, S., & Turner, J. (2010). Therapist training and supervision in clinical trials: Implications for clinical practice. *Behavioural and Cognitive Psychotherapy, 38*(3), 291–302. https://doi.org/10.1017/s1352465810000068

Rothwell, C., Kehoe, A., Farook, S. F., & Illing, J. (2021). Enablers and barriers to effective clinical supervision in the workplace: A rapid evidence review. *BMJ Open, 11*(9), e052929. https://doi.org/10.1136/bmjopen-2021-052929

Rousmaniere, T. G., Swift, J. K., Babins-Wagner, R., Whipple, J. L., & Berzins, S. (2014). Supervisor effects on client outcome in routine practice. *Psychotherapy Research, 26*, 196–205. https://doi.org/10.1080/10503307.2014.963730

Schilling, L., Dearing, J. W., Staley, P., Harvey, P., Fahey, L., & Kuruppu, F. (2011). Kaiser Permanente's performance improvement system, Part 4: Creating a learning organization. *The Joint Commission Journal on Quality & Patient Safety, 37*(12), 532–543. https://doi.org/10.1016/s1553-7250(11)37069-9

Schoenwald, S. K. (2016). Clinical supervision in a quality assurance/quality improvement system: Multisystemic Therapy® as an Example. *The Cognitive Behaviour Therapist, 9*, e21. https://doi.org/10.1017/S1754470X15000604

Sewell, K. M., Kao, D., & Asakura, K. (2021). Clinical supervision in frontline health care: A survey of social workers in Ontario, Canada. *Social Work in Health Care, 60*(3), 282–299. https://doi.org/10.1080/00981389.2021.1880532

Snowdon, D. A., Leggat, S. G., & Taylor, N. F. (2017). Does clinical supervision of healthcare professionals improve effectiveness of care and patient experience? A systematic review. *BMC Health Services Research, 17*(1–11). https://doi.org/10.1186/s12913-017-2739-5

Tomlinson, J. (2015). Using clinical supervision to improve the quality and safety of patient care: A response to Berwick and Francis. *BMC Medical Education, 15*(103). https://doi.org/10.1186/s12909-015-0324-3

VA Office of Inspector General. (2018). Veterans Health Administration. Audit of veteran wait time Data, Choice Access, and Consult Management in VISN 15. *American Review of Public Administration* 1–14.

VA Office of Inspector General (2020). *Veterans Health Administration.* Appointment management during the COVID-19 pandemic. https://www.va.gov/oig/pubs/VAOIG-20-02794-218.pdf

Vaughn, V. M., Saint, S., Krein, S. L., Forman, J. H., Meddings, J., Ameling, J., Winter, S., Townsend, W., & Chopra, V. (2019). Characteristics of healthcare organisations struggling to improve quality: Results from a systematic review of qualitative studies. *BMJ Quality & Safety, 28*(1), 74–84. https://doi.org/10.1136/bmjqs-2017-007573

Wampold, B. E., & Holloway, E. L. (1997). Methodology, design and evaluation in psychotherapy supervision research. In C. E. Watkins (Ed.), *Handbook of psychotherapy supervision* (pp. 11–30). Wiley.

Watkins, C. E. (2019). What do clinical supervision research reviews tell us? Surveying the last 25 years. *Counselling & Psychotherapy Research, 20*(2), 190–208. https://doi.org/10.1002/capr.12287

Watkins, C. E., & Milne, D. L. (Eds.). (2014). *The Wiley International Handbook of Clinical Supervision.* Wiley-Blackwell.

Weigl, M., Stab, N., Herms, I., Angere, P., Hacker, W., & Glaser, J. (2016). The associations of supervisor support and work overload with burnout and depression: A cross-sectional study in two nursing settings. *Journal of Advanced Nursing, 72*(8), 1774–1788. https://doi.org/10.1111/jan.12948

Weisz, J. R., Ugueto, A. M., Herren, J., Alpert, W., Marchette, L. K., Bearman, S. K., & Weissman, A. S. (2018). When the torch is passed, does the flame still burn? Testing a "train the supervisor" model for the Child STEPs Treatment Programme. *Journal of Consulting and Clinical Psychology, 86*, 726–737. https://doi.org/10.1037/ccp0000331

Wheeler, S., & Richards, K. (2007). The impact of clinical supervision on counsellors and therapists, their practice and their clients. A systematic review of the literature. *Counselling and Psychotherapy Research, 7*, 54–65. https://doi.org/10.1080/14733140601185274

Whipple, J., Hoyt, T., Rousmaniere, T., Swift, J., Pedersen, T., & Vaughn Worthen, V. (2020). Supervisor variance in psychotherapy outcome in routine practice: A replication. *SAGE Open*, *10*(1). https://doi.org/10.1177/2158244019899047

White, E., & Winstanley, J. (2011). Clinical Supervision for mental health professionals: The evidence base. *Social Work & Social Sciences Review*, *14*(3), 77–94. https://doi.org/10.1921/095352211X623227

Wilkins, D., Khan, M., Stabler, L., Newlands, F., & Mcdonnell, J. (2018). Evaluating the quality of Social Work supervision in UK children's services: Comparing self-report and independent observation. *Clinical Social Work Journal*, *46*(4), 350–360. https://doi.org/10.1007/s10615-018-0680-7

Williams, N., & Beidas, R. (2019). Annual research review: The state of implementation science in child psychology and psychiatry: A review and suggestions to advance the field. *Journal of Child Psychology & Psychiatry*, *60*(4), 430–450. https://doi.org/10.1111/jcpp.12960

11

Conclusions: What Do We Now Know about Resolving Critical Issues in Supervision?

Introduction

Some 20 years since clinical supervision was deemed a distinct professional competency (Falender et al., 2004), the complexity and challenges of the role continue to grow, driven by the ever-expanding demands within healthcare organisations (Milne & Reiser, 2020). How are supervisors to cope? How should healthcare systems, including supervisees and clinical managers, support and guide supervisors' coping efforts? How can we make supervision 'compute' (Watkins, 1997)? Our fundamental approach has been to develop answers to such questions through the process of evidence-based practice (EBP), drawing inspiration from relevant theories, the best-available research evidence, and expert consensus statements. Following Parry et al. (1996), we sought these answers through an inclusive version of EBP, accepting a broad spectrum of research evidence, by integrating continuing professional development activities and resources, and by encouraging a scholarly and contextualised approach to supervision (including expert consensus statements). Constructing individualised formulations of critical issues enabled us to suggest ways in which supervisors can understand and resolve the most common critical issues within normative supervision. Throughout this book, we have relied on these underpinning assumptions:

- **Critical issues are common in supervision:** In Chapter 1, we scanned staff surveys, statistics, research reviews, neighbouring literatures, and expert consensus statements. This allowed us to define stressors as arising primarily from workplace demands (e.g., high workloads), from personal misconduct (e.g., unethical behaviour), from incompetence, and from relationship problems (e.g., communication breakdowns). In Chapter 2 we delved more deeply into problematic supervision relationships, then investigated ethical issues and legal dilemmas, such as vicarious liability.
- **Critical issues are wide-ranging, yet poorly defined in the literature:** As we could not find a definitive list of critical issues, we created a preliminary classification scheme (following Milne, 2020). This helped by yielding a description of the most common or likely issues. But such schemes cannot capture all such critical issues, as many are highly subjective in nature, arising from the ways that people make sense of events unfolding around them.

Resolving Critical Issues in Clinical Supervision: A Practical, Evidence-based Approach, First Edition.
Derek L. Milne and Robert P. Reiser.
© 2023 John Wiley & Sons Ltd. Published 2023 by John Wiley & Sons Ltd.

- **Critical issues can be formulated as stressors requiring a response:** Therefore, reflecting this interaction between work environments and individuals, we defined critical issues in supervision as those events that supervisors appraise as requiring a response (i.e., they are subjectively perceived as stressors). This definition meant that such issues could also include opportunities for professional growth, called 'positive' stressors (e.g., a supervisee's questions that challenge and stimulate the supervisor). But we did not address positive stressors in any detail in this book, as our priority was to tackle the most pressing concerns.
- **Critical issues should be viewed systemically:** We considered the system surrounding supervision, recognising that critical issues can also concern the supervisor, as supervisors may themselves behave in ways that represent critical issues for other stakeholders (e.g., managers or supervisees). In this sense, it is effective supervision that has been our focus, and not solely the supervisor. Furthermore, these are issues about which supervisors may have limited awareness, or may lack motivation to resolve (e.g., abusive relationships or unethical conduct). Unfortunately, supervisors are not always models of good professional practice, nor are they always expert in coping with their own stressors, and so these difficulties do arise in practice (e.g., Ellis et al., 2014; Milne, 2020).
- **Critical issues are understandable and can be resolved through an evidence-based formulation:** after dealing with ethical and legal issues, from Chapter 6 on we addressed each of remaining common issues (i.e., untrained supervisors, incompetent supervisors, challenging supervisees, ineffective treatments, and dysfunctional organisations). Our approach was to define and describe the issues, applying theories so that we could better understand them. These formulations were the foundation for our suggested resolutions, drawn from several different professions and from neighbouring literatures, such as 'direct' supervision in the medical literature (e.g., Galanter et al., 2014), and expertise development across diverse groups (Rousmaniere et al., 2017). In this way, we sought to empower supervisors and others so that their critical issues could be resolved in an efficient and constructive manner, making supervision ever stronger.
- **Critical issues in supervision matter:** Supervision is a clinically valuable and professionally satisfying activity, and should be properly organised. There is much at stake: supervision benefits the supervisees (e.g., competence development and confidence enhancement (Wheeler & Richards, 2007)), benefits the supervisors (e.g., validation and collegial support (Milne & Reiser, 2020)), benefits the patients (e.g., improved care processes and outcomes (Snowdon et al., 2017)), and even benefits the host organisations (e.g., job satisfaction, job retention and ability to manage workload (Watkins, 2019)).

Limitations of Our Approach

Reflection occupies a hallowed place within the supervision literature, so we should ourselves pause to consider whether our approach has always been sound. What are the main threats to our understanding of the critical issues, and to our suggested resolutions? We have selected these examples because of the most common reactions we have received from others.

Weak Research Foundations

Taking Chapter 6 as an example, in identifying the critical issues in training supervisors we relied heavily on relevant theory, extrapolation to neighbouring literatures, and expert consensus. This was adequate in some respects, such as clearly supporting the use of a blend of didactic and experiential training methods (e.g., Roth & Pilling, 2007; Rousmaniere et al., 2017). However, to date research on supervisor training has been narrowly focused on participant reactions and immediate learning outcomes, meaning that we actually know very little about what actually happens during or after training. Specifically, there are very few process evaluation studies of the actual delivery of supervisor training (i.e., manipulation checks), being studies which measure which training methods are used, how competently they are conducted, or other questions concerning training fidelity. Rare exceptions include the exploratory observational study by Culloty et al. (2010). Therefore, one weakness in our approach is that we have not been able to define the selected critical issues empirically, meaning that we may have ignored some critical issues that are actually common, but not yet identified.

We must also acknowledge that our awareness of the extant, multi-disciplinary research literature on supervision in general has been limited by the fact that we are both clinical psychologists, working within the mental health field. These biases will no doubt have blinded us to a greater fund of empirical evidence.

Over-inclusive: Treating Supervision within All Healthcare Professions as Similar

In Chapter 1 we stated that this book aimed to help supervisors from all healthcare professions to find better ways of resolving critical issues arising in their supervision, enabling them to become better supervisors. Throughout the book, we tried to take this inclusive position through the use of examples from the different professions, and more importantly by emphasising the fundamental similarities that we see between healthcare groups. Treating all healthcare professions as if they were essentially one discipline can be seen as a flawed assumption, as there are clearly some marked differences between them, alongside some strong professional traditions indicating an exclusive position: 'Currently, supervision has a profession-specific focus and varies greatly within and across professions' (Health Education England, 2020, p. 3). Examples include the ways that the different professions prefer to learn about supervision (Snowdon et al., 2017), and the variable resourcing of supervision (e.g., placement providers for medical students receive ten times more funding than in nursing: Reynolds & Mortimore, 2021). Attitudes to supervision also vary, as social workers may struggle with the reduced professional autonomy (Kadushin & Harkness, 2002), while nurses traditionally viewed supervision as a form of management surveillance ('snoopervision': Beddoe & Davys, 2016).

On the other hand, the way that we all understand supervision is similar across disciplines and professions (Vandette & Gosselin, 2019), as reflected in the fundamental methods that are used, and the common issues faced across healthcare (Health Education England, 2020). Therefore, while we do acknowledge the distinctiveness of the way that different professions approach supervision, we believe that there is more to be gained than lost by seeing past the differences to the underlying commonalities and core principles. We accept that this comes at the price of a related criticism, unwarranted extrapolation.

Unwarranted Extrapolation: Jumping to Conclusions

Throughout our work on an evidence-based approach, we have argued that extrapolation offers a particularly valuable tool in resolving critical issues in supervision. This is because it partially offsets the scarcity and generally poor methodological quality of research within the supervision field. Therefore, we have repeatedly turned in need to the literatures from neighbouring fields, such as instructional design, staff training, expertise development, and education (Milne, 2007). For example, such extrapolation allows us to assume that the principles of effective feedback apply roughly equally across individuals, whether one is considering the education of physicians or the supervision of nurses. That is, feedback is one of the general principles of human development, regardless of whether one is a musician, a surgeon, or a supervisor (Rousmaniere et al., 2017). This is not to ignore the risk of jumping to faulty conclusions, but rather to strike a balance in which some carefully reasoned extrapolation may be judged preferable to the rigid exclusion of neighbouring literatures. This belief has been strongly supported in writing this book, as our goal to provide a broad approach meant that we delved more thoroughly than before into the non-psychology literatures. This could have falsified some of our cherished assumptions about supervision, but instead we can say that wherever we looked we instead found verification (e.g., regarding the optimal use of feedback within medical education: Kogan et al., 2017).

Nonetheless, we realise that extrapolation needs to be used with care, such as considering whether or not the parallels that are being drawn are truly similar, are from closely related fields, and are plausible (Kretz & Krawczyk, 2014). We also agree with our critics that it is preferable to have explicit research evidence.

Myopia: Ignoring Important Topics

Many of the most cherished supervisors were highly rated not because of their technical expertise, but on account of their capacity to inspire (Sutkin et al., 2008). In this sense, in this book we may have been blinded by the technical aspects of supervision, when we perhaps should have adopted a greater emphasis on the interpersonal processes that can be seen as the 'primer' for learning and development (Kogan et al., 2017). Similarly, we have surely omitted some critical issues of significance to others, alongside possible resolutions. For instance, Fickling et al. (2017) conducted a content analysis of counselling supervisors' and supervisees' descriptions of significant events within one USA training programme, noting that both groups cited placement logistics as one of the critical issues, alongside time management during supervision sessions. We accept that these are perfectly suitable topics for this book, but our prioritisation of other issues was ultimately decided by the frequency with which issues were presented in the literature (see Chapter 1). However, we feel that a strength of our broad problem-solving approach is that we have hopefully provided the tools for understanding and resolving some of the issues that we never addressed, such as the distinctive issues within private practice.

Action Implications

In Chapter 1 we said that we would draw out the conclusions that follow from this book, pinpointing corrective actions for the main stakeholders in supervision. This list is only illustrative, a brief reminder of the examples that can be found at the end of earlier chapters.

Supervisors

Throughout this book we have provided a methodical approach to identifying and formulating critical issues in supervision, with a main goal of enabling supervisors to negotiate challenging problems utilising an evidence-informed approach. Our hope is that supervisors (and their trainers) can use this approach to systematically identify and proactively address problems. The other main action implications for supervisors are to be more assertive in seeking the necessary resources (especially ongoing training and support), and to minimise experiential avoidance during supervision (exemplified by the flawed arrangement of peer supervision: Martin et al., 2017). The goal should be to work on expertise development and quality control, within a supportive context.

Supervisees

Supervisees also have a major stake in making supervision successful and we have outlined critical issues that can inform and enable them to identify and address problems in supervision. In particular, the literature indicates that supervisees can engage in a number of maladaptive and problematic behaviours, often incorporating some form of experiential avoidance during supervision. A common issue is the avoidance of direct observation, despite the educational benefits. Supervisees are probably best-placed to address this through user-friendly technologies (e.g., handheld devices or other electronic platforms: Kogan et al., 2017). Another promising option is to work towards more frequent, low-stakes, formative observation.

Managers

Executive, clinical, and strategic leaders are critical stakeholders in establishing a workplace environment where supervision is a routine and valued part of the job, one that is properly resourced. Critical issues can be tackled through action research projects, or by forming a project steering group to oversee a supervision development programme (Moran et al., 2014). The aim is to develop a positive organisational climate, including affirmative performance monitoring and feedback, to facilitate quality improvements, and so that poor performance can be identified and resolved (Francis, 2013). Leaders should prioritise training and supporting supervisors in their professional specialisation, entailing continuing professional development. Proper training requires the application of sufficient resources, including allowance for time off, loss of productivity and investment in high quality training and consultation. The pay-off is substantial. The inspirational work of Buus et al. (2016), Clark (2018), Lynch and Happel (2008), and

Schoenwald (2016) illustrate how barriers can be removed and how supervision systems can operate effectively.

Researchers

Researchers must treat supervision seriously, starting by providing descriptive data on its role in clinical research (Roth et al., 2010), and moving on to study supervision directly, including the systematic observation of its processes and outcomes. We believe that research will increasingly indicate the vital role played by supervision in high-quality clinical care.

Conclusions

In Chapter 1 we defined the methods of normative supervision as workload review, education and training, awareness-raising, plus evaluation, monitoring, and feedback (following Kadushin & Harkness, 2002). These methods aim to enhance the supervisee's work performance, so as to encourage adherence to professional standards, to improve quality control, and to promote patient safety. In the ensuing chapters we described the wide range of critical issues that commonly arise within normative supervision, suggesting ways to resolve them. Our own guidance came primarily from relevant theories, research studies, and expert consensus statements, which we combined following our trusted EBCS strategy (initiated by Milne & Westerman, 2001). This kind of scientific approach to normative supervision is rare, and we were initially unsure how well it would work. But we are relieved to conclude that normative supervision can also be firmly evidence-based, alongside the formative and restorative functions of supervision (Milne & Reiser, 2017; Milne & Reiser, 2020), so completing our EBCS journey.

We hope to have played a useful part in illustrating how normative supervision can be collaborative and constructive, fostering an improved 'literacy' for understanding and resolving normative critical issues in the complex business of supervision. Similarly, we need improved literacy on many other aspects of supervision including the use of feedback, modelling, behavioural reversal, direct observation, and other specific experiential supervision techniques (Molloy et al., 2020). This literacy should foster a greater willingness to 'engage in difficult conversations' about critical issues (Beddoe & Davys, 2016), one of the most neglected aspects of supervision, and surely one of the greatest barriers to improved supervision and higher-quality healthcare.

References

Beddoe, L., & Davys, A. (2016). *Challenges in Professional Supervision*. Jessica Kingsley Publishers.

Buus, N., Lisa Lynch, L., & Gonge, H. (2016). Developing and implementing 'meta-supervision' for mental health nursing staff supervisees: Opportunities and challenges. *The Cognitive Behaviour Therapist*, 9, e22. https://doi.org/10.1017/S1754470X15000434

Clark, D. M. (2018). Realising the mass public benefit of evidence-based psychological therapies: The IAPT programme. *Annual Review of Clinical Psychology, 14*, 159–183. https://doi.org/10.1146/annurev-clinpsy-050817-084833

Culloty, T., Milne, D. L., & Sheikh, A. I. (2010). Evaluating the training of clinical supervisors: A pilot study using the fidelity framework. *The Cognitive Behaviour Therapist, 3*(4), 132–144. https://psycnet.apa.org/doi/10.1017/S1754470X10000139

Ellis, M. V., Berger, L., Hanus, A. E., Ayala, E. E., Swords, B. A., & Siembor, M. (2014). Inadequate and harmful clinical supervision: Testing a revised framework and assessing occurrence. *The Counseling Psychologist, 42*(4), 434–472. https://doi.org/10.1177/0011000013508656

Falender, C. A., Cornish, J. A. E., Goodyear, R., Hatcher, R., Kaslow, N. J., Leventhal, G., Shafranske, E., Sigmon, S. T., Stoltenberg, C., & Grus, C. (2004). Defining competencies in psychology supervision: A consensus statement. *Journal of Clinical Psychology, 60*(7), 771–785. https://psycnet.apa.org/doi/10.1002/jclp.20013

Fickling, M.J., Borders, L.D., Mobley, K.A., & Wester, K. (2017). Most and least helpful events in three supervision modalities. *Counselor Education and Supervision, 56*, 289–304. DOI: 10.1002/ceas.12086

Francis, R. (2013). *Report of the Mid Staffordshire NHS foundation trust public inquiry*. The Stationery Office.

Galanter, C. A., Nikolov, R., Green, N., Naidoo, S., Myers, M. F., & Merlino, J. P. (2014). Direct supervision in outpatient psychiatric graduate medical education. *Academic Psychiatry*. https://doi.org/10.1007/s40596-014-0247-z

Health Education England. (2020). *Recognition of Trainers: Standards & Guidance*. HEE.

Kadushin, A., & Harkness, D. (2002). *Supervision in social work* (4th ed.). Columbia University Press.

Kogan, J. R., Hatala, R., Hauer, K. E., & Holmboe, E. (2017). Guidelines: The do's, don'ts and don't knows of direct observation of clinical skills in medical education. *Perspectives in Medical Education, 6*(5), 286–305. https://doi.org/10.1007%2Fs40037-017-0376-7

Kretz, D. R., & Krawczyk, D. C. (2014). Expert analogy use in a naturalistic setting. *Frontiers In Psychology, 5*, 1–8. https://doi.org/doi:10.3389/fpsyg.2014.01333

Lynch, L., & Happel, B. (2008). Implementation of clinical supervision in action: Part 2: Implementation and beyond. *International Journal of Mental Health Nursing, 17*(1), 65–72. https://doi.org/10.1111/j.1447-0349.2007.00512.x

Martin, P., Reiser, R., & Milne, D. (2017). Peer supervision: International problems and prospects. *Journal of Advanced Nursing, 74*(95), 998–999. https://doi.org/10.1111/jan.13413

Milne, D., & Reiser, R. P. (2020). *Supportive Clinical Supervision: From burnout to well-being, through restorative leadership*. Pavilion.

Milne, D. L. (2007). Developing clinical supervision through reasoned analogies with therapy. *Clinical Psychology and Psychotherapy, 13*(3), 215–222. http://dx.doi.org/10.1002/cpp.489

Milne, D. L. (2020). Preventing harm related to CBT supervision: A theoretical review and preliminary framework. *The Cognitive Behaviour Therapist, 13*(e54), 1–15. https://doi.org/10.1017/S1754470X20000550

Milne, D. L., & Reiser, R. P. (2017). *A Manual for Evidence-based CBT Supervision*. Wiley-Blackwell.

Milne, D. L., & Westerman, C. (2001). Evidence-based clinical supervision: Rationale and illustration. *Clinical Psychology and Psychotherapy, 8*(6), 444–445. https://doi.org/10.1002/cpp.297

Molloy, E., Ajjawi, R., Bearman, M., Noble, C., Rudland, J., & Ryan, A. (2020). Challenging feedback myths: Values, learner involvement and promoting effects beyond the immediate task. *Medical Education, 54*(1), 33–39. https://doi.org/10.1111/medu.13802

Moran, A. M., Coyle, J., Boxall, D., Nancrow, S. A., & Young, J. (2014). Supervision, support & mentoring interventions for health practitioners in rural and remote contexts: An integrative review and thematic synthesis of the literature to identify mechanisms for successful outcomes. *Human Resources for Health, 12*(1), 10. http://www.human-resources-health.com/content/12/1/10

Parry, G., Roth, A.D., & Fonagy, P. (1996). Psychotherapy research, policy and evidence-based practice. In A.D. Roth & P. Fonagy (Eds.), *What Works for Whom?* (2nd ed., pp. 37–56). New York: Guilford Press.

Reynolds, J., & Mortimore, G. (2021). Clinical supervision for advanced practitioners. *British Journal of Nursing, 30*(7), 422–424. https://doi.org/10.12968/bjon.2021.30.7.422

Roth, A. D., & Pilling, S. (2007). *A competence framework for the supervision of psychological therapies*. University College London. The full set of competences referred to in this document are available for downloading from the CORE website www.ucl.ac.uk/CORE

Roth, A. D., Pilling, S., & Turner, J. (2010). Therapist training and supervision in clinical trials: Implications for clinical practice. *Behavioural and Cognitive Psychotherapy, 38*(3), 291–302. https://doi.org/10.1017/s1352465810000068

Rousmaniere, T., Goodyear, R. K., Miller, S. D., & Wampold, B. E. (2017). *The cycle of excellence: Using deliberate practice to improve supervision and training*. Wiley-Blackwell.

Schoenwald, S. K. (2016). Clinical supervision in a quality assurance/quality improvement system: Multisystemic therapy® as an example. *The Cognitive Behaviour Therapist, 9*, e21. https://doi.org/10.1017/S1754470X15000604

Snowdon, D. A., Leggat, S. G., & Taylor, N. F. (2017). Does clinical supervision of healthcare professionals improve effectiveness of care and patient experience? A systematic review. *BMC Health Services Research, 17*(1), 786, 788. https://doi.org/10.1186/s12913-017-2739-5

Sutkin, M. D., Wagner, E., Harris, I., & Schiffer, R. (2008). What makes a good clinical teacher in medicine? A review of the literature. *Academic Medicine, 83*(5), 452–466. https://doi.org/10.1097/acm.0b013e31816bee61

Vandette, M.-P., & Gosselin, J. (2019). Conceptual models of clinical supervision across professions: A scoping review of the professional psychology, social work, nursing, and medicine literature in Canada. *Canadian Psychology, 60*(4), 302–314. https://psycnet.apa.org/doi/10.1037/cap0000190

Watkins, C. E. (Ed.). (1997). *Handbook of psychotherapy supervision*. Wiley.

Watkins, C. E. (2019). What do clinical supervision research reviews tell us? Surveying the last 25 years. *Counselling & Psychotherapy Research, 20*(2), 190–208. https://doi.org/10.1002/capr.12287

Wheeler, S., & Richards, K. (2007). The impact of clinical supervision on counsellors and therapists, their practice and their clients. A systematic review of the literature. *Counselling and Psychotherapy Research, 7*(1), 54–65. https://doi.org/10.1080/14733140601185274

Index

a
accountability 24
acid test 156, 185
action implications 200–201
action research 186
adherence (see also *drift*)
adverse triggering events 6–7
A&E (accident & emergency department) 165–166, 180–181
alliance 3, 50–64, 70–71, 149–152
  rupture 3
anxiety 115
appraisal (cognitive) 8, 11
audit 126
authority of supervisor 22, 50–64, 118, 142
autonomy of supervisee 22, 50–64
awareness-raising 143

b
barriers and boosters to supervision 32–34, 187
Beddoe & Davys 3, 201
benefits of supervision 197
best evidence synthesis (literature review method) 14
bias (cognitive) 91, 162
bug-in-the-eye technique 74
bureaucracy 173
boundaries to relationship 70

c
capability 72–73
case-study illustration: see also *illustration*
CBT (cognitive-behaviour therapy) 28
challenging 71–72
character 50–51
clinical oversight 23–24, 75
clinical responsibility 39–48
clinical supervision (see supervision)
coaching 118
cognitive bias 91, 162
Cognitive Therapy Scale (Revised) 161
collaboration 161–163
collusion 119
communication problems 3, 158, 160
competence & incompetence 3, 5, 91
  framework 116, 120
  Dreyfus scale (competence levels) 116, 144
conclusions 196–201
confidence 165–166, 181–182
conflict resolution 149
consensus 122–123
consent (informed) 5
consultancy 28–30, 118, 121, 123–125
  guidelines 127–128
context 9, 130, 172–190
continuing professional development (CPD) 25, 47, 92, 98–99
contract 24–30, 47, 50–64,
coping (personal coping strategies)
  diagram 10
  formulation 60–63
  strategies 9, 143
  theory 8–10

Resolving Critical Issues in Clinical Supervision: A Practical, Evidence-based Approach, First Edition.
Derek L. Milne and Robert P. Reiser.
© 2023 John Wiley & Sons Ltd. Published 2023 by John Wiley & Sons Ltd.

vicious cycle   8, 10–11, 61–62
virtuous cycle   10–11
counselling   94–95
critical issues   1, 3–4, 6–8
  change mechanisms/processes   13
  framework (classification scheme)   5–6, 6–8
  illustration (case study; see also *illustration*)   11–12, 28–30
  outcomes   12
  resolution   12–13
  techniques   12–13, 50–64
cultural competence   161–162

d

DAR approach   149
decision-making   162, 166
delegation   24
deliberate practice (DP)   90, 114–131, 146–148
demonstrating (modelling)   72, 75
de-skilling (destabilization)   29–30
developmental processes   13
disaster in healthcare   174–175
discussion   71
distress   10
Dreyfus (competence levels)   116, 144
drift (non-adherence)   115, 119, 121, 129
due process (procedural justice)   5, 80

e

economic factors   173
education   72–73, 124
emotional intelligence   62
Ellis   136, 138
environmental factors (see also *context*), 157, 163–167
Ericsson   116, 118, 146–147
ethical conduct
  defined   50
  standards   50–51
  consequences   57
  destructiveness   58–59
  documentation   57
  due process   5

  ethical versus legal issues   51–52
  illustration   59–60
  misconduct (transgressions)   52
  principles   57
  resolving ethical issues   68–83
  sanctions   55
  unethical supervision
    defined   56
    understood   61
  whistleblowing   52
ethical issues   50–64
  action implications   64
  boundary violation   57–58
  bullying and harassment   54
  classification and specification of ethical concerns   4–5, 53–54, 56–60
  coping strategies   54
evaluation   78–80
  acid test   156, 185
  action research   186
  causal pathway   185
  outcome   156
  structure-process-outcome   119, 184
evidence-based clinical supervision (EBCS)
  definition and nature   13–15, 89, 201
  evidence   89
evidence-based practice (EBP)   13–14, 124, 167–168, 196
experiencing   151
experiential learning   13, 16, 29–30, 72–73, 75–76, 92, 99–100, 118–119, 123
  avoidance   119–120
expert consensus see *consensus*
expertise   90, 116, 118 *see also* deliberate practice
external examiner   79
extrapolation   6, 199

f

feedback   75–76, 122, 189
fidelity   167
  framework   6, 186
fitness to practice   50–51
  unfitness   52
force-field analysis   186–188

formulation 14, 31–35, 60–63, 90–94, 116–118, 141–142, 158–159, 161–165, 186–188

g
game-playing (negative interpersonal transactions) 31–34, 69, 141–142
gatekeeping 78–82
guided discovery 71–72
guidelines 34–36, 98, 100, 121–122, 142–151

h
Haarman 3, 51, 79
Harm to patients 6
Health & Care Professions Council (HCPC) 77
healthcare disaster 174–175
humility 159

i
illustration 11–12, 28–30, 39, 43, 94–95, 124–125, 128–129, 150–152, 165–167, 175–177, 180–183
imposter syndrome 166–167
Improving Access to Psychological Therapies (IAPT) 75, 90
incompetence 58, 114–131
  formulation 116–118
interpersonal process recall (IPR) 151, 159, 162

k
Kadushin & Harkness 23, 25, 32–33, 46, 69, 91, 101, 104, 139–140, 142, 201
Kolb 13, 84

l
leadership 120, 177–178
legal aspect 39–48
  liability (vicarious; 'strict/direct') 30, 40–42
  negligence 41
  risk management 46–48
limitations of book 197–199

m
malpractice 58

managers (line managers; clinical leaders; executives; administrators) 7, 14, 16, 34, 45, 62–63, 82–83, 93, 101, 117, 164, 175, 177–179, 188, 200–201
Manchester Clinical Supervision Scale (MCSS) 126
manual (supervision) 2, 14
mentoring 78, 121
metacognition 148–149
meta-supervision 121
modelling (demonstrating) 72
monitoring 160, 189
moral principles 50
motivation 144–145

n
normative supervision 1
  definition 2–3
nudge theory 80

o
observation 73–74, 120
organizational system 7
outcome monitoring 125–126
oversight (clinical) 23–24

p
patient factors/characteristics 157, 160–163
  adherence 160–161
peer supervision 2, 33, 93, 179–183
power 23–24, 33, 141–142
problem-solving 76–77, 125
proctor 121
protocol 166
psychiatry residents 28–30

q
quality control/improvement 172–190
questioning 71, 143

r
rating
  bias 74
  self 74
reflection (see *illustrations*), 76
relationship issues 3, 50–64, (see also *alliance*)

authority of supervisor   22
boundaries   5, 57–58, 69
collusion   119
dual relationships   57, 77
research (see also *evaluation*)
    action research   186
    best evidence synthesis (literature review
        method)   14
    weak literature   198
resolving critical issues   12
    process   70
    techniques   68–83
    challenging supervisee behaviours   139
resources   175
responsibility   24, 27
    clinical responsibility   39–48
restorative supervision   143
risk management   46–48
role induction   160
Roth & Pilling   75, 96, 116, 120, 122, 136, 150

S

SAGE see *Supervision: Adherence and Guidance Evaluation*
scandal   183–184
Schoenwald   167
self-awareness   122–123
self-care   77, 124
self-monitoring   122, 124–126
self-regulation (inc. metacognition)   63–64, 148–149
self-supervision   126
social support   77, 117, 164
    observed   164–165
supervisee,
    autonomy   22, 50–64,
    challenging   136–152
        classification table   139
    co-construction   136
    de-skilling (destabilization)   29–30
    feedback   122
    learning expertise   144–145
    motivation   144–145
    personal factors   157–160
    power   33
    role   73

self-regulation   159
supervision
    barriers and boosters   187
    benefits   197
    co-construction   136
    contract   24–30, 50–64, 123
    definition   2–3
        empirical   3
    direct   74
    disciplinary (mandated)   76
    drift (non-adherence)   115, 121
    effectiveness   185 (see also *evaluation*)
    functions   2, 197
    guidelines   34–36, 98, 100, 121–122, 126
    harmful   76
    inadequate   76, 123
    incompetent   114–131
        definition   114
    managing/structuring supervision   68–69
    outcomes   197
    peer group   120–121
    peer supervision   2, 33–34, 179–183
    professional approach   46
    quality   184
    remedial   80
    responsibilities   25–30
    restorative   143
    supervision-of-supervision   80, 118
    terms & scope (duties &
        responsibilities)   25–30
    training   7, 47, 88–106, 198
    unavailable   178
    unethical supervision defined   56
Supervision: Adherence and Guidance
    Evaluation (SAGE)   102–103, 120,
    122, 123
supervision-of-supervision   80
systemic (see *context*)

t

Thomas   70, 76
training   73, 88–106, 198
    absent   91
    definition   90
    deliberate practice   90
    design (e.g. ADDIE)   95–104

evaluation   102–104
　fidelity framework   103
formulation   90–94
goals (objectives; intended learning
　　outcomes: ILO)   96–97
gold standard   101–102
inadequate   92
insufficient   92
in supervision   7, 47
manual   96–98
methods   92
misguided   92–93
necessary   88–89
reaction evaluation   102
resources   99–101
standards   98
unsupported   93

u

understanding   125 (see also *formulation*)

v

Veterans Administration (VA)   183
vicarious liability: see *legal*
vicious cycle   61–62 (see also *coping*)
video demonstrations   68

w

waiting list scandal   183–184
Watkins   88, 104, 196
Watkins & Milne   68
well-being   10, 77
work (workplace: see *context*)
　barriers and boosters   187
　stressors, listed   4